THE NATURAL ARTISTRY OF DREAMS

THE NATURAL ARTISTRY OF DREAMS

)) ● ((

*Creative Ways to Bring the Wisdom
of Dreams to Waking Life*

Jill Mellick

Foreword by Marion Woodman

CONARI PRESS
Berkeley, California

Acknowledgment of permission to reprint previously published material can be found on page 289, which constitutes an extension of this copyright page.

Conari Press books are distributed by Publishers Group West
Cover design: Leigh Wells Design
Cover illustration: Jill Mellick, Wild Geese

ISBN: 1-57324-019-2

Library of Congress Cataloging-in-Publication Data
Mellick, Jill.
    The natural artistry of dreams : creative ways to bring the wisdom of dreams to waking life / Jill Mellick; foreword by Marion Woodman.
       p. cm.
    Includes bibliographic references and index.
    ISBN 1-57324-019-2 (trade paper)
    1. Dreams. 2. Creative ability.   3. Dream interpretation–Social aspects. 4. Symbolism (Psychology)   I. Title
BF175.5.D74M45   1996
154.6'3–dc20   96-4577

Printed in the United States of America on recycled paper

10 9 8 7 6 5 4 3 2 1

I dreamt another bird and I were flying
in the silence of the night.
The other bird was flying just below me,
accompanying me, supporting me,
yet both of us sustained by soundless currents of air.

   —Dreamer

At birth, it enters into us, that bird. . . .
It dwells in our deepest depths.

   —*Hamsa Upanishad*

In genuine metaphor
the illuminating image arrives from another world,
like a bird through the window of your room,
to quicken the transposition of natural appearances
and their power of significance.

   —Jacques Maritain
   Creative Intuition in Art and Poetry

For J and J,
strong-hearted companions on the path,
and for Letty and Stanton,
my parents, who gave me so much for the journey

Table of Contents

)) ● ((

Acknowledgments

What a community of loving, generous, and astute people I have had around me during the writing of this book:

Judith Armenta's professional intuition put me in touch with Conari Press; Ashi kept me quiet company; Martha Casselman, my agent, believed in an earlier manuscript, which indirectly led to this book: Jennifer Clements assisted with valuable research background; the Conari Press family made its publication a delight; Joan Heyden provided sensitive, creative work and commentaries; Jan Fisher assisted with impeccable editorial and permissions work and prepared the index; Helen Tait accompanied me in friendship and assisted with research; Peter Hirose, librarian, quietly obtained the unobtainable; June Matthews' wisdom and wit provided a creative matrix for the work; Stanton and Letty Mellick modeled creative lives for me, encouraged my creativity, and provided a restful environment in which the first pages were written; Paula Reeves and her discerning and loving eye offered ways to flesh out the manuscript, and she was an inspiring companion in the spiral process of writing; Mary Jane Ryan offered me the rare opportunity to write a book about what I wanted and in the form I wanted; Jacques Rutzky's writer's eye offered many valuable perspectives; my Sha Sha sisters' courage and creativity in talking about their lives and dreams inspired me to continue my search for new ways to express our images; Dyane Sherwood brought her discernment and wide Jungian background; Jeanne Shutes introduced me to Jung, has actively supported all visible and invisible dimensions of my writing, and also reviewed each page and idea with the eye of an experienced therapist and fine writer; Barbara Smothers provided courageous personal art and reflections; Jeremy Tarcher believed in what I wanted to say and his kind, steady support encouraged me to keep looking for the right publishing house for my odd work; Judith A. Vaughn took the photograph of hands molding clay; Helen Wickes provided me with helpful references and books; Marion Woodman's work and friendship have inspired me for years, and Marion generously wrote the foreword; Chrysanthe Zantis' wise words as we walked along the river encouraged me to write from a deeper place.

I also wish to acknowledge the inspiration of those writers, theorists, and practitioners whose work has enriched and furthered mine greatly. Their wisdom and words appear and reappear in this book. I mention particularly the work of Fraser Boa, Robert Bosnak, Robert Johnson, James Hillman, Harry T. Hunt, C. G. Jung, June Matthews, Carol McRae, Arnold Mindell, Sylvia Brinton Perera, June Singer, Leonard Shlain, Rina Swentzell, Marie-Louise von Franz, and Marion Woodman.

A Special Acknowledgment to the Dreamers and Artists
I am grateful to the many people who have seen me for psychotherapy over the years. They have been superb, lov-

ing, and patient teachers. Their integrity, courage, and creativity continue to inspire me.

Many of those whom I am currently privileged to see in therapy indicated that they would be happy to have me include their dreams or aspects of their inner work in this book. However, when it came to actually incorporating their invaluable material, I found myself unable to use it. Inner material changes when it is exposed to others, regardless of whether the dreamer is identified. Our work together is still evolving and, I believe, still deserves a sheltered place in which to grow.

Instead, I have used, with permission, material from workshop participants and people whose therapy with me ended several years ago. Each example amalgamates various psychotherapeutic experiences; each is true to the spirit and experience of therapy but has been fictionalized to preserve the privacy of the dreamer. Each dream represents a wave in an ocean of deep and treasured work to which I was a privileged witness. I am deeply grateful to these dreamers for their wisdom, trust, and generosity, and to the dreamers who currently explore with me and teach me about the creative wisdom of the heart and soul.

About the Artwork
The painting on the cover and all mandalas at the beginning of sections were painted by the author. All other artwork was provided to the author for use in this publication.

)) ● ((
Foreword

Some people say, "Of course, I honor my dreams, even if I don't know what they are about." Some say, "I never dream," or "I dream, but I can't remember my dreams." Others say, "I dream, but I can't make any sense of my dreams." Still others may say, "I think I understand my dreams, but I know I'm not getting to the heart of them."

Beginners, veterans, therapists, and counselors—anyone who has experienced any of these responses, yet genuinely yearns to explore dreams in their full beauty and intricacy—will surely treasure *The Natural Artistry of Dreams.*

Jill Mellick is a musician, artist, and psychotherapist who honors the unconscious in the poetry of her own life. She has also lived among people of cultures not bound by linear thinking. She recognizes the power of the metaphor in the creative process and the power of the creative process in healing. In this book, she has woven her perceptions of music and painting with her understanding of psychotherapy and other cultures. The ideas she offers weave a tapestry that speaks directly to the healing powers of the unconscious as it compensates for the one-sidedness of consciousness. Immediately, it senses new possibilities in *playing* with a metaphor, possibilities that may lead to buried feelings, lost connections, new resonances in the psyche and in the cells of the body.

Jill understands the innate structure of a dream. She also understands how people lock themselves into one specific way of working with a dream and thereby limit the full flowering of the images. Whatever is innate is far too multidimensional to be bound to a one-dimensional, fixed mode of perceiving it. In *The Natural Artistry of Dreams*, she finds alternative structures related to dance, music, painting, poetry, and sculpture that can act as a container for the dream. At the same time, they provide ways of working with the images without restricting them to the linear thinking that, until recently, has dominated Western culture.

In any dream, as in any poem, the image is the content and the structure. Perhaps other cultures understand the dream story more easily than do we with our linear minds. Thus, their ways of working with dreams, as Jill sensitively demonstrates, are worthy of our attention. As we experiment with other approaches, we will find new ways of relating to the psychic reality of the metaphor upon which the coherence of the dream depends.

Metaphor is the literal language of the soul. Poets do not try "to think up metaphors." They are not interested in making up riddles for the rest of us to figure out. They *think* in metaphors. In his poem "The Tyger," for example, William Blake poses an immense theological question in one simple line: "Did he who made the Lamb make thee?"

Organic images are destroyed if we subject them to linear thinking. How often we judge them as "bizarre" or "weird." They need to be allowed to grow like plants in a spiraling movement. They carry emotional and imaginative energy as well as intellectual meaning, and as they spiral they are illumined with nuances of feeling. Hence their power to bring wholeness. Momentarily, we may suddenly think, feel, and imagine at the same instant. We may experience ourselves as whole, with a moment of goose-flesh that says "Yes." We may lose the sense of totality almost at once, but the psyche and body have experienced what wholeness is. They can then reconnect to that still point as to a tuning fork. Where consciousness and the unconscious intersect at the still point, that is where we are whole. That still point, as Jill demonstrates again and again throughout the book, is discovered in bringing to the dream's unconscious process an unobtrusive consciousness that cherishes rather than judges.

This book is a delight. As image transforms into image, we are reminded of Blake's butterfly:

> *He who binds to himself a joy*
> *Does the wingéd life destroy*
> *But he who kisses the joy as it flies*
> *Lives in eternity's sunrise.*

The dream carries within it what Samuel Coleridge calls "the sacred power of self-intuition." Those who can recognize in their dreams the unconscious operation of this power are those, as Coleridge suggests in *Biographia Literaria,* "who within themselves can interpret and understand the symbols, that the wings of the air-sylph [butterfly] are forming within the skin of the caterpillar; those only, who feel in their own spirits the same instinct, which impels the chrysalis of the horned fly to leave room in its involucrum for antennae yet to come. They know and feel, that the *potential* works *in* them, even as the *actual* works *on* them!"

In dreams the *actual* that works on us by day becomes the *potential* that works in us by night. This conversion of the actual into the potential (the waking state into the dream) vastly enlarges our sense of the actual, and by doing so vastly enlarges our life. The actual carries through the dream a potential for meaning that without the dream might never be discovered. In this book, Jill explores, in a wide-ranging series of perspectives, the dream potential in the actual. The result is a sense of the actual as a perpetually expanding universe that is always already situated "in eternity's sunrise."

—Marion Woodman
London, Canada, 1995

A Woman's Hands

Shape a Clay Pot

I have taken this time to write, this week in the tropics. Until now, I have been writing in the early morning and then leading a full day, personally and professionally. I have brought my laptop computer with me, but I also need to rest. My eyes wander away from the computer screen to the slow undulations of the palm, to the fearless cardinal meticulously mauling the papaya skins I put out on the patio, to the sudden gathering of a wave as it gathers, shines, and thumps on the shore. I want to "go tropo," forget everything, but am loath to stop writing. This is an ideal time to write—especially about dreams—in this dreamy environment.

I have brought many books with me: cognitive psychology books that view dreams as a complex grammar; books that offer instant answers to dream mysteries; books that provide instant symbol translations; books that ascerbically critique all other stances, yet offer no alternative other than working with an analyst five times a week; books that interpret, analyze, romanticize, historicize, categorize—by culture, by function, by content, by effect, by language, by image.

More and more books on dreams. I am wearing out my kind librarian. I am using up forests of recycled page markers. And I am diluting the mystery. When I move too far or too long from the dream itself, I lose the feel of its magnetic energy field. I can still describe the pattern of iron filings the magnetic field might make on a piece of paper. I can still draw the magnet. But I can no longer *feel* its energy. I am disquieted. Perhaps my delight in writing is vanishing. Surely not, and yet . . . I need to stop reading and start listening, watching, and trusting again.

After a long walk and a long swim beyond the waves

The dream comes from the world of the eternal, the great "I Am," and the language of that world is very different. A dream is a picture, a spiritual condition. Its language uses the details of the day but complements the details with a whole system of emotions and feelings—a totally different language. And there's no way the language can be reduced to a two-dimensional reality.

—Marion Woodman
Dreams: Language of the Soul

to the rocky point, I doze over my book. I awake with a single image. A painterly image, a Rembrandt. Neither a story nor a drama.

What we take out of dreams, what we get to use from dreams, what we bring up from dreams, is all to the surface. Depth is the invisible connection; and it is working with our hands on the invisible connections where we cannot see, deep in the body of the night, penetrating, assembling and differentiating, debriding, stirring, churning, kneading— this constitutes the work on dreams. Always we are doing precision work, but with invisibilities, with ambiguities, and with moving materials.

—James Hillman
The Dream and the Underworld

I am looking down at the dark olive skin of a woman's round arms and plump, tapered hands. Her hands are forming the inside of a round clay bowl. The light on her skin is soft and warm. All else is in darkness. It is silent. As I recall the image, I realize that I am looking down—not at—this woman's arms. I am looking from the position of being in her body. There is only one way I could be in that position: if they were my arms. They are mine yet they are not mine. The woman making the pot is not me, yet I see through her eyes.

How often have I seen round, dark arms like hers, selling me an elegant, simple, clay pot like this dream pot under the portal of the Palace of the Governors in Santa Fe? How often have I been enveloped by arms like hers when I have visited my old friend from the Pueblo Indian village of Santo Domingo, her embrace always so soft and enveloping that I feel as though I am falling into feathers and am embraced by the Great Mother herself?

I feel—I don't know—I feel how this dream potter dwells within me, quietly going about things in her own time, in her own way, gathering earth from secret places in the hills of her soul, sifting it, coiling serpent upon serpent of clay, firing it in the dung of her inner darkness. The potter's is a slow, patient process done with attention to the spirit of the clay and with tender love. The potter knows that eventually her pot will be held by other hands, but that is not what must inform her heart or determine its

shape. The clay will tell the woman how to shape it—but she must wait quietly and listen.

The dream is a gift. It helps me recognize that once again I am getting lost in outer concerns. It helps me realize again—and again reluctantly—that I cannot write this book to order. It must form itself out of my own lived knowledge. I cannot make a list of clever things to do and check them off as I write up each one. The dream world is in charge here, and I have become accountable to it and its logic in a way I had not anticipated. I am not concerned about planning how I shall continue now. I must wait quietly and listen. This book must create itself from the clay of my own experience and in its own way.

Part One

Opening Up to Your Dreams and Creativity

1

Entering Your Dream World

A New Culture

I desire to accept
myself fully

Unbidden Gifts: Dreaming as a Creative Art

Some dreams haunt us with their images, words, sounds, and feelings. They often influence our inner and outer lives. They disturb, amuse, intrigue, haunt, and inspire. They are messengers from another realm with their own logic antithetical to waking logic. Dreams use the narrative structure of the soul, an acausal logic that exists in a timeless, spatially unbound universe. At times in our dreams, we occupy two time frames or places at once: We are our current age but in our childhood home; we change our sex; we are older, younger; we may occupy the consciousness of two people at once, seeing events from different perspectives simultaneously; we are in the future; we are both dead and alive. Wiser and more humorous than we, dreams remind us that we are subject to larger forces and influences than we tend to acknowledge on a daily basis. Many of our most profound images surface from dreams.

What happens if we let this dream world constructively intersect with waking life? What happens if we pay creative attention to our dreams, consciously allowing their imagery, patterns, and forms into waking consciousness? The wisdom of the dream can balance or affirm our waking attitudes. The heartbeat of the dream can beat in our actions and in the presence we bring to situations.

We do not always need to fully "understand" or interpret dreams to receive their gifts to heart and soul. Rather, we can circumambulate them, respect them, let their images feed our imagination and lead us onward, just as a glimpse of ocean or lake renews and orients us on a long drive. Fine plays and films leave images hovering in awareness—the hand reaching out across the car seat, the old letter being opened, the long shadow across the lawn. They

Our culture, following the Greeks' vision of a rational universe, used space, time, and mass as basic elements, but ultimately came to see the universe in terms that went beyond these elements.... With the quantum physical discovery of the effects of the observer on subatomic systems, the mind became part of the universe, entwined with mass, space, and time.

Today, our position is close to the one discovered by basic tribal peoples.

—Fred Alan Wolf
The Dreaming Universe

also engender feelings that linger in the heart—inspiration, paradoxical whimsy, poignancy. Even a film in an unfamiliar language can still touch something universal in the depths of the heart.

I was once told that it wasn't important if I understood my dreams. What was important was that the dreams understood me. My attitude toward my dreams would determine their attitude toward me. It's a living dialogue. When we listen to dreams, we change, and when dreams are heard, they change.

—Fraser Boa
The Way of the Dream

Dreams prove us creative artists, natural poets capable of simile, metaphor, symbol, and sheer imagery unbound by the cognitive restrictions of waking life. Dreams prove us painters, sculptors, superb storytellers, and myth makers. Dream images are sketched in fugitive ink, however. If we don't reexperience them immediately, they fade to invisibility on the fast-turning pages of waking consciousness.

In the ocean of the unconscious, dreams are swells that rise and pause and break on the shores of personal consciousness, only to suck back, leaving precious flotsam and jetsam on the beach of waking awareness. We cannot influence the tides or the currents, but we can ride the crest of the wave into shore and gather the treasures to us as we walk at dawn.

We cannot make a contract with our dreams. And dreams do not make contracts with us. Dreams promise nothing. They don't give answers. They don't even promise us their remembered presence.

We can, however, make a covenant with our dreams. Dreams ask trustworthy questions, questions from our deepest selves, perhaps deeper. We can choose to have a passing acquaintance or a deep, long friendship with them. We can promise them we shall be with them, record them, sing them, dance them, laugh with and weep for them, draw them. If we are willing to make this covenant, we can then receive what comes from our dreams as unbidden gifts. Two separate, trusting people in a loving, conscious relationship cannot demand reciprocity. They can only offer each other the possibility of being together in ways that allow their best selves to fly accompanied into an unknown, often moonless sky, sustained by quiet air currents of acceptance.

Like lovers, all we can do is promise to be there for our dreams—with heart, soul, intellect, body, and discernment. If we can let go of demanding, we can begin to learn the dream's language of love.

FLYING OUT THE CLERESTORY WINDOW: APPROACHING THE DREAM WORLD AS A NEW CULTURE

My approach to dreams has its roots in curiosity about my own dreams since childhood and my many cherished years working with dreamers in my capacity as a clinical psychologist in private practice. The wisdom and work of Carl Jung, Jungian theorists, and other selected theorists, have deeply watered and fertilized those roots and shaped my understanding. So has a lifelong interest in and involvement with other cultures' world views.

My first undergraduate anthropology class was held in a dreary, regulation beige and brown basement auditorium of one of the formal sandstone buildings bordering the University of Queensland quadrangle. February marked the humid height of summer in Australia. High, small windows at grass level framed the sky. As I listened to the lecturer talk about how we could observe and understand different cultures, something irrevocable happened to me: My spirit soared out of my hot, uncomfortable body, escaped through those high windows into the cloud-

If we think back on any dream that has been important to us, as time passes and the more we reflect on it, the more we discover in it, and the more varied the directions that lead out of it. . . . The depth of even the simplest image is truly fathomless. The unending, embracing depth is one way that dreams show their love.

—James Hillman
The Dream and the Underworld

less noon sky, and hovered momentarily over the map of Australia.

Even though I had been raised with an active appreciation for other cultures, at that moment I saw with silent shock that I still had a culture-bound, ethnocentric world view. I began to understand that I could look *at* my own culture as well as look out from it. I felt freedom and rumbling anxiety: I could never again put on cultural blinkers and trot unthinkingly through my environment. I did not forget that moment; at the first opportunity, between undergraduate and graduate studies in English Literature, I traveled to Papua and New Guinea, where I spent time with the Atzera and Foré tribes.

When my spirit escaped through those windows that blistering summer day and flew around, peering down at my own and other countries, I did not know that the experience would eventually inform the way I would look at dreams. Years later, I came to realize that dreams, too, are a different culture and that even the ways we treat and tell our dreams are culturally determined.

I do not believe that we can use one culture's norms and belief structures to view another without clouding the cultural integrity of each. The context in which we live, in which we dream, in which we tell our stories, is central to our inner and outer world views. And the structures of our lives, dreams, and stories are inseparable from their content.

This approach runs contrary to the beliefs of many Freudian theorists, who psychoanalyze dreams from third-world cultures assuming that the narrative structure and content of the Oedipus myth are universal templates for any culture's psyche and dreams. This approach also runs

For the Mae Enga [of New Guinea], the dream is not inside the individual but rather the individual, finds himself inside the dream. This concept of the dream is not unlike that which Piaget finds common in young children.
—Carl W. O'Nell
Dreams, Culture, and the Individual

contrary to contemporary groups who lift spiritual rituals from one culture and reenact them within their own, divorced from the unique cultural context that engendered these rituals.

I do believe, however, that we can stand back from our own culture and also be receptive to others. We can better understand how we construct our templates for realities, both inner and outer. We can also add new awarenesses from other cultures' perceptions, cultures more sensitized to certain experiences than our own.

My personal heritage includes several cultures and, having grown up in Australia and lived most of my adult life in the United States, I consider myself bicultural. I have also been fortunate to travel widely and to work in other cultures, including many years with the Pueblo Indian communities of the southwestern United States. However, no matter how many ceremonial dances I attend in the Pueblos, I shall always be a welcomed visitor, never a participant in the ritual. Nor shall I have more than a superficial understanding of the religious context of that dance, no matter how many books I read or how much form and feeling I absorb. I can better appreciate, however, the role of ritual drama, the spiritual impact of slow, repetitive dance and low singing, and the appearance in religious ceremonial costumes of nature symbols—rain, cloud, mountain. I can breathe in the experience and feel it enrich the breath of my own culture. I can include ritual, dance, art, nature, symbol, and song with more care, intent, depth, and fidelity in my life.

Our dreams, too, enact themselves in a different culture that we can only partially understand. So we must be wary of the preconceptions we bring to our dreams from

To experience the world, we invent ways to move about in time and space, to change matter into energy, to turn chaos into order; to survive.

—Fred Alan Wolf
The Dreaming Universe

our waking culture or from other cultures. However, by learning from other cultures' ways of structuring and receiving stories, dreams, images, and experiences, we can enrich our perceptions of and responses to dreams. Free of the constraints of our answer-addicted, deterministic culture, we can open to new secrets, new themes, new ways of listening and attending.

[We] should in every single case be ready to construct a totally new theory of dreams.

—C. G. Jung
Collected Works

AUNT MABEL AND THE POTATO PEELINGS: OPENING TO NEW WAYS OF EXPERIENCING "THE OTHER"

In *Keeping Slug Woman Alive*, a study of Native American narrative, Greg Sarris, a part-Pomo ethnographer, demonstrates that, after listening to a story, different cultural groups remember different elements of the story. In one culture, for example, listeners value the facts of the story; in another, listeners value who told the tale and in what circumstances; in yet another, listeners value not the objects appearing in the story, but their color.

Sarris describes his friendship with Mabel McKay, a Pomo Indian basketweaver and medicine woman. He was recording her life story. One day when he visits her, relatives Violet and Frances are peeling potatoes. He quickly observes that they are making perfectly round, peeled potatoes. He works at making perfectly round potatoes, gets good—and fast—only to see Violet glance with a small smile at the peelings. He looks, too. The women's peelings are fine and transparent and have wasted no potato. Greg's peelings are chopped off bits of dense potato. Sarris realizes he has missed the point of the exercise. Aunt Mabel simply says, "My life is like that." She quietly teaches Greg to be wary of attending to the wrong thing in the stories she tells.

Like Aunt Mabel and Sarris, each culture peels the skin off the dream differently, although almost all cultures, across seas and time, have regarded dreams as guides for unmapped spiritual, emotional, and physical—even cultural—territories. There is wide cross-cultural agreement, too, that "big" dreams carry special significance for the individual, and even for a whole community. In the Senoi tribe of Malaysia, for example, individual dreams are important to the whole group. In classical Greece, visitors to the healing center at Epidaurus slept in a dream chamber until they had a special dream that opened the way to psychological or physical healing. In other shamanic tribes, those desiring a big dream or an encounter with their guardian spirit set themselves aside to fast until a dream guide appears.

Sigmund Freud considered dreams the "royal road" to the unconscious, to inner worlds of personal history, trauma, and primitive need. Carl Jung believed that dreams draw from not only a personal well of experience, but also a vast reservoir of universal human experiences, responses, images, metaphors, symbols, and mythology. Jung observed, from extensive and deep analytic work with his patients and himself, that dreams perform restorative, corrective, compensatory, prophetic, and developmental roles in the psyche. To attend to our dreams is to attend to the cry of the soul through image. While putting forward the most comprehensive, culture-sensitive, and open system of dream theory, Jung also believed that it is wiser and more personally fruitful to approach individual dreams with humility and unknowing.

For the Tikopians [a Polynesian people] the dream is an adventure of the spirit. Dream experience, in fact, is taken as evidence of the spirit world to which everyone has access. The dream is a creation of the spirit world, being the outcome of what is enacted there.

—Carl W. O'Nell
Dreams, Culture, and the Individual

Life is not a (Western) drama of four or five acts. Sometimes it just drifts along; it may go on year after year without development, without climax, without definite beginnings or endings. Or it may accumulate climax upon climax, and if one chooses to mark it with beginnings and endings, then everything has a beginning and an ending.

—Trinh Minh-ha
Woman Native Other

Through the window of Jung's experience, we see dreams speaking on many levels at once, just as a piece of art does. Michelangelo's *Pietà* has many levels of meaning: one sculptor's rendering of two individual human models; the portrayal of a scene significant to Christian cultures; the depiction of a universal emotion; the unbearable grief in the loss of a child. What the sculpture evokes is not only personal but archetypal: people from all cultures looking at that sculpture touch their own experiences of loss.

Familiarity with the work of Freud or Jung or another coherent dream theory consonant with your personal acculturation, is helpful but not crucial for fruitful dreamwork. In fact, interpreting dreams by exclusive and unquestioning application of a template from one theoretical system can be dangerously misleading at times. The theory must take into account the culture, the individual, and *the nature of the individual dream with which we are working*. To apply a theory blindly is to make assumptions about the dream culture without traveling with an open mind. We become souvenir hunters, missing engagement with the vibrancy and mystery of the unknown culture, bent only on collecting and carrying a heavy suitcase of artifacts that will fit into our predetermined decor.

Most theorists assume that the dream's narrative structure exists almost independently of its substance, like a frame waiting for a painting or a survey for answers. Many even believe that if the dream (as it is reported in *words*) lacks a defined beginning, middle, and end; something is awry or unformed in the dream or dreamer.

In *Woman Native Other*, Trinh Minh-ha, a writer, filmmaker, and composer, points out that stories from different cultures are told in infinite ways. Each story creates its own structure. She adds that it is not only self-limiting but also oppressive to force Western "beginning-middle-end," cause-and-effect story structure onto another culture and then to evaluate the narrative or retell it in that mode.

We often oppress dreams in the same way. We separate their content and structure. In order to retell our dreams with some verbal, linear coherence, we unthinkingly use Western story structure to make the dream comprehensible to waking consciousness. Unconsciously influenced by telling stories that have a beginning, middle, and end, that wrap up loose ends from certain events or characters, that make one thing lead to the next, we make our dream tales conform to our storytelling habits, to our need to place them within a familiar narrative framework.

Aunt Mabel showed that we can miss the point by our preconceptions or by restructuring experience. A well-known author and creative-writing teacher asserts that he makes his students tell their dreams in class, whereupon other students deem the dream a good story or a bad story! They are to critique the dream for having no ending or beginning or for being boring or uneventful!

Who said that all dreams are stories? And according to whose definition of story? Undoubtedly, many dreams are indeed stories. And it is even possible that our ways of storytelling can actually influence the original formation of certain dreams. Yet many dreams are not stories at all but natural plays, paintings, poems. Would we "analyze" a poem as though it were a novel? Would we analyze a novel as though it were a painting? Would we expect an Aboriginal tribal member to produce a dance ritual in the classical form of a Shakespearean play—or a Noh drama,

A dream is not a story, not a movie or text or a theater play. A dream is a happening in space, an articulation of space.
—Robert Bosnak
A Little Course in Dreams

or a nineteenth-century novel in which every character is accounted for and *The End* is printed on the last page? Why, then, do we do this with our dreams?

Beautifully woven rugs from Newlands, a remote area on the Navajo reservation, have one pattern of overlaid threads on one side and a slightly different pattern on the other. Because we expect both sides to look the same, it's easy to miss the difference. At a recent exhibit of fine paintings, one was suspended in a clear, double-sided frame; there was a drawing on both sides. Used to looking for what we look for, we rarely expect this. We stop too soon and miss the beauty of the other side of the rug, the painting. We miss the transparency of the potato peelings.

Even Harry Wilmer, one of my favorite writers, who brings such an original perspective to dreams, draws the lines at some structures:

the on-and-on dream
The on-and-on dream goes off here and there
in curlicues without plot to hold sequences together . . .
It's hard to find a story line
when all is told . . .
Don't get sucked in to the quicksand of words and images.

Like Wilmer, I too have difficulty with these kinds of dreams—both others' and my own. But my difficulty is my difficulty. I suspect I lack the sensitivity to be present to the dream in the way the dream needs. Perhaps I have difficulty because these dreams are like stories from another land, spiraling stories, requiring a different ear, a unique imaginative response, a deeper patience.

If we can allow the dream to be what it is, rather than immediately compare it to what it is not, we can allow the

The text of a dream may be similar to that of any poem, painting, or narrative: "a system of internal energies and tensions, compulsions, resistances and desires." . . . But it may also be a single image —visual, auditory, and/or kinesthetic— to be enriched in the web of associations, explanations, and cultural/mythological amplifications . . . that inevitably radiate out from the node of psychic energy that the image expresses in sensate form for (partial) revelation.

—Sylvia Brinton Perera
"Dream Design"

dream its own structural integrity, which is probably best expressed through an art form more fluid than conventional story. We need to let dreams paint themselves, dance themselves, sculpt themselves, begin at the end and end at the beginning, spiral in on themselves, meander without climax or major turning point. Perhaps then, when content and structure are seen as an indivisible whole, we can truly begin to appreciate the elegant sagacity of the dream.

Delighting in Diversity: Approaching the Material in This Book

The more I read dream theory, the more convinced I am that opting for a single approach to dreams usually excludes other valuable approaches. Those who impose universal truths ignore cross-cultural diversity. Those interested solely in cross-cultural differences miss archetypal patterns. Those who believe the dream is basically verbal dismiss the possibility that dreams use *synæsthesia* (the mixing of the senses) or originate in the visual area of the brain. Those who focus on narrative and content can forget that the way we tell stories in our culture is just that: the way we tell stories in *our* culture. Dream theorists also take oppositional positions, of which the following are a sample:

- Dreams don't exist.
- Dreams are meaningless productions of the brain.
- Dreams mean the opposite of what they say.
- Dreams are all about the past.
- Dreams are all about the future.

- All dreams are ordinary.

- All dreams are sacred.

- Most dreams are ordinary and some are sacred.

- Dreams are only about and for the dreamer.

- Dreams are only products of and produced for the community.

- Dreams preserve the culture.

- Dreams create the culture.

- Dream images use clear symbols that we can interpret.

- Dreams images are not symbolic but purely imagistic.

- We must know the personality and history of the dreamer before we can understand the dream.

- We need only to understand the symbols to understand the dream.

- Dreamers' concerns can be interpreted the same way across cultures because the underlying psychological dynamics are the same.

- We need to know about the dreamer, the culture, and universally generated symbology to fully understand a dream.

- We understand the dream when it just "clicks" inside.

- Feeling a dream "click" is suspicious—sometimes we just make it fit what we want to believe.

- Dreams should always be grounded in daily life.

- Dreams are their own world and should never be co-opted to serve daily life.

- Dreamer's concerns can be interpreted only within their cultural context.

Let's get back to your dream. What does your dream say?

—C. G. Jung
In Mary Ann Mattoon's
Applied Dream Analysis

- All dreams have the same underlying structure.

- Each dream creates its own structure.

- Dreams are primarily verbal.

- Dreams are primarily visual.

In view of this wide and well-argued dissension in dream theory, entertaining many possibilities but taking none as absolute truth seems wiser, perhaps. There is a time for understanding the implications of dreams for waking life, for making travel to dream country purposeful; we come to learn, to interpret, to understand the symbols, to learn the language, to understand the customs. But there is also a time when traveling to a country is an end in itself; we can let the journey nourish and sustain without needing the experience to change our lives.

Not all books on dreams are rooted in experience and wisdom. Many simplified and illustrated guides to dreams and their symbols have the sensitivity of an elephant on ice skates and the reliability of politicians' economic predictions. The Jungian theory of archetypes and other symbolic theories are easily mimicked but rarely accorded the subtlety or spirit of inquiry they deserve. It is easy to seduce with gross generalities. It is even easier to be seduced by them. They give certainty where there is none. Be wary of books that offer easy and authoritative solutions, particularly to approaching dreams. Jung believed that we must be ready at any moment to construct an entirely new theory of dreams. He maintained a spirit of inquiry and eternal curiosity about his research. For him—and for us— the dream itself is the final authority on itself and we are forever the students.

I think these [dream dictionary] books are very, very bad. They get you off the track because they give a static interpretation. . . . You can sometimes be inspired by looking at one of these . . . to see what all the possibilities are . . . but then you have to return to the dream and ask, "What does it mean to the dreamer?" and that is always much more specific.
—Marie-Louise von Franz
In Fraser Boa's
The Way of the Dream

Eventually I moved away from interpretation—at least immediate interpretation. I came to feel that immediate interpretation of the dream image is a resistance phenomenon. Then in Japan . . . someone said, "It's very interesting what you're doing, but you're interpreting so much." Since then I've been trying more and more to postpone interpretation.

—Robert Bosnak
In Michael V. Adams'
"Image, Active
Imagination, and the
Imaginal Level"

Be wary. Be critical. Be curious. If you are unfamiliar with dream theory, I recommend Robert Johnson's *Inner Work*, Robert Bosnak's *A Little Course in Dreams*, and Fraser Boa's interviews with Marie-Louise von Franz in *The Way of the Dream*. They are practical, imaginative introductions founded in clinical experience, and containing a welcome absence of quick fixes. If you are familiar with and appreciate Jungian approaches to dreams, read further in Marion Woodman's many books and tapes including *Leaving My Father's House* and *Dreams: Language of the Soul*; Karen Signell's *Wisdom of the Heart*; and June Singer's books including *Boundaries of the Soul*. These, among other fine books, unfold, with wisdom, grace, and psychological depth, how dreams are worked with in analysis.

There are also available several excellent cross-cultural reference books on symbols. Review the qualifications of the author(s) before you purchase their work. Refer to these books last rather than first when you work with dreams. Let your personal associations carry the ultimate weight. The reference list at the end of this book includes other works you might consult. Also watch for two forthcoming books that approach, with skill, experience, and depth, ways to work with images from the soul in and through the body: Marion Woodman, Mary Hamilton, and Ann Skinner's book on imagery and bodywork, and Paula Reeves' *Stepping into the River*.

A WAY, THE WAY:
TO INTERPRET OR NOT TO INTERPRET

This book refrains from discussing dream interpretation. Rather, it offers only ways to ask questions. I don't know answers and I can't give you any about your dreams. Trust your lived experience of what is fitting, creative, and ethical for you. We all choose *a* way, but it is unlikely that it is *the* way. It may be the way for us, but when we begin to think that ours is the only way, we blind ourselves to the rich coloration of others.

Western culture has difficulty holding contradictory beliefs about the world. Other cultures easily hold paradoxical world views. Many Pueblo Indians, for example, are faithful followers of Pueblo religious practices and also devoted Roman Catholics. From a Western perspective, these two religions run counter to each other. However, my Pueblo friends who live this "contradiction" calmly demonstrate that this discomfort itself is determined by acculturation.

This book provides you with many lenses through which to view your dreams. Often, these lenses contradict each other. For example, many dream theorists and practitioners work with dreams with the traditional techniques noted below on the left; others, in the innovative ways noted on the right. This book focuses on the innovative activities and attitudes, but also draws heavily on the rich offerings of the traditional approaches.

Sick interpretations,
a Jungian bag of tricks,
a Freudian bag of
tricks,
any kind of bag of
tricks
is the hallmark of the
trickster archetype.
—Harry Aron Wilmer
Practical Jung

Traditional (doing)	Innovative (being)
analyze	nourish
interpret	explore
identify	imagine
hypothesize	associate
work on	be with, play with
get a handle on	fly with
apply to life	give life to

Traditional (doing)	Innovative (being)
theorize	inquire
break down	connect
defuse	infuse
think about	create around
figure out	sustain the mystery of
assimilate	accommodate
categorize	allow to evolve
understand	appreciate
study	learn
observe	participate
research	experience
translate	learn the language
decode	delight in
tell, write down	paint, dance, mime, sing, sculpt . . .
denote, connote	imagine, amplify
simplify	enrich

The difference between a coherent theory and a consistent attitude is that the latter is both more modest in its ambition and more daring in its practice. . . . Any theory will do so long as it does not disturb the consistent underworld perspective of the dream as image. We stick with tactics, the imaginative, soul-making work with the dream.

—James Hillman
The Dream and the Underworld

There is nothing inherently right or wrong about any of these approaches. Personality, training, beliefs, and cognitive style determine which selection we make at different times.

How do you work the material in this book, then, if different ways of exploring your dreams are paradoxical? Practice holding this paradox without resolving it; practice seeing several "oppositional" approaches as worthy. Exercise Samuel Taylor Coleridge's "willing suspension of disbelief." Entertain one idea as if it were the only approach that had worth and work with that perspective for a while. Then choose another.

Trust your own experience. Experiment with as many ideas in this book as possible. Determine which are helpful to you now. Return to ideas you have set aside after a few months. What works now might not be what works later. For example, you might find painting helpful for several weeks, but one day it loses its potency. Don't hold on and force a painting. Experiment with poetry or sculpture or some modality that previously did not attract your attention. Be wary of locking permanently into one approach or belief to the exclusion of others. Choose a frame for viewing your dreams, realizing that the frame is not the view.

Embrace approaches (and their underlying theoretical assumptions) that bring richness, meaning, and growth to you. Not everyone is suited to deep and extended Jungian symbolic work, or to active, dramatic Gestalt work. Ensure that the approaches you choose do not run counter to your inner direction. For example, acting out a figure in a dream might feel too confrontational at a time when you are feeling stressed. Perhaps you need to draw the figure or do a mandala to lower your stress. If an approach runs upstream from your inner movement, it does not indicate that the approach itself is bad. It simply means that, at this time, this particular approach is too far removed from your world view for you to derive benefit that would not be clouded by discomfort. You would not be able to constructively integrate it into your life. In the same way, offer possibilities to others based on your own experience, but withhold directives about theirs. Because one way works well for you does not mean that it will work well for your partner, child, parent, therapy client, or friend.

Integrate your time with and understandings from your dreams into your own life, keeping in mind that dreams

The dream world and the unconscious psyche show their positive face to us only if we go with life, if we don't refuse to live.

—Marie-Louise
von Franz
In Fraser Boa's
The Way of the Dream

I do believe that dreams have a function. I don't see anything that has no function, not anything that has been created. . . . The brain is so strange and wondrous in its mystery. I think it creates a number of things for itself—it creates launching pads and resting places— and it lets steam off and it reworks itself. It re-creates itself almost every minute.

—Maya Angelou
In Naomi Epel's
Writers Dreaming

have eternal world views, cultural norms, and customs, so you cannot make your life consistent with your dreams. You can weave the threads of your understandings from your dreams into the fabric of your life, however. You can acknowledge the sense of hurry that was in your dream, for example, and slow down a little in daily life.

When I first went to Japan, I fell in love with the simplicity of architectural spaces. No chairs, no tables, no shoes—just a single vase, a single scroll. When I returned to my house, jet-lagged and suffused with the Japanese aesthetic, I took one look around my house and wanted to put everything away. I wanted to take down every painting but one in every room, remove every sculpture, pot, and beloved artifact but one from every surface, and ban family photographs from the kitchen. I'm relieved I was too exhausted to act on my impulse. I would have substituted what little I understood of the Japanese aesthetic for my own without a thought for the fact that my daily life has a different context from that of the Japanese, just as dreams have a different context from waking culture. After I recovered both my energy and my personal aesthetic, however, I did decide that I could pay homage to the beauty I had seen in Japan by simplifying my visual world a little. I cleared clutter (sometimes). I changed paintings in the house according to season. I took more time to do simple flower arrangements. I continue to slowly integrate those ideas into my daily life.

If you are in therapy, talk with your therapist about which approaches to your dreams you are exploring. Some will fit better with your work than others. Few therapists work equally well with all approaches to dreams. Some will suit your therapist better; others will suit you better.

As well as pursuing those approaches that work for you, look for others that provide a common ground of experience. If you have been going through a stressful time, talk with your therapist about which approaches might be most helpful and least stressful. It is easy to unearth new material within us, but harder to integrate it into heart, mind, and life. If you are symbolically inclined, for example, loading yourself down with more symbolism, imagery, and inner work might be just what you *don't* need during a stressful time. You might need to read a detective novel or go to a light movie. Be patient. The time for more symbolic work will return.

The dream is its own interpretation.
—The Talmud

The dream is more often the companion of the soul than the lackey for daily life. Use pragmatic discernment about the "advice" from dreams. Although you can be responsible about and responsive to anything you suspect your dreams are indicating to you about your waking life, be wary of *always* co-opting the dream into the service of your daily life and thought.

We would not embark on an African safari without an experienced guide, plenty of provisions, a way of protecting and defending ourselves, familiarity with the risks and environment, ways home, people to call if the going got rough, and good places to wait out a stampede or storm. The same respectful entry into the dream world is imperative. Do not dismiss its strength, do not go lightly, do not go literally, and know how to find your way home. Too much time spent in the dream world leaves you disconnected in your daily world, wandering around in imagination without a ticket home or cognizant of the basic necessities and mutable, tangible demands of daily life. Take the journey dead seriously, but do not take yourself too seriously. Worlds other than the safari need you just as much. Keep balance and visit civilization a lot.

Most of all, distrust fixed interpretations. As Harry Wilmer, Jungian analyst and author, points out, any bag of tricks is suspect. Preface your interpretations with: *This is a way I currently understand this dream* . . . Otherwise, you risk turning your dream into a robot guru who dispenses unquestioned wisdom. When I do dramatic improvisations with friends and when I teach psychotherapy skills, I sometimes use gibberish games. For example, one student is the therapist; another, the client. Each talks in gibberish (nonsensical speech). A third student "interprets" into English what each is saying. The students always do remarkably well. Their interpretations are credible and creative. When I ask observers how they would have interpreted the words, answers vary widely, yet each has coherence and credibility. When I ask the two actors what they were "saying," their responses often differ. Closed-ended interpretation of subjective phenomena is risky. Listen with open ear and eye to the many intimations of heart and soul.

Some practices in this book presume the value of symbolic interpretation. Others provide ways to bring understanding from dreams into daily life. Others offer ways to nurture imagination. Still others focus on narrative threads that weave dream fabric. Many break out of story line (especially conventional story line), inviting you to experience your dream as poem, painting, myth, play, ritual, sculpture, or body experience. If you suspend disbelief and embrace each new approach as a possible lens, you can discover those practices that most enhance both your dream and waking lives.

2

Closer Than Breathing

Freeing Your Creativity for Dreamwork

THE SAME SOURCE:
THE CREATIVE ARTS AND DREAMING

All cultures value creativity and its expression through the arts. How strange, then, that we undervalue our individual needs to express ourselves creatively.

The food of and for the soul is our imagination. When we do not feed the soul, we die a little. Denying ourselves the fertile inner realm of visual, auditory, and kinesthetic imagery disconnects us from our deepest, most sensitive, and most solid sense of who we truly are. Image, metaphor, symbol, and myth carry and translate messages between outer and inner worlds, and among the different domains of our inner world—personal, cultural, and archetypal. The arts express, evoke, and mirror these inner images. By creating and contemplating simple art pieces, we can focus the energies of our personal and archetypal experiences.

Poetry and the arts come from the same source and illuminate the same interface as do dreams. Both derive from the formative power of the archetypes, which manifests to some extent in time/space and psyche in the form of images.

—Sylvia Brinton Perera
"Dream Design"

Sometimes it takes a traumatic event to bring us home to our imagination. For several years, I redirected my creativity away from painting, writing, and music into my teaching, graduate work, and psychotherapy practice. Then I had an extended illness for which there were no quick cures. Just as I was realizing that I probably needed to design my own healing program, I had a hammer dream! A *hammer dream* is one that has to make its message particularly obvious because I am being particularly dense. In this dream, I saw a college catalogue in which this class was listed: *The Chemistry and Alchemy of Poetry, Art, and Music*. The listing was illustrated with a photograph of a tall, elegant, mixed-metal sculpture. I felt in my bones that this dream was showing me in blunt terms that I needed to express myself creatively again. It seemed to be inviting me to heal body (chemical) and soul (alchemical) through creative pursuits—which for me had always been sources of joy. I enrolled in an art class the next day and others soon after. Reestablishing my creative pursuits became vital to my healing. And ever since, I have taken classes in painting, drawing, poetry, improvisation—but only with teachers who do not emphasize skill, performance, or product.

A question remained: How could I have let myself lose touch with these old passions? I noticed, too, that I was not alone in having neglected them. What happened to us?

A SPECIAL KIND OF ARTIST: THE NATURAL CREATIVITY OF CHILDHOOD

Creativity flows naturally in children. We were young; we took it for granted. It was as central to our early lives as breathing. We wanted a friend? Voila! A "pretend" friend. We wanted our stuffed animals to talk? They prattled endlessly. We wanted to sing, so we sang. We painted paper, each other, walls. We wanted to make up a story or change a story, so we did it—even tales about who really spilled the orange juice. We wanted to play-act with friends, so we improvised a play and used some hapless adults' best clothes before they caught us. We happily drew stick pictures of family or friends, giving them blue hair and a yellow face and finding them beautiful. We didn't think about whether our creations had aesthetic merit.

Most children have what Marie-Louise von Franz calls "no unconscious doubt" about their creativity, no barrier between impulse and expression. Children don't naturally wonder whether they have talent; they don't naturally

I certainly think you should listen to your dreams, take account of them, but don't be bound by "this is the way to interpret or decode your dreams" books. . . . Water means a different thing for somebody who doesn't like wine than it does to somebody who almost drowned as a kid.

—Clive Barker
In Naomi Epel's
Writers Dreaming

do things based on successful outcome. Outcome is not at issue. They embrace these activities with confidence, trust, and delight. They don't ask themselves, *Am I creative?* They just have fun and *are* creative.

What happened between childhood and adulthood? When did we lose our unfettered creativity? Few of us became full-time artists, writers, or dancers. And even though we might have developed avocations in the arts, we often negatively assessed, hid, or qualified our work. Somehow, we left our spontaneous, uncritical selves behind with toys and supple, young bodies.

I made a monster out of paper and glue. I gave it sex organs. My teacher sent me out of the room and told me I always did the wrong thing.

—Andrew

Was our creativity a shooting star in a summer sky? Did all our artistry channel itself into work and home, making us creative teachers, counselors, businesspeople, athletes, parents? Certainly creativity is needed in many adult arenas. But what happened to the creativity that didn't need to produce anything except its own delight, the creativity whose sole purpose was to express and delight us?

Unofficial initiation into adolescence usually included obeying overt or covert constraints: We were often rewarded—if not at home, then at school—for setting aside "childish" things, such as imagination and play, in order to attend to the "real" world of work and responsibility. Creative energies succumbed to negative comparison, to performance demands, to unhelpful comments from well-meaning adults bound by limited vision.

In every workshop and class I have led, participants remember teachers, family, or others who valued academic excellence to the exclusion of creative expression, who told them they had little or no creative potential in one or more artistic fields. These incidents forever clouded the

We were supposed to cut out pre-drawn shapes and stick them on cards for Valentines; but I picked up all the leftover paper off the floor and stuck it on the window in the shape of a tree. I got sent to the principal's office.
—Ingrid

children's self-perception. They learned the lesson well: to survive childhood, adapt where necessary. To a greater or lesser extent, they conformed, giving priority to behavior that would gain acceptance. If they did continue creative pursuits, they usually considered them extracurricular, coming after time with friends, homework, and family. Creative expression ceased to be an integral part of daily life and eventually became unnecessary or inaccessible. Many sacrificed imaginative freedom to the intense demands of families where hypervigilance was the only way to survive psychologically, where demands to be someone other than their natural selves were overwhelming and rewarding. Being intelligent, they adapted and became someone else. The natural, creative self went underground.

We need to unearth and restore this buried treasure no matter how deeply it lies under the rubble of adaptive self-concept and behavior.

Several years ago, I was fortunate to spend a month studying with master watercolorist and sculptor Nancy Graves. At times, we talked about our experiences as artist and psychotherapist and reiterated what others have noticed: the artist's experience of drawing from inner creative resources closely resembles the psychospiritual journey toward wholeness. Nancy observed that many great artists seemed to be psychological orphans; lacking a healthy childhood world, they had to create their own through their art.

Parents are human, extraordinary, and imperfect, so each of us has capacities that went untended or unrecognized in childhood. As adults, we need to create a world in which to care for the parts that fell by the wayside.

Alice Miller, psychoanalyst and writer on the long-lasting effects of parenting, describes her own journey to recover this childhood self. In the preface to a book of her own paintings, *Pictures of a Childhood*, she describes the failure of two long analyses to touch the forgotten experiences of the child she once was. It was not until she returned to the artistic pursuits she had buried in the face of her mother's harsh expectations that she found that child in hiding. She needed to give this "forgotten child of long ago the right to her own language and her own story" through painting.

By exploring our dreams through the creative arts, we can reconnect with our innate capacity to creatively express our inner worlds and widen the path to our soul.

PO-WA-HA: CREATIVITY AS A LIFE PROCESS

Rina Swentzell, an architect and Native American from Santa Clara Pueblo in New Mexico, explains that there is no word for art in her language, because Tewa people do not experience art as an activity separate from any other in life. The word that most closely approximates the artistic process is *po-wa-ha*, which translates as "water-wind-breath," the creative force that moves through the waters and the earth. For the Tewa, artistic creativity is closer than breathing; it is the spirit of life itself moving endlessly through its cycle. The potter making a pot does not need to separate herself from family life or make special time for her inner life; in creating art in the seamless context of her daily world, she is simply living her life! Being and doing are one, because she is experiencing the movement of life within her as it flows through hands and eyes.

The implications of this are simple and far-reaching:

Creativity from the source . . . the [Tewa word] po-wa-ha, literally "water-wind-breath." It is that energy that flows from everybody and everything—plants, stones. . . . In connection with the po-wa-ha there is still a special way of bringing the clay, of working with it, which takes you into a spiritual connection. You are an incredible part of the process that is still very satisfying and a very good thing to happen for whatever end it happens.

—Rina Swentzell
"The Butterfly Effect"

Every person is a special kind of artist. Children are treated as people who have all the capabilities of anything that's ever happened in the world. Creativity just begins to flow out of people. . . . And that's a really different sense of creativity— not creativity as a limiting or exclusive sort of thing, but as that idea in life which breaks through limits and limitations and flows through from the very source of life.

—Rina Swentzell
"The Butterfly Effect"

po-wa-ha is larger than you or I; *po-wa-ha* takes us back to the inexhaustible source of life itself; it connects us directly to the creative energy. For the Tewa, art is a process, not a product. There is a product, of course; however, to the traditional Tewa potter, the product is incidental—the experience, essential and always available. The real product is inner renewal, a sense of oneness with the life force.

Widespread Western attitudes toward the creative arts derive from beliefs contradictory to the Tewa's. Many people carry unexamined negative beliefs about their creativity, beliefs that leave them disconnected from self-expression. Their attitudes toward creativity often resemble their attitudes toward other sources of energy in life, such as time, love, money, and relationship. They believe they cannot generate enough to meet their needs and ideals. And too often, because they are blind to their own innate expressive capacities, they idealize talent in others.

For example, after a successful career, Ian had finally decided to make time to sculpt. It was now or never. He was entranced by and spoke frequently about several younger women artist friends whom he described as "incredibly creative." He deeply wished he could be as creative as they. I asked him what he imagined his experience with sculpting might be like. His response was frightening: "In my room, alone, struggling with stone and clay, resisting impulses to play golf, be with friends, relax with my family; burning the midnight oil, starting all over again. Wresting from my depths exquisite forms that will transform others . . ."

Small wonder he spent more time talking about his sculpting than sculpting! Who would want to engage in such an agonizing process? When Ian reflected more on *why* he wanted to sculpt, he saw that he had competing goals: to nourish his soul and to be recognized. He believed his goals could coexist but that only one could take priority.

As we talked further about his painful assumptions, my imagination (without my conscious consent, I might add) created a strange scenario in a matter of seconds: I saw Ian beside a sunlit river in early morning with young women who had priestly duties to perform, yet who were also laughing and carefree. I saw him walking down to the stream to pay them homage and offer help. As Ian and I had a solid and trusting working relationship, I told him what my imagination had invented while my conscious awareness was absorbing his dilemma. He wanted to explore the scenario. We came to see the women as Ian's muses, the energies of creativity *within* him. When he recognized that his muses were inside him, he realized that he had idealized their outer, unattainable form in his women friends and disowned the muses within. The good stuff and the joy of creating was beyond; all the inadequate stuff and the suffering was enveloping him.

Ian began to free himself from an assumption he learned early, along with tying his shoes and obeying the work ethic: that anything worthwhile is painful and difficult, and anything painful and difficult is worthwhile. As he freed himself, he began to see that living in service of these priestesses of the imagination could be an inner affair of utmost and daily delight. Ian eventually decided that recognition would have to be a side benefit if he were to engage in this work with spiritual integrity. He also saw that what he had seen as competing goals—nourishing his soul and being a recognized sculptor—could be subsumed

Dreams point to your back, to what you don't see, and you have to stand on your head . . . to understand your own dreams. That's the great difficulty. And that causes so many errors.

—Marie-Louise von Franz
In Fraser Boa's
The Way of the Dream

under and transcended by a third force, the reintegration of his own creativity.

Helen had a similar challenge. After experimenting for the first time with painting several watercolors based on her dreams, she had no further inspiration for weeks. She sadly resigned herself to a quick end to her watercolor experience. Yet she still hoped for one more strong dream image that might inspire her to paint. None came.

Eventually, she began to view her creative energies differently. She realized that she had been waiting for her creativity to present itself to her like the all-enfolding embrace of a loving parent who would always take care of her. Helen had thought that this was what "surrender," "trust," and "feminine consciousness" meant: passive waiting. After a period of introspection, she realized that, on the contrary, conscious surrender meant to *actively* wait, to *actively* feed this delicate, newborn capacity without attachment to its turning out the way she wanted.

Helen decided to make a covenant not only with her dreams but with her creativity. She decided to feed the work daily. She added doodling to her journal-keeping and carried oil pastels and a small notebook so she could idly draw, wherever she was. She fed her imagination without expectation. Eventually, watercolors emerged out of the doodles and sketches. She was delighted. Then, just as she was growing accustomed to doing watercolor, her creativity dictated a new direction and she found herself drawn to clay work. By then, she knew enough to trust her inner impulses and follow them.

Ian and Helen both accepted the challenge to feed, serve, and actively participate in their surrender. We need to make similar covenants with our creative energies, to

*. . . the soul
Remembering how she
felt, but what she felt
Remembering not,
retains an obscure
sense
Of possible sublimity.*
—William Wordsworth
Prelude, Book II

give without expectation of return. Serving the creative self means acknowledging it daily in small ways: noting the sheen of a leaf on the morning walk, recording the vanishing point of a dream, sketching a craggy face on the commuter train, humming the strange melody from childhood that plays over and over in the mind, following the movement that wants to emerge from the body or fingers as we listen to music.

It takes only an eyedropper full to feed the imagination.

AFTER THE SILENT GATHERING: THE CREATIVE CYCLE

The Tewa people are not alone in knowing that creativity and breathing are closely related. Both repeat the cycle of life itself: birth, life, death.

The first phase of breathing, *inspiration*, is the drawing in of the breath, of inspiration, of life. The second phase is a moment of pausing so that the fresh air and spirit exchange with the old. The third phase, *expiration*, is the release of the old breath, spirit, life, so that a new cycle can begin.

These cycles follow the natural cycles of creativity. In creative pursuits, we often assume that the only valuable force is the first—inspiration—because it is unmistakably "creative." However, creativity uses all three forces. We draw in our creativity, bring it into awareness. Moments of quiet or rest follow, when nothing seems to happen but much happens inside, out of awareness. This quiescence is followed by death, active surrender, release—either through completion, sacrifice, or transformation of a

Thus it is that after the silent gathering a breath arises, coming not from the outside, but from the center of the soul—sometimes a breath which is almost imperceptible, but compelling and powerful, through which everything is given in easiness and happy expansion; sometimes a gale bursting all of a sudden, through which everything is given in violence and rapture; sometimes the gift of the beginning of a song; sometimes an outburst of unstoppable words.

That is the phase of diastole, and of "inspiration" as it manifests in its most apparent and usually recognized forms.

—Jacques Maritain
Creative Intuition in Art and Poetry

project—so that the cycle can begin anew. Rina Swentzell explains that, for the Tewa, art is like a song: It must be released into the atmosphere—breathed out and released, not clung to or deified.

Breathing teaches us something else about our creativity. Breathing is the one activity in our bodies that can either be unconsciously or consciously regulated. When we meditate, sing, and speak, we consciously direct our breath; when we sleep and engage in daily activities, we leave breathing up to natural impulse; at still other times, we combine conscious and unconscious direction. So, too, with creative expression: There is an ever-changing balance between conscious and unconscious activity.

To breathe that po-wa-ha makes you the most of who you are. And that expression is the most essential thing in the world. To have that kind of connection is basically what the Pueblo world is about—or was about traditionally.

—Rina Swentzell
"The Butterfly Effect"

INTEGRATED CREATIVITY: ATTENDING TO THE FOUR PHASES OF CREATIVE WORK

Whereas pure creativity is the expression of the soul without conscious interference from ego-bound goals, those committed to psychospiritual development know that understanding when and how to move from conscious intent to unconscious freedom and back again is crucial.

Most practitioners of integrated creativity notice that their experience develops through four phases: an intentional departure from ordinary awareness, an inner journey into the imagination, a return to ordinary awareness, and a reflection on the journey.

The artist who paints extraordinary material in a drugged stupor may indeed be creative. However, this artist's creativity is operating in a psychological vacuum and has not been welcomed into the body or into consciousness. Overidentifying with or staying either in strategic artistry or complete unconsciousness during creative sessions diminishes the creator's ability to harness these experiences and learn from them. Such an artist becomes a prisoner in the strange realm of the gods instead of a free traveler.

What distinguishes integrated creativity from this artist's experience are the first and last phases. Other altered-state experiences, such as meditation, active imagination, and shamanic journeys, also require this kind of integration. So if you are committed to undertaking your inner journeys consciously, including journeys into dream arts, there are several important elements to which you will want to pay attention.

Set aside time and place. Create a protected and private context. Release yourself temporarily from normal awareness, from personality boundaries. Do this with respect for the power of the dream and other imaginal material that might arise. With intent and context set, undertake your creative work with your dream. Allow material from deep within to surface; commune with the symbol or image. Your whole person—and its creative tools—becomes a vehicle for the symbol or image to move from unconsciousness to consciousness, just as it does for all creators, both professional and lay. When you are ready to leave the inner realm, carefully allow the experience to come to a close and reenter "normal" awareness. This conscious completion and departure creates the distance from the experience that you need for later reflection, insight, and integration.

Both dreams and the ritual arts manifest and mediate transpersonal energies. Both are forms of enactment, expressing the depths of existence and the energies flowing from the source through life. . . . To use processes suggested by one to illuminate the other may permit us to relate to the dream in terms that do not lurch it from its matrix, yet facilitate and develop participant witnessing in the dreamer.

—Sylvia Brinton Perera
"Dream Design"

THE MOST OF WHO YOU ARE: LETTING GO OF GOALS, INTERPRETATION, AND JUDGMENT

But what can a man create if he doesn't happen to be a poet? . . . If you have nothing at all to create, then perhaps you create yourself.

—C. G. Jung
Collected Works

When you consciously decide to undertake an inner journey to explore your dreams creatively, do not set goals for how that journey will evolve or express itself. Let go of the need for certain outcomes, particularly those involving excellence, performance, or specific content. The mind provides apparent reasons and directions for what you are doing, but the soul provides the deeper reasons and directions. If you stay attached to the ostensible, you miss the real.

That momentary alignment of will and grace, of conscious intent and unconscious energy, requires detachment from goal. I once attended an art class with a teacher who talked incessantly. He would engage me just as I was beginning to contemplate and sketch the figure of the silent, patient model in front of me. Although I was frustrated, I would always stop and listen. One evening, I felt so helpless in the face of my compulsive politeness that I let go of my wish to do a good drawing and doodled absentmindedly as he talked. Suddenly, he interrupted his solipsistic flow and exclaimed, "Look at your drawing!" It was the most spontaneous piece I had done all quarter. I had finally let go of my attachment to making a good sketch and surrendered to the process.

In this kind of personal art work, jettison any idea that you can help yourself or others by interpreting, praising, or criticizing. These have no more place in this work than telling a mother that her child would look better with different colored eyes. These kinds of creative pieces and experiences are only for *being* with. The only helpful response is to nourish the imagination and the piece by associating other images to it and noticing what feelings it evokes in you. Leave a creative piece and its maker richer for exposure to your consciousness, not poorer. Constructive interpretation can often give a creator a momentary sense of being appreciated and understood. The long-term results of interpretation are less satisfactory, however; interpretation too often preserves the piece in intellectual formaldehyde when it could have led a long and vibrant life.

Even positive comments (your own or others') contaminate this kind of creative experience. Why not praise? Because one end of the praise continuum evokes the other. When we receive praise or criticism for a personal expression that was never meant to be a performance, we unconsciously use self-deprecation to try to restore a state of equilibrium in which we are neither too impressed nor depressed by our performance. In trying to rebalance, we forget that we should not be evaluating at all.

As I was writing this, some children came to my door. They showed me colorful paper flowers and drawings they had made. Clearly they had delighted in making them. Then they told me each piece cost three cents. Did I help or hinder their pleasure in their creativity by "buying" one from each? Perhaps this street-sale creativity marks the beginning of their departure from pure joy into performance concerns. Perhaps, at their age, they are still so in touch with their creativity that asking for three cents doesn't detract from the intrinsic joy in the making. Yet perhaps not.

Adults are even more at risk than children in this regard. Ellen was painting a dream in a simple way when her neighbor, who was passing by her open door, commented, "What a beautiful painting." Ellen felt momentarily

Only when I make room for the voice of the child within me do I feel myself to be truly genuine and creative. I use every means now at my disposal . . . to help this child to find the appropriate way of expressing herself and to be understood. . . . I have been able to give the silent child of long ago the right to her own language and her own story.

—Alice Miller
Pictures of a Childhood

pleased, and then immediately experienced silent, painful self-criticism that negated the neighbor's comment. Her mind repeated its old songs: *She's saying it to be nice. It's awful . . . No one tells you the truth. You're a fake.* Ellen needed to better protect the vulnerability that her creative side engendered. "I was wide open when I was painting. When my neighbor praised me, I felt exposed, silly." What Ellen did with these painful feelings was wise, however. She painted them—big black circles and red X's—until her divided focus reunified and she could return to the original work.

This whole realm of symbol connects consciousness and unconsciousness. It's the realm of poetry, the whole extension of the soul—music, architecture, painting, sculpting—all the arts.
—Marion Woodman
Dreams: Language of the Soul

I often encourage people not to prepare what they want to talk about during a therapy session. When they can accommodate spontaneity, they sometimes begin with a dream or image or make passing reference to a metaphor as they describe their feeling state. Usually, the image reappears elsewhere in the session, often without their being aware. The unplanned, repeated image is a gift from the unconscious, and there is usually a moment when it is ready to reveal itself to consciousness. Christopher, for example, arrived at a session wearing black and white, recorded a dream about laying a black-and-white floor, and then related an intense story about a situation requiring him to act in a way that he viewed as either all right or all wrong. When I eventually mentioned the black-and-white theme, he started laughing and saw, without my belaboring it, how his unconscious had already been showing him how he had been restricting his responses.

Just as the prepared session leaves little room for discovery, so does overplanned creative work around dreams—or other images. Discovering a repeated image, metaphor, or symbol is usually satisfying and energizing—

no matter how shocking. We see how our unconscious has more insight, more coherence than we thought. Observe these recurring images, ideas, colors, shapes, and textures without judgment. The soul is making itself known to you through your unique mythology. Images nourish you and your journey. They are wellsprings of wisdom when contemplated. Their efficacy and longevity, however, lie in preserving some of their mystery. Take away all their mystery and you take away their power and life. Experience. Do not evaluate.

Dreams, creative expression, and soul are inseparable. They operate in an endless cycle. Each plays a crucial role in your inner life. Each needs, nourishes, and leads into the other. Treat each with the quiet, curious, and loving respect it deserves.

3

A Map for the Journey
Traveling Alone and Accompanied

"A FREE AND SHELTERED SPACE:" PREPARING YOURSELF FOR CREATIVE EXPLORATION

The Greek word *psyche* means "butterfly." It is also denotes "soul." Dreams give your soul wings. And images from dreams are the exquisite patterns on the wings. Hold your dream as you would hold a butterfly—in your open, quiet palms. Make sure none of the delicate wing dust brushes off onto clumsy hands. Pinning the dream down with interpretation will tear the wings off the butterfly and kill it. We can put the dead butterfly under glass, study it, admire its uniqueness, and also let others admire it (if they like butterflies). But it will never, never, never fly again. Hold your dream images gently enough so that they can still fly.

We have a dream experience. Then we reconstruct the dream in memory. Still later, we use words to represent the memory of the dream. The actual dream gets farther and farther away. Language reduces dreams from several dimensions to just two, and customarily reduces perception to linear descriptions of past, present, and future.

So often, we treat the words as though they are the dream. Sometimes, they are vitally connected to the life force of the dream. More often, they are a pale and flat record of a rich and timeless experience. We are used to using this one artistic medium (words) in one particular form (story) to express dreams. However, there are other, more flexible ways to "re-member" and express dreams than conventional storytelling. We can express them in the art form that best suits them, in the art form whose structure is most akin to their innate structure.

When we can loosen our attachment to the linear structure of the sentence by exploring cross-cultural arts, we

I love that story about the old [Pueblo Indian] woman who [when asked about how she learned to be creative] says, "First of all I would feed cornmeal of all colors to the butterflies. . . ." To watch and do or to be like the butterflies . . . think about the way in which butterflies make themselves beautiful. Human beings might learn from them— whether butterflies themselves do it, or butterflies allow who they are to come through them.

—Rina Swentzell
"The Butterfly Effect"

open ourselves to new ways of nourishing and being nourished by our dreams.

SETTING CONTEXT FOR CREATIVE DREAMWORK

A dream that is not understood remains a mere occurrence; understood it becomes an experience.

—C. G. Jung
Collected Works

Dora Kalff, Jungian analyst and developer of sand play therapy, described this optimal environment in which unconscious images can emerge, pattern themselves, and transform as "a free and sheltered space." Creative dreamwork needs a similar temporal, physical, and psychological environment. It needs right time, right place, and right state of consciousness.

Given your already full life, can you provide these? It is a challenge, but possible. The unconscious usually doesn't require much in order to open up; it has learned to settle for less than optimal, even if you haven't!

The physical space you choose needs to be as private as possible. Find a space in the garage or a small space in the family room or bedroom that you can declare your own. Alan, for example, lived in a small, two-bedroom apartment with his wife and young son. He tried working in a small space in the living room. At the end of his first session, his son walked by and said disparagingly: "Dad, your hands aren't even dirty!" His son was right. Alan had set up this place with several provisos: He couldn't permit himself or the surroundings to get grubby. He was asking his uncensored creativity to emerge in heavily censored conditions. The next evening, at his son's suggestion, he spread plastic over the floor of his son's bedroom and halfway up the walls, and, together, they took turns making a mess! If, like Alan, you don't have a permanent space, buy yourself large, cheap trays and plastic to cover a floor area.

In minutes, you can bring trays out of storage, lay down plastic, and create work space.

Now that you have space, you can attend to the rest of the environment. Turn down your phone; don't even listen to it ring while you work—this is a time for which your answering machine was designed! The more quiet you have, the better you can unfetter your imagination. When you have reduced the noise level, consider whether you would like to listen to music. If you live in a small space or with others, use or borrow a tape recorder with earphones. Choose contemplative music to play while you work. I once took my Walkman and music tapes to a figure-drawing class. I was delighted with how my body's response to the music changed the way I drew. The lines of the drawing moved the way the music did.

When you set up your space, plan on using more than one medium during one session. Leave easily accessible: paper and pencils for writing, paints or crayons for sketching, clay for modeling, a tape recorder for verbal notations, and old magazines and glue for collage.

The element of play puts us in our true selves. Play takes us back to how we can be.

—June Matthews, Child Studies Seminar, C. G. Jung Institute, San Francisco, 1993

EXPLORING ALONE: CONTEMPLATIVE PLAY

Better to do five minutes of something than *not* do twenty!

The creative practices in this book have been designed for simplicity and completion in as short or as long a period of time as you wish. Sometimes, when I look in a bookstore at workbooks on art or self-development, my imagination runs wild. It runs so wild and ahead of itself that I complete the project in my head in a few breaths. I have already *made* that beautiful journal from hand-pressed paper; already laid my body out on newsprint, drawn all around it, and colored it in with eerie colors (that would in reality, necessitate several trips to the crafts store); already gone to the ocean and made that life-sized symbol in the sand. If I allow my leaping intuition to rule me, I am sunk. I promise myself a wonderful experience whose experimental logistics are designed for those with more time than I—for those who don't do household tasks, earn a living, spend time with family or friends, exercise, or just vegetate without guilt at regular intervals.

This book assumes that you would probably like to spend more time exploring your dreams than you do or can and that you don't want to spend much money or time buying supplies. Most of the practices, too, can be completed in less than fifteen minutes or can be expanded into a longer session, should you wish or should the dream demand. Refer to the time estimates in the appendix so that you can choose a practice that fits your time frame or plan the time you want to devote to a particular practice.

The purpose of spending more time is not to perfect your work. Neither the soul nor the dream responds in proportion to the linear time you spend on it, so there is no inherent virtue in allocating endless periods to your dreams. "More time" does not necessarily affect quantity or outcome, but the quality of the experience: more nourishment for the dream, for the image, for the soul; a more relaxed and contemplative approach; the probability of deeper integration. You are accountable to no one other than yourself for the time you spend on these practices. Allocate what you have and bring your full attention, even if just for five minutes.

Many North American Indian tribes . . . attach great significance to dreams. Of special significance . . . were guardian-spirit dreams. . . . Guardian spirit dreams are also found in other parts of the world. For example . . . a young man [of the Sea Dyak tribe of Borneo] who does desire such a spirit guardian, will attend to his quest in much the same fashion as does the Plains Indian youth. The young Dyak will deliberately detach himself from the group, fast in seclusion, and await the response of his guardian spirit in dreams.

—Carl W. O'Nell
Dreams, Culture, and the Individual

Play First, Work Later!

Making creative dreamwork the reward for having done everything else you were supposed to do leads to instant defeat. If possible, do it first—for instance, early in the morning. Feed your soul first; then you will do less-replenishing things with better grace, a fuller heart, and more presence.

Some people work at paint or clay or music—anything to say "yes" to the soul.

—Marion Woodman
Dreams: Language of the Soul

Warm Up

Writing, painting, and sculpting use the whole body; the hands are just the final extension of a whole-body response. As you begin your session, stretch arms, legs, torso, neck, fingers, and facial muscles. There's no need to "dance." Just move freely to music. The music might take you to the ocean, up onto a cloud, into the jungle, or to a formal French garden. Welcome these images. Words or sounds might also come. Watch them come and go. Don't hold on to them. They are bright-eyed, darting fish in the fast-flowing stream of consciousness.

Use Unfamiliar Media and More Than One at Once

Arnold Mindell, trained as a Jungian analyst and now the originator of Process Work, reminds us that the more sense channels through which we absorb an experience, the more chance it has of being integrated into consciousness and the more fully we are able to live it. Verbal description helps to move the insights into waking consciousness, but not all insights are verbal. We do not need a cognitive, coherent, verbal presentation of dream wisdom for it to work its healing. So moving from one medium to another is also crucial to free-flowing creative dreamwork. For example,

Susanne Langer has introduced a distinction . . . between representational symbolism, best illustrated by language and most formalized in mathematics, and the presentational forms of symbolism that predominate in the expressive arts and apparently (less formalized and finished, of course) in at least some dreams.

—Harry T. Hunt
The Multiplicity of Dreams

by translating the image and feeling of the dream into a body sensation and then transferring this into an abstracted visual form with color and gesture, the dream transforms through different sense channels, giving us several opportunities to nonverbally absorb the experience.

Choose media in which you are *not* competent. When you use a familiar medium, you run the risk of confining yourself to old habits and of becoming too self-critical. Each medium is a fine teacher, with subtle lessons for certain times. Watercolors teach about the mutable elegance of water as it is made visible through color; they teach about letting go, about the uniqueness and evanescence of the moment. Oils teach about the luscious, substantial flow of color; they teach trust in being able to change direction midstream without apology; they teach patience while they dry over weeks. Pastels teach about blending of color, about responsiveness and delicacy; they are also forgiving, allowing rework and change of intuitive direction from moment to moment without fear of retaliation.

I am unrepentantly fickle when it comes to the arts. I have fallen in love with musical instruments, fat tubes of thalo blue watercolor, fragrant green tea rice paper, a person-sized sumi brush. The fortunate thing about falling in love with media is that they are faithful. They hang around quietly until I am ready to be with them again. They don't lie about their capacities. They understand that I love them all. They accompany me into the unknown without criticism or praise.

Use Your Nondominant Hand Occasionally

On days when your self-judgment is thriving and criticizing everything, use your nondominant hand. This shift removes any possibility of your being invested in performance, competency, or outcome. It also makes you more aware of how you use your hands and arms and takes you back to the childhood sense of the enormousness of things like crayons and pencils. It invites you into body awareness in the present.

Treat Your Completed Work with Respect

Date the piece, title it, and sign it. As soon as you have finished it, make notes on the back or on a separate page about your experience of making it. Then photograph the piece. Later, put photographs and notes in a portfolio (see "Creating a Dream Portfolio") so that you have an evolving record. Many people find this to be central to their experience. They gain new perspectives when they see their work through the lens of the camera.

Leave Work Visible and Protected for Contemplation

Images that emerge from deep in the unconscious sustain special energy for a long time. On their odd wings, they carry secret messages to personal awareness. Often it takes daily contemplation—even as you walk by them—to comprehend their messages. Choose places to leave your pieces out. Meditate on your work with eyes half open in a still gaze. Play with the retinal patterns the lines and colors make, with eyes open, then closed.

Make "display" space as private as possible. If necessary, hang a sign: NO COMMENTS PLEASE, GOOD OR BAD; NONARTISTIC DREAMER AT WORK! It's a reminder for you, too.

Some of the Indians from the Colorado River Basin attribute great significance to the dream. The Mojave look to the dream for validation of cultural change. The Yuma believe that the dream reveals whatever has happened or will happen in human experience. In both cultures, dreams constitute an important mechanism, if not the most important, for legitimizing religious belief and practice, interpreting tradition, creating new expressions in song and dance, confirming shamanistic power and curing ability, and validating authority in individuals.

—Carl W. O'Nell
Dreams, Culture, and the Individual

INTERSECTING WORLDS:
SHARING DREAMS WITH TRUSTED OTHERS

There are two schools of thought on telling dreams: One says we should and one says we shouldn't. The Senoi people pay such communal respect to dreams that they tell them to each other regularly. Our society rarely has time for or values this kind of gift. How many of us have friends, family, children who are going to pay rapt attention to our fuzzy sagas in preference to reading the comics over breakfast? Although our dreams are of interest to us, they are rarely actively valued by anyone else except our dream group or therapist.

Telling a dream to an unreceptive or insensitive audience is like feeding pâté to a puppy; it's a waste of good spiritual food and diminishes dream and dreamer. When I was in Nugini, many villagers were wary of my camera, believing their spirits might be captured and whisked away. And though their reasons for not wanting their photograph taken might evolve from a different world view from ours, they were wise in wanting to protect their souls. Be wary of letting unappreciative people snap up your dream and either dismiss it, ride over it roughshod, or analyze it to death (usually in their best interests, not in yours).

I shudder when I see people in large workshops share intimate, important dreams. Right atmosphere, respect, and understanding are rarely present. Most people have not learned to listen to others' dreams with enough sensitivity to accept their individual, community, and cultural value. Be cautious. You can rarely go wrong by not sharing your dream, but you can often lose its spirit or energy by telling it too soon or to the wrong person. Although you might love your partner, family, and friends dearly, they are not

I was naturally much interested in the natives' dreams, but at first could not get them to tell me any. . . . I suspect the reason was fear . . . that harm may come to them from anyone who has knowledge of their dreams.

—C. G. Jung
Memories, Dreams, Reflections

automatically the most sensitive audience for your dreams. Here are some criteria for sharing dreams with others—either one person or a group:

- Do the receivers really want to hear?
- What do I want from sharing it? Have I been explicit?
- If I just want a receptive audience, have I been clear about that?
- Do these people have a lived sense of the reality of the inner world?
- Do these people have a developed sense of the symbolic realm, or will they take my dream literally (or personally)?
- Do they really have time to hear my dream and reflect on it?
- Am I willing to hear their dreams as well? Do I want to? If not, is it acceptable that one of us might tell and one might not?
- Have we all set a considerate context in which to do this, or are we finishing up lunch in a noisy restaurant, driving in commuter traffic, or rushing somewhere?
- Do these people know anything about dream theories and creative approaches to dreaming? Does that matter to me?
- Does it matter that they share the same approach to dreaming that I do?
- Can they keep my dreams confidential?

Setting the Context for Sharing Dreams with One Person

Sometimes you will be fortunate enough to be able to explore your dreams with one special person: your spouse, partner, close friend. Sharing dreams with one valued person adds spice to the soup that requires careful handling! So, in addition to the criteria just listed, you can consider following these basic guidelines:

- Set aside ten minutes for each dream.
- Alternate going first.
- Ensure a quiet, uninterrupted environment. Answering a telephone call or doorbells disrupts the flow of attention and the capacity to imaginatively enter the other's world.
- Be in harmony before you begin. If you are at odds with each other, don't exchange dreams. Your partner will be tempted to receive the dream more like a surrendered weapon than a delicate newborn.
- If you believe that a dream can offer a peaceful solution to a current difficulty with your partner, share the insight first. Follow later with the dream.
- Save discussion of dreams for this time only and refrain from either telling new dreams or commenting on earlier ones at other times. There are always exceptions, but be sure that you both agree about them. Otherwise, it renders the time set aside less precious.

Exploring Rather Than Interpreting Your Partner's Dream

Interpretation itself is delicate, skilled, and uncertain surgery, even in experienced hands. If your only goal is to gain insight into daily life, you will probably focus on co-ordinate points between waking and dreaming states—an approach that bypasses most archetypal and cross-cultural approaches. If you want clues for waking life, then, by

Dreams are . . . important to Mayans . . . and public dream narration and interpretation are commonly practiced. All over the Mayan region it is routine to awaken one's spouse, or other sleeping companion, in the middle of the night in order to narrate a dream . . . and in some communities mothers ask their children about their dreams every morning. . . . Among adults, important dreams are shared with initiated shamans who are dream interpreters.

—Barbara Tedlock
"The Role of Dreams and Visionary Narratives in Mayan Cultural Survival"

all means, look for them, but don't take dream "clues" literally. Dreams can't be literal; they can *appear* logical and causal and related to daily life—but so can a film. Dreams can be analogical, metaphorical, alchemical, and all kinds of other *-als*, but they won't ever be lite*ral*, so beware of taking concrete advice from a dream figure. And even if you're fortunate enough to have a prophetic dream, it's unlikely that you'll know it. So, insatiable curiosity, creativity, and humility are the best guides.

If you wish to do more intrapsychic and analytic work with your own and others' dreams, make sure you agree upon and are well versed in a particular approach, such as Jungian or Gestalt. In dreamwork, a little knowledge spread thinly is dangerous and much knowledge laid on too heavily is suffocating. Both accord false authority to the interpreter, and diminish dreamer and dream.

Better still, unless you are in a group devoted to working with dreams in a defined context with clear parameters, eschew interpretation. Rather, develop a series of questions along the lines of the following, questions that help a dreamer go more deeply. You and your dream partner or group can ask each other such questions. Clearly, you won't ask all. (Some dreams take ten minutes in the telling!)

- What was the feeling with which you awoke?
- What questions do you have about the dream now?
- Do you have any immediate sense of a message or situational reading from the dream?
- How might you explore this dream creatively? What media might you use to explore this dream further?
- What are the most arresting images in this dream for you?

In the presentational side of symbolism . . . meaning resides directly in the felt qualities and rhythm of the expressive medium—to the point where material in the visual arts, poetry and music and certain imageries in altered states of consciousness . . . resist any full or complete narrative formulation. Presentational meanings . . . depend on a full and even contemplative experiencing of the formal qualities of the expressive medium, . . . a "receptive mode" involved in meditation and contrasting with . . . ordinary language use.

—Harry T. Hunt
The Multiplicity of Dreams

- What are your strongest associations to any of the objects or people in this dream?
- Do any of the objects or people seem to symbolize something to you? If so, what might they symbolically evoke cross-culturally, archetypally?
- What would your title for this dream be?
- What would you most like me to remember about this dream?

Small dream work is no high art, filled with masterful insight and Olympian-sized success for either interpreter or dreamer. To work with small dreams, one must cultivate humility and the ability to tinker, to seize the opportune moments. We must, as Rilke said of the artist, ". . . learn to love the enigma."

—Stephen A. Martin
"Smaller Than Small,
Bigger Than Big"

Choose questions that encourage you and the dreamer to hold the dream respectfully. Once again, remember to receive without judgment, without clever interpretation, but with quiet attention, curiosity, and caring dispassion. Too often, it is easy for us to unconsciously drive points home that we have been wanting to make. ("I see a weight issue in this dream. . . ." "*Hmm*, forgetting things again? . . ." "I *thought* your sexual attention was elsewhere! . . ." "I *knew* you were upset about that dinner party—see it's right there!") If you are going to treat your partner's dreams with the respect they deserve, you won't use them to benefit your position in the relationship.

Receive the dream as a human gift. It doesn't matter how dark or how bright the dream is. It is still a gift of trust and imagination given to you from another's inner life, an opportunity to walk in your partner's inner world for a few moments. In certain improvisation games, participants practice being grateful for whatever wild opportunities are thrown their way by fellow actors. This attitude of active receptivity is crucial. Appreciate what your partner has given, no matter how hard, boring, scary, or disconcerting listening to it was for you. You are being given a unique creation—just like a painting, sculpture, or poem.

MAKING A PLACE FOR THE UNIQUE AND THE UNIVERSAL: FORMING A DREAM ARTS GROUP

A paradox of the inner path is that the more individualized and individuated our responses become to our experience, the more universal they seem to become. Think of poetry you have read or paintings you have seen: both reflect one person's experience of the world as well as a universal truth. When we receive, copy, or merge our experiences with others', we end up with stereotypical images; when we accept our uniqueness, we vitalize archetypal images.

So sharing our uniqueness with others provides them and us with ways to connect on a universal level. Talking about dreamwork with a group of trusted others reminds us of wider, deeper dimensions of human experience. Dream arts groups can be successful with as few as three people or as many as ten. When we talk simply and honestly about what we are learning from our own experience, others also learn. Even when we describe something painful, talking about it *with dignity and self-respect* can be deeply healing for others as well as for us. I have seen group members talk in one meeting about creative pieces that came from dreams they associated with joy, humor, death, abortions, shame, separations, guilt, playfulness, healing, confusion, and fears. The members' willingness to accept all experiences and their loving observation of their own humanity allows all member participants to view themselves with dignity and to remember that pain and joy may be drawn from separate wells but spring from a common artesian river.

Find fellow explorers to form a group. If you are seriously interested in forming a group to explore dreams through

A thousand and one reasons occur to you for not working on your dreams today, especially after your first enthusiasm has waned. Thus it is important to work on dreams together with others. . . . With their help, your habitual consciousness can stay with images that it would otherwise flee from in subtle ways.

—Robert Bosnak
A Little Course in Dreams

If merely writing out and interpreting one's dreams over time can change them . . . how much more might dreaming be transformed in . . . [tribal] societies, as the public mirror of personal and social concerns?

—Harry T. Hunt
The Multiplicity of Dreams

creative expression or some other approach, do some reading on dream groups in addition to what I outline. Robert Bosnak's *A Little Course in Dreams* has sound guidelines for groups. Then find four to six like-minded peers who wish to explore together.

Give the group a ritual form. Establish a two-hour period to meet weekly or bimonthly at a regular time (the unconscious seems to like regular rhythms). The beginning of your time together can be simple—sitting in a circle in silence or listening to quiet music for two minutes helps everyone quiet themselves and focus. The ending can repeat the opening. It doesn't have to be complicated. It simply needs to be there. Without an ending, the group can take longer to shift mood, feelings, and attention from the inner world to the outer.

How do you structure the time in the middle? Plan it however your group wishes. Your group might like to consider some of the following approaches. Of course, the format needs to simplify with increasing numbers.

Use many response levels. Working with a group that is exploring creative expression both deepens and broadens possibilities for interaction. When you sit and talk with one other person, there is only one avenue for learning: your mutual interaction. When you meet and share creative work with a group, you can choose to respond to the art piece itself, to its creator, and/or to the whole group.

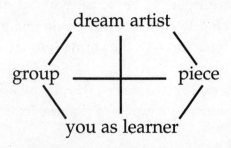

Practice loving acceptance and nonjudgment. Your group is not engaging in psychotherapy, dream therapy, art therapy, or art criticism. However, you can attend to the inventiveness, mystery, wisdom, and humor of dreams. Your group can focus on ways to integrate dream material. Knowing that this is neither therapy nor an art class can free you; there is nothing for you to *do* with someone's pain, puzzlement, or joy other than to acknowledge, accept, and hold it with loving respect. Retain a spirit of nonjudgmental receptivity, respectful curiosity, openness, and appreciation. Clearly, if someone seems at risk, help him or her find professional assistance.

When you listen to or watch other group members share something, receive them and their work with an attitude of loving acceptance and nonjudgment. This sounds difficult, but, with few exceptions, group members are amazed at how their capacity for nonjudgment is evoked by someone else's speaking truthfully from the heart. Something about dreams and the arts evokes larger responses from us, regardless of our limitations.

Establish a framework. At your first meeting, determine clear guidelines for your group work.

Be confidential. Agree at the beginning that everything shown or discussed in the group is private and will not be discussed elsewhere without explicit permission.

Take turns. Ensure that everyone has an opportunity to share pieces.

Allocate time when appropriate. Check at the beginning of each meeting how many people would like to share pieces or speak.

Respect diffidence and quietness. Feel free not to bring or share something, and accord others the same freedom.

A story in Africa may last three months. The storyteller relates it night after night, continually, or s/he starts it one night and takes it up again from that point three months later. Meanwhile, as the occasion rises, s/he may start on yet another story. Such is life.

—Trinh Minh-ha
Woman Native Other

Share the experience as well as the content. Talk about the process of making a piece as well as the content. Sometimes the process was effortless but the content painful; sometimes the process was difficult and the content full of delight.

Feel free to share dream art pieces without commentary. Don't push someone who wishes to show a piece of dream art without talking.

Feel equally free to discuss the experience without sharing content. Sometimes you might want to talk about the experience of making something, but neither show it nor talk about the dream because it still feels too private. Trust your reticence. If your intuition tells you a piece needs to gestate before sharing it, wait longer. Trust your timing.

Don't withhold out of shame. Feeling ashamed of a piece, however, is no reason to withhold it. Paint the shame, sculpt it, talk about it—do anything rather than identify with it.

Ban spoken and unspoken praise and criticism. When you focus on another group member's piece, don't even silently praise or criticize it. Oddly, when one is engaging in silent assessment of another, the other picks up a "performance aroma" and begins to self-deprecate. Moreover, withholding judgment from others is good practice for that harder task: withholding judgment from your own work. When judgment arises spontaneously, watch it and let it go. Judgment is a habit.

Never apologize. Never preface your work with apologies. Don't apologize after, either.

Ask for what you would like. Invite the group to respond to your work in one of the ways suggested, or ask them simply to receive it in silence. You might have brought a

The Iriquois . . . had special dreams that they interpreted as messages for the group. Most such dreams were believed to originate with mythological beings or cultural heroes who were protecting the interests of their people. Even a very ordinary person could have such a dream.

—Carl W. O'Nell
Dreams, Culture, and the Individual

dream painting of difficult events that are almost too hot for you to handle. You might just manage to share the work, but it would be too much to talk about it. This is good judgment. In an informal group without a professional facilitator, it is wiser to say too little than regret having said too much. Never ask for critical feedback, positive or negative. If criticism is asked of you, gently remind the asker of the purpose of the group.

Offer a variety of responses where appropriate. There are several responses you can offer. Remember that the presenter is the center of the group's attention right then; if the presenter's piece reminds you of something in your own life, only talk about it in a way that respects the current focus on the *presenter's* experience. You could also thank the presenter for putting words or images to something you have experienced but not articulated. Certain responses can help presenter, piece, and group:

- *Associate to the piece.* Give the creator three descriptive, sensate adjectives that come to mind as you look at the work. These are not adjectives of praise or criticism but ones that describe a mood or movement, for example, "sinewy," "flowing," "jagged," "bright."

- *Allow others' imagery to nurture yours.* Allow other dreamers' pieces to jog your sensitivities about your own dreams and experiences—do they help you understand yourself better? For example, "Until I saw your sculpture of that demon, I never thought demons could have a comic side. I'll look at mine anew now!"

- *Add your imagination (not interpretation) to the piece.* Does it look like something—a forest? a mask?

[Jung] rightly felt that the reality of the soul is eruptive and dangerous. His warnings are important. But the fact that something is dangerous doesn't mean it should be avoided. The soul has been professionalized by psychotherapy. I'm all for taking back this dangerous territory. Dream groups are helpful because we can catch each other when we fall. . . . Danger demands careful, slow approaches, not a turning away. . . . I would suggest to anybody who uses active imagination in dream work with groups not to push too hard.

—Robert Bosnak
In Michael V. Adams's "Image, Active Imagination, and the Imaginal Level"

If the dream artist is willing—and only if:

- *"Dance" the piece as a group—that is, move to it.* Follow its lines or let its mood move you.
- *"Sing" the piece as a group.* Even paintings can be "sounded" if you put your rational mind aside—it won't sound harmonious but it will generate energy! Again, let your voice follow the lines or express the mood of the piece.

Read poems twice. If a dreamer has written a poem, invite someone else to read the poem a second time so that the writer can hear its cadence and rhythm afresh. This is a gift to the writer and surprisingly moving. Invite the writer to read the poem, also, in his or her native language if it is not the first language of the group. The speaker can usually feel much more at one with the message and mood of the poem in his or her first language.

Don't compare—even internally! Professional artists use others' work to inspire, not to discourage themselves! They plagiarize with proud abandon and in the most honorable of traditions!

Make room for silent appreciation. Don't say something for the sake of speaking. If you have a feeling with no words to accompany it, just say so. When we are vulnerable presenters, we sniff out insincerity or forced comments like old bones! Some of the most receptive moments are moments of absolute quiet after a presentation. Don't fill them!

Pay full attention. Do give the creator the gift of your attention. Receptivity, respect, nonjudgment, and active, unspoken acceptance create the charged atmosphere through which the transpersonal can quietly permeate. In

Interpretation of dreams and their associations is familiar to all [Senoi] adults and an essential part of bringing up children. The daily dream clinic opens at breakfast time when the male adults of the family interrogate and interpret dreams. Subsequently the men of the community gather to report, analyze and discuss their own dreams.

—Kilton Stewart
"Dream Theory
in Malaya"

this atmosphere, each of you can hear the other speak for you in a quite uncanny way.

Don't allocate turns. Let whoever feels like going next present next. Going around in a circle heightens anxiety and encourages rehearsing.

Acknowledge and provide transition. Always acknowledge a presenter for bringing and/or talking about a piece. Then allow a moment's silence to change focus from one person and mood to the next.

Treat yourself with the same care and respect as you treat other members. Give your dream art the same respect, impartiality, and loving interest you give others'. This is a far cry from cold dispassion, disdain, or objectivity; it is also a far cry from overinvolvement or overidentification. This is a spiritual practice. Whether alone or in a group, you have a responsibility to be your own compassionate witness!

4

Stepping into the Unknown
Drawing from and Nourishing
Your Imagination

CREATING A DREAM PORTFOLIO: PRESERVING DREAMS IN VISUAL AND VERBAL FORM

Intrigued at the magical reality of my night life, I began to record my dreams when I was eleven. They told me stories, gave me images that comforted and intrigued. For twenty years, I kept them in small notebooks—many kept while traveling. The containers varied in size and quality. And each had a history.

In more recent years, I felt confined by lined books and paper that made it difficult to draw, so I bought spiral-bound, blank books. Then I moved to blank sheets that I later placed in a binder. This less structured format gave me more flexibility. I could write large or small. I could interweave associations with recording. I could add poems. I could doodle or draw.

Three-ring binders work well. If these are too expensive, you can use manila folders. In this way, you can keep odd pieces of paper and table napkins as well as the dreams you have written by hand, typed, or printed out. Clear plastic sleeves can hold odd bits of paper. You will probably go in and out of being well organized. Sometimes pages can pile up for weeks or you can't be bothered doing anything with them. Date these fragments and pages; otherwise, you will have no idea how to order them later. It's inconsequential to anyone else, but it will matter to you.

Title your dreams and start each dream on a new page. It's easier to experiment with such groupings if dreams are separate. Sometimes you might wish to group dreams by subject, symbol, or image. Leave space between lines and after each dream. Leaving space underneath lets you write or draw associations and note anything you, your

The Chinese contemplative painter becomes one with Things, not to be carried along by their generative torrent, but to seize upon their own spirit. He draws them in; he suggests their spiritual meaning, leaving aside the whole glut of sense-satiating, flesh-and-blood forms and colors, luxuriant detail, or ornament; he endeavors to make Things more impressively themselves, on his silk or paper, than they are in themselves, and to reveal at the same time their affinities with the human soul; he enjoys their inner beauty, and leads the beholder to divine it.

—Jacques Maritain
Creative Intuition in Art and Poetry

group, or therapist might imagine about your dream. A friend of mine records her dreams in black with large spaces between lines. She later adds in turquoise possibilities that she and/or her analyst generate. Keep blank paper available for paintings, mandalas, and doodles that you might use to record or express the feeling of the dream.

Photograph your dream projects, if you can. If a two-dimensional piece is small, you can simply slip it into a three-hole plastic sleeve or glue it to a larger three-hole piece of paper and clip it in. Small pieces can disappear in the Sargasso Sea of the garage or spare room, however, so it's helpful to include a photograph right in your portfolio. If the painting is large, definitely photograph it.

Start a new dream portfolio whenever you run out of room. Dreams are not concerned about whether the new year is beginning or not. Note the beginning and ending dates on the inside of the binder.

So long as we turn to dreams as a primary source for inner exploration, we owe them what we owe other valued friends and esteemed teachers: loving attention, commitment, and constancy. Keeping a portfolio can provide an excellent opportunity to value our dreams in this way.

BEYOND STRAIGHT LINES: A NEW WAY TO WRITE

A woman showed me her dream journal one day. Her elegant, small script was laid out diagonally across the page. "I'm writing about my waking life horizontally and my dreaming life diagonally!" she declared with a creative freedom that delighted me. What a simple yet vivid way to acknowledge that dreams operate on a unique time line that can intersect our waking lives!

Just as we tend to tell stories within a linear framework, we also usually write dreams in horizontal lines. Some people even apologize to me for the messiness of their paper scraps—as though they are half expecting me to give them a demerit. I, too, often behave like a good elementary school child, taking my visual cue from the paper's margins and making my writing parallel and horizontal.

Why not be deliberately "messy" about keeping dreams? We can free up our writing to take whatever form it wishes— including three-dimensional forms as well as two-dimensional ones.

- Forget sentences.
- Forget paragraphs.
- Group parts of the dream according to their movement in internal space within the dream.
- Group parts of the dream according to moments in time or special feelings.
- Write the dream in a spiral or a square, or concentric or intersecting circles.
- Let the lines of the narrative meander over a blank page.
- Write out sections of the dream on different pieces of paper and then move the pieces around on a blank page, deliberately altering their order.
- Hang the sections of your dream vertically on a long piece of cloth, like a scroll.
- Make a miniature book. Write each part of the dream on a small, square piece of paper, and staple these together so that each piece stands by itself and can also be read as a whole.
- Emphasize certain words by writing them in larger script than or in a different style from others.

Then, in that dreamy state [when you first awake from a dream], somehow you can reach in the darkness and find something like a treasure that is hidden in this storage room. And that is what your dream is about. It's bringing back information to your conscious mind that has always been there because you wouldn't dream about it if you didn't have it already within you. So it's yours.

Isabel Allende
In Naomi Epel's
Writers Dreaming

- Substitute line drawings for easily rendered figures.
- Make a map of the dream and write beside each area what happens there.

Mapping the Dream

Ian took a nonlinear dream narrative and decided to write it out both in conventional lines and then in whatever form and groupings his intuition decided upon. Here is the linear version of this nonlinear dream:

The Gods in the Whale

I go across to the [family vacation] island to say good-bye to my family. I embrace my mother in the water. I swim away easily with effortless grace until I get close to shore, where the current seems to pull me back. The people on shore explain that it must be the submerged whale. I finally get to shore and look down into the crystalline waters. There, dead on the floor of the lake, is the submerged whale. In its mouth are a colored goddess figure, a dog, and a stone god. I realize how valuable they are and that I have seen them first so I might have first claim on them. Then it is decided: I say, "Let's get the dog up." Someone dives for the dog. When it is brought up, water pours from its mouth. I am about to say, "Turn it on its side," but I can tell that it needs no further resuscitation. It is breathing.

Ian wrote out the nonlinear form of his dream in less than two minutes, as shown in the illustration on the following page.

Ian responded strongly to writing out the dream in this nonlinear form:

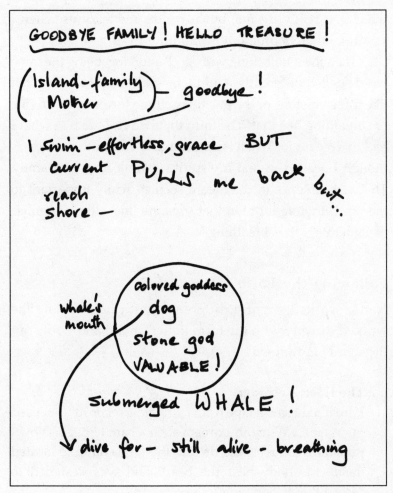

GOODBYE FAMILY! HELLO TREASURE!

(Island - family) - goodbye!
Mother

I swim - effortless, grace BUT
current PULLS me back but...
reach
shore —

whale's
mouth

colored goddess
dog
stone god
VALUABLE!

submerged WHALE!

↓ dive for - still alive - breathing

The Gods in the Whale

"I hadn't felt aware of the significance of the pull of the current as strongly until I wrote the dream out this way. It made me think about how strong the pull is for me to go back to family—how hard it is to swim away from that comfortable place and be an independent adult.

"And it made me really think about the relationship my mother and I have. We were in the water together—somehow in the same emotional lake together. I don't know what that really means, but it makes me anxious when I say it, so there's probably something in it!

"Then the whole thing with 'god' and 'dog' being the same word spelled differently. And then, 'god-dess,' too. They felt like three versions of the one thing, three forms of the divine or something like that. The form that had *real* life was what I had to dive for and then it miraculously came alive again, as though I needed to find my spirit separate from my family. That last sentence in the dream seemed really important to me when I wrote it out in that separate line—like a promise of something: 'It is breathing.'. . ."

Following the Form

Nadia worked slightly differently with her dream. She worked directly with the form in her dream and wrote out the words in that way:

The Heart Recorder
I dreamed I saw a tape from a tiny tape recorder that used microtapes. Why did I dream such a banal image? Now I remember more of the dream: the tape could be located inside the body near the heart, and was designed to record things happening deep inside.

Writing out the words of her dream in this spiral form gave Nadia a different sense of its levels of meaning:

"When I wrote the dream out this way—in the tape form—I saw the symbol of the spiral emerge so clearly! It's an important symbol for me: It represents my own inner growth, it reminds me of the Celtic designs that have so much mystery and fascination for me, and it reminds me of my Celtic ancestry. It just seems to fit the way the

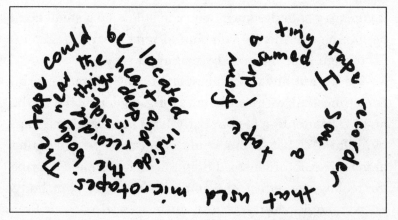

The Heart Recorder

Like the forms gener-
ated by chaos theory
and the dream itself,
Celtic art concerns
itself with translating
energy into precise
design. It use forms
expressing process,
linear analogues of
cosmic libido.

—Sylvia Brinton Perera
"Dream Design"

heart records its responses to situations, too—never straightforwardly but always in a roundabout way. I think about this symbol a lot now during the day, when I have an emotional response to situations. I just *feel* that tiny tape recorder inside me circling and circling. Somehow just re-membering the image makes me pay more attention to my feelings."

These two dreamers discovered for themselves what po-ets and writers of illuminated manuscripts, advertisers, and graphic artists know: that the placement of words on a page has a lasting impact. Because the message enters into our awareness in two ways—verbally and visually—we receive it more fully, a capacity that can only enhance our dreamwork.

I AM AN AIRPORT:
WORKING WITH DREAM FRAGMENTS

"I don't dream," many people say. Yet research shows that we all do, indeed, dream. Often, we do not remember. Even if you are a "nondreamer," you can still keep a small book beside the bed in case you should remember a fragment. Encourage your memory by making it easy.

We do not always remember dreams in image form. Sometimes, all we recall is a feeling. If you wake in the night, pay attention to your body. Is it tense? anxious? happy? relaxed? That feeling could be a dream reverberating in the musculature instead of in the imagination. Describe the feeling, the effect, the emotion suffusing your body. Even a single word—*excited, anxious, restless*—can be a dream. Note that one word. Over time, you'll accumulate a body-feeling record that will tell you something about your silent preoccupations during the night.

Every dream has its own atmosphere, just like the heavenly bodies. Often such an atmosphere is the only thing that is left behind from a dream.
—Robert Bosnak
A Little Course in Dreams

Sometimes, we don't have a residual feeling in the body but a sense that we have just arrived from another realm where we were doing or experiencing something. That, too, can be the tip of a dream. By writing it down, we can nudge memory into recalling more.

Many "nondreamers" readily acknowledge that they sometimes remember fragments. And some dreamers seem to need only fragments. Here are what I consider to be some "complete" dreams that others might consider fragments:

- An arm and a hand—hairy
- Chopin—no images, just Chopin—piano concerto, maybe
- I'm in an airport—noisy

These dreams are not stories. Some are not even fully realized visual images. They are partial visual or auditory constructs. But they are complete dreams and can have import for the dreamer if floated up to consciousness. Many people have had rich results from letting a fragment reveal its associations.

Simple visual practices can also open the way into the wealth of a dream fragment. Let's explore the first dreamer's image of a hairy arm and hand. Imagine that you visit a highly respected art gallery. You see a six-by-six oil painting of a hairy arm and hand. It is the only painting on display. Wouldn't you pay attention to it? Wonder what the painter had in mind? Register your feelings about the arm and hand? How would you have painted it? What medium? What colors? Taking this evanescent image and giving it artistic focus like this can deepen appreciation.

Let's take the second dreamer's image. Imagine you enter an empty room and a famous pianist is playing a Chopin concerto. This performance has been arranged for you and you alone because it has been determined that this is exactly what you need at this time in your life. You sit down in the large auditorium. The pianist begins. Your body is filled with this concerto. How do you feel? Imagine who is playing. Why are they playing this especially for you?

Wanting to emphasize the paucity of her dream life, the third dreamer mentioned her noisy-airport dream to me in passing. "See? I don't have real dreams to speak of! I mean, I'm in airports every week. It's always just leftover stuff from work." Yet, when I asked her what it *felt* like to be in a noisy airport, how *she* felt, what went through her mind, what airports symbolized in her life, what they symbolized in general, and what she associated to them in particular, a scroll of helpful material unrolled for her.

She began to think of the ways in which her profession as a financial comptroller resembled an airport manager's: Everything was siphoned through her. She also remembered that she was the "family bus station" when she was

"Why is it difficult to remember one's dreams?" I asked, prompting Nyima to quip, "Ah, this guy asks everything from head to foot! Because a dream is like the wind, just coming and going," Latu continued, stirring the fire with a stick. "It is not part of our body; it is like a guest, not staying long, and so it is difficult to remember so well. As with watching a movie, one can remember some thing, but forget most."
—Robert R. Desjarlais "Dreams, Divination, and Yolmo Ways of Knowing"

growing up, always the one to run interference between warring siblings and her sister and her mother. We explored the Gestalt technique of *being* the object in her dream— *being* a noisy airport. As she did this, she saw how her personal and professional lives had a common theme: She saw herself as the one to whom everyone else came in order to move ahead in the right direction. She always felt responsible, intruded upon, unable to abdicate her predestined role, yet she also realized that she unconsciously encouraged this situation.

All this out of a small dream image! We were amazed and amused at how astute her unconscious had been to offer her such a homely yet rich image.

Record and work with snippets, fragments, partial images, sounds, tastes, smells, and colors, as carefully as you would a longer dream. Most of us live in countries that tend to equate quantity with value and meaning, but dreams are subject to no such values in their country. Working through any sense, they send us telegrams, put one flower in the vase of sleep, offer a single, timely image to our waking selves.

"I DON'T DREAM–WHAT NOW?": ACTIVE IMAGINATION

What if you don't remember even fragments but would like to work with dreams personally or in therapy? An excellent alternative to dreaming is what Jung called *active imagination*, a practice he formalized and describes in his collected writings. The practice is too rich to explain fully here. Comprehensive guidelines and examples are found in several books. A practical description of how to engage in active imagination is given by Robert Johnson in *Inner Work*. Barbara Hannah provides a more theoretical analysis in *Encounters with the Soul*. Marion Woodman and June Singer also provide fine descriptions of this process in their works.

Active imagination is just that: active. It differs from passive fantasy and daydreaming, in which you allow the play of your imagination to do anything it wishes with you. In active imagination, your waking, daily self is an active player in the inner drama. You retain a firm connection to your everyday self with its ethics, limitations, capacities, preferences, intellect, and emotions. That everyday self then enters into dialogue with inner figures or energies who are the autonomous products of your imagination (rather than people whom you know or know of).

Some of the flavor of the technique is evident in the experience of Robert, a man who rarely remembered his dreams. He described his incessant perfectionism like this: "It's as though I have this *thing*, almost like a little animal with big teeth and big eyes that gnaws at me when I don't do things perfectly. He gnaws away at my gut and nags at me when I'm tired and want to go home. And the faster and harder I work, the faster he runs and the more he finds wrong."

I asked Robert whether he would be willing to do an experiment. Would he—the daily, waking Robert—be willing to grow quiet, go within, and imagine meeting this fierce little creature? He thought this was "pretty weird" but, at that moment, his description was so real to him that his curiosity was awakened (and his perfectionism, he readily acknowledged, extended to his trying to be the perfect recipient of therapy, too). I told him I'd keep track

[In active imagination, Jung] stumbled upon, as many had before him, the irreducible reality of the soul world: dreamtime.

—Robert Bosnak
In Michael V. Adams'
"Image, Active Imagination, and the Imaginal Level"

of time. I also gave him the choice of relating what was happening as it happened or describing it afterward. He closed his eyes and grew quiet. He went within and was still for twenty minutes. I was about to tell him that the time was drawing to a close, when he opened his eyes and looked right at me.

For us, the golden rule in touching any dream is keeping it alive. Dreamwork is conservation. . . . Conservation implies holding on to what is and even assuming that what is is right.
—James Hillman
The Dream and the Underworld

"It was just like the fairy stories! This stuff is crazy! But it works! That was so real! I stayed myself but I certainly couldn't control what he did—he kept surprising me—turning up under tree trunks and bushes in a jungle—laughing from branches—cackling. How did that happen? I just watched—I mean, I wasn't making it up—I was watching!

"Anyway, finally I got sick of his taunting me all the time as I tried to make it through this forest I was hacking away at, so I swung around and yelled, 'Damn it, have the guts to come down here and face me—be a man—don't be a wimp! You hassle me all the time but you don't have the courage to face me directly!' Well, I heard this rustle (I don't believe I'm saying this—I'm an MBA!) and there he was—squibby little guy with an ugly face. Before he could do or say anything, I picked him up by the scruff of the neck (I would've shot him but you told me to do only things I'd really do in real life, so I held off). Picked him up by the scruff of his disgusting little neck and told him that we had to live in the same body, so we'd better find a better way of getting along.

"When I said this, he started to cry. He said he was only trying to goad me into doing things well so I wouldn't make a fool of myself and would finally get Dad's respect—that he didn't know any other way of getting my attention, and that I wouldn't listen otherwise. He said he'd been around since I was six!

"Well, I told him that he could remind me about doing things well but that he knew nothing about the office or about my personal life and *I* had to be the best judge of that. Then I also found myself telling him that Dad was *never* going to be satisfied and we might as well stop. And suddenly, when I said that, we both got really quiet—and I was out of the scene and back here."

I made no comment. Unnecessary commentary or interpretation intrudes on this work. If done with consciousness, delineated time frames, and the realization that the inner symbolic world does not translate literally into the waking world, it is its own vehicle for insight.

Not all active imagination is as fully realized or understood as Robert's. One image of a cliff or an eye or a blue vase is enough to work with and amplify. Sit quietly. Allow an image, the first bar of a song, a catch-phrase, or a feeling to come. Encourage yourself to interact with this image or symbol. You can engage in conversation or move with it or allow it to show you things. Just stay yourself while you interact with it.

Active imagination is a rich alternative to dreaming and provides for a form of invention that has nothing to do with conscious intent or control. It gives the imagination free play while still keeping the silver thread of awareness tied to the waking personality.

FROM MUNDANE TO MAGICAL: THE CARE AND FEEDING OF DREAM FIGURES

The practices in this book work with a variety of dream energies, from human figures to animals, from inanimate objects to themes, from colors to patterns. Most commonly appearing, however, are human figures and animals.

In dreams, we are visited by the daimones, nymphs, heroes, and gods shaped like our friends of last evening.

—James Hillman
The Dream and the Underworld

Each theory offers a different perspective on dream figures. However, the most common question all theories address is: Do these figures really represent their counterparts in the outer world or do they represent parts of us? It is probably the *or* in this sentence that is confusing. It forces us to decide between alternatives.

A less dualistic position frees us to see dream figures on a continuum. At one end are strange, unknown creatures who seem to personify some unfamiliar aspect of our psyche. At the opposite end appear known figures who act like themselves in waking life, and with whom we seem to move through ordinary situations. Most figures, however, slide along the continuum: Familiar figures act "out of character" or in magical fashion (coming alive, when they are dead in waking life; being generous in the dream, whereas in waking life they are selfish); unfamiliar figures act like "real people," yet they are pure products of the dramatist within.

We need to exercise a "both . . . and" approach to these figures. They are at once built from the clay of everyday interchange and experience, but fashioned by the unconscious in such a way as to make them unmistakably symbolic of some known or unknown part of ourselves.

Jung's theory is probably the most comprehensive in its treatment of the psyche's personifications of itself. Just as the Hindu world view provides endless names for and personifications of the forms of the divine, thus permitting subtle differentiation among the personalities of gods and goddesses, so, too, Jung's theory provides for differentiated energies within the psyche. If you are familiar with or interested in Jung's approach to archetypal figures—such as the anima, the animus, the persona, the shadow, the mother, the father, the senex, the wise old woman, the puer, and the puella—consult Jung's *Collected Works* and some excellent contemporary introductions, such as Harry Wilmer's *Practical Jung*, June Singer's *Boundaries of the Soul*, and Robert Johnson's various books such as *He, She, and We.* These are but a few of the clear and succinct books on these subjects. There are equally fine studies of single archetypes—too numerous to mention here.

A brief introduction to these archetypes would create several unhelpful outcomes: It would do the theory a disservice, it would frustrate those who know more, and it would frustrate those who want more. So, instead, let's review some general ways to view and work with dream figures.

Is the figure someone I know? If so:

- What is/was my connection to this person?
- If I were to describe this person in three adjectives, what would they be?
- Do I like/dislike this person, or am I indifferent?
- When do I feel like, act like, or look like this person?
- What do I know about this person that stands out at this instant from all the things I know about him or her?
- What positive and/or negative aspect(s) of myself does this character remind me of or introduce me to?

The paradox in a dream is that while these presences, these beings that people the dream world, are entirely independent—part of the same world I live in, but just as little a part of me as you are a part of me—they are subpersonalities of my very being as well. The dream figures have a life of their own, totally and utterly different from mine, and they are elements of my soul. They are myself and not myself at all. Of course, this makes no logical sense, but psyche cares about Wirlichkeit, as Jung calls it: "effective reality," not logic.

—Robert Bosnak
In Michael V. Adams'
"Image, Active
Imagination, and the
Imaginal Level"

- Is this person behaving in ways that are atypical of waking life?

If this is a person I do not know:

- How fully can I describe the figure?
- What three adjectives would I choose to describe this figure?
- What is my relationship to this figure?
- What role does the figure play in sustaining or changing the direction of the dream?
- What feeling tone does this figure add to the dream?
- Does this figure have a name? What name would I give this figure?
- If this figure had to represent one quality alone, what would it be?
- What is the age of this figure in the dream? What is my age? How would the dream feel different if the figure were a radically different age from the figure currently in the dream?
- What can I imagine this figure's personal history to be?
- What aspect(s) of myself does this character remind me of or introduce me to?

If this figure is the same sex as I am:

- What is our relationship in the dream? Does this remind me of waking relationships?
- What about our personalities is notably alike, either positive or negative or both?
- How are our personalities and our actions quite different, either positive or negative or both?
- If I were to employ this person in real life, the most constructive position for this person would be . . .

One dreams in the first place and almost to the exclusion of all else, of oneself.
—C. G. Jung
Collected Works

- How would my feeling about this figure change if the figure were to turn up in the same dream as the opposite sex? So what does the figure's being the same sex add to the dream for me?
- The task for which this figure would be least suited would be . . .
- If this figure had to represent one quality alone, what would it be?
- What is the age of this figure in the dream? What is my age? How would the dream feel different if the figure were a radically different age from the figure currently in the dream?
- What might this figure's personal history be?
- What aspect(s) of myself does this character remind me of or introduce me to?

"Threatening Shadow Woman Reappears" Newspaper Collage

If this figure is the opposite sex from me:

- What is our relationship in the dream? Do I have this quality of relationship with waking-life people of the opposite sex?
- How would my feeling about this figure change if the figure were to turn up in the same dream as the same sex? So what does the figure's being the opposite sex add to the dream for me?
- What are this figure's most outstanding characteristics? What three adjectives could describe this figure?
- What is the age of this figure in the dream? What is my age? How would the dream feel different if the figure were a radically different age from the figure currently in the dream?
- When do I act/feel/imagine myself to be seen like this figure in waking life?
- What might this figure's personal history be?
- What aspect(s) of myself does this character remind me of or introduce me to?

If this figure is magical, mythical, or divine:

- What is the nature of this figure's special powers or qualities?
- How can I describe them as fully as possible?
- If I were to imagine that I have been apprenticing with this figure for a long time, what have I learned (both good and bad) from this figure?
- What might this figure's personal history be?
- What aspect(s) of myself does this character remind me of or introduce me to?
- If this figure were to appear in a gathering of gods and goddesses and were to be given a name that described

One should always first ask, "What is it in me that does that?" instead of taking the dream as a warning against other people.

—Marie-Louise von Franz
In Fraser Boa's
The Way of the Dream

his or her essential nature, what would the figure be named?

- Do I feel familiar with any aspect of myself that sometimes is able to exhibit this quality?
- Does this figure represent something in me that feels very far from who I am? Can I imagine taking some aspect of that figure inside of me and letting it operate? How would it feel?

The Life Cycle of Unicorns and Griffins: The Care and Feeding of Dream Animals

So much fine (and mediocre) material has been published on the symbolic meaning of animals in our dreams, inner journeys, meditations, and active imaginations. If you are not already familiar with this material, visit your local library or bookstore and leaf through these books. But before you get absorbed in reading about the symbolism of elephants, rabbits, and spiders, first reflect on your own associations to the animals who visit you in the night.

Meditate on your perception of the animal spirit. Explore your personal associations to the animal. Then write down everything you know (or think you know) about all aspects of this animal:

- Character
- Habitat
- Food choices
- Method of getting and eating food
- Elimination
- Procreation
- Gestation

The idea that Jungian dreamworld will lead to "big dreams" is similar in kind to the vague, though tenacious, presumption that when individuation is completed, at some mythical future time, one will glow in the dark with a bodhisat-tvic luminosity.

What typically occurs is something quite different, quite the opposite from this rather ideal fantasy. When we build a bridge from the conscious mind to some further shore of unconscious content, the first denizens of that dark country to cross over are usually the mundane impression and perceptions that we consign to the unconscious mind simply because they are in conflict with our self-image.

—Stephen A. Martin "Smaller Than Small, Bigger Than Big"

- Birth
- Life span
- Sleep patterns
- Relationships with other animals
- Vulnerabilities to the environment

Asking for associations is one of the essential parts of work on dreams. It makes for connections between the dream and the daily life of the dreamer. Next to these personal associations, each work creates a kind of electromagnetic field of meaning that is usually associated with that word. After the personal associations, we can enter the fields surrounding the words.

—Robert Bosnak
*A Little Course
in Dreams*

Include what you might think are positive as well as negative descriptions. This list represents your subjective-objective take on the animal. Circle information that seems to parallel aspects of your character.

Research the life cycle of the animal in its living form. Read up on the facts about each of these categories. Note down anything that attracts, or deeply bothers, or amuses you.

Work with group imaginative perceptions of the animal. If you are working with a group of dreamers, spend time with your group brainstorming about what they associate with certain animals that appear in your dreams.

Understand the animal's life span as symbols and mythological characters. When you have finished with the actual remembered or researched aspects of the animal's actual life, use reliable reference books to research this animal's cross-cultural associations in mythology, heraldry, religious ritual, and world views.

By doing this, you can create a delicate web of associations, a double helix of connotations that moves in and out at the same time. One spiral moves from your dream image upward into the conscious associations you and others have with this image. The other spiral moves downward; each outer association you discover flows back into the psyche and waters and fertilizes the roots of the image in the psyche. Don't expect to see flowers. You are fertilizing the root system of your image and other images that are rooted and growing close by. Amplifying your dream images is an excellent way to enrich the image. Keep returning to the original image as home base.

When you have finished enriching the image, write a story for children that includes some of the mythical qualities your animal had in your dream and some of the real qualities you have researched.

Part Two

Dream Expressions and Practices

5

Widening the Window
on Dream Time and Space

AMARANTA SUNSET: CARING FOR AND FEEDING DREAMS–IN FIVE MINUTES

It's late but you've had an important dream. You don't have time to write it out in detail and you'll be too tired to remember or explore it tonight. So do you just ignore it or give it a few minutes? It is better to *do* five minutes of something than *not* do twenty minutes of it. So, how can you work with your dream in such a short time?

Just to have a small knowledge of how dream process works is so enriching.

—Marion Woodman
Dreams: Language of the Soul

Have Materials on Hand

Some dreamers keep tape recorders by their beds. If you or your partner can't stand your maundering on into your recorder, keep a small notebook and pencil beside the bed—a cheap, sturdy notebook. Most writing and art teachers suggest we use cheap materials for spontaneous creative pursuits; we are less in awe of the blank page and more willing to be messy and free if the paper is not bound in elegant leather.

Capture the Essence

When you haven't much time and you've had a long dream, consider shortcuts. These are not desirable but they are realistic:

- Omit articles; for example: *an, the, a* . . .
- Omit pronouns where possible; for example: *she, he, we, I, they* . . .
- Abbreviate names after the first mention; for example: *David = D; Sara = S; Mother = M; the tall man in the yellow raincoat = YM (yellow man)*
- Omit transitions; for example: *then; the scene changes* . . .
- Use an asterisk to indicate a change in time, place, scene,

or logic; for example: *Horse rears head, gallops into ocean.* * *In auditorium—woman singing.)*

- If you have an association in the middle of writing, put it in parentheses and keep writing; for example: *Weeping child (Carola? Me at 7?) holds up rag doll (film on depression?) . . .*

- Omit approximations; for example: *It seemed as though . . . it was as if . . . looked somewhat like but really wasn't . . . almost but not really.*

- If you must include approximations, precede them with a tilde; for example: *blonde ~Aunt Betty* is briefer than saying, *It was someone I don't know but she looked a bit like Aunt Betty except she was blonde.*

- If possible, don't abbreviate conversation, but omit all the *he said/she said* additions. Begin new lines for a change of speaker and put the speaker's abbreviated name on the left. For example:

  D: Where's the river?
  Me: I don't know but the star might tell us.
  D: You're the leader.

- Include details that feel charged. Omit those that carry no overt charge, if necessary. This is not advisable as a general practice; all dream details have purpose. However, if omitting details makes the difference between your recording the dream and not, then omit. For example, if the room is square, unless the fact that it *is* square becomes important later in the dream, omit mentioning it. If the room is shaped like an egg, include it.

- Abbreviate words in whatever way makes sense. Be obvious and consistent; in two months you'll have no idea what marvelous mysteries you have concealed in forgettable hieroglyphics. List repeated abbreviations in the back of your journal, or use the word in full the first time with the abbreviation listed after it.

- Punctuation subjugates elements that were never meant to be subjugated from the viewpoint of heart and soul. Use dashes instead. They are actually more appropriate for indicating dream structure, logic, and time. Read Emily Dickinson's poetry with the *original* punctuation to remember or learn how eloquent dashes can be.

In the following example, Mark took less than a minute to write out the essence of his dream (in bold type). The full version (in ordinary type) shows what he omitted.

Amaranta Sunset

I walk downtown. When I get down there, everyone is beginning to gather to watch the special sunset. I bump into Paula, who has come down to see it. She begins talking immediately about the sunset, not greeting me but just treating me as though it's fine to see me.

Downtown—people gather—special sunset—Paula—doesn't greet me but it's OK.

Paula says something about the sunset and then says, "Of course, I know you're not supposed to use that word for this particular day but I have such difficulty with the word 'amaranta.'"

P: "I know you're not supposed to use that word for this particular day but I have such difficulty with the word 'amaranta.'"

[I know it is Spanish (?) but have no idea what it means, nor have I ever heard about this sunset.] Paula is articulating extremely consciously, not an English

So it looks as if there is within us a superior intelligence which we could call an inner guide or a divine inner center which produces the dreams, and that the aim of dreams seems to be an optimum of life for the individual.

The dreams cannot protect us from the vicissitudes and illnesses and sad events of human existence. But they do give us a guiding line on how to cope with them, how to find a meaning in our life, how to fulfill our own destiny, how to follow our own star . . . in order to realize the greater potential of life within us.

—Marie-Louise von Franz
In Fraser Boa's *The Way of the Dream*

articulation but one that clearly has some esoteric superiority that I had failed to recognize in the past because I didn't know enough. I feel lowly. Paula walks away to watch as the sun begins to descend.

Spanish? No idea re meaning of sunset. P speaks carefully—not English—esoteric—can't recognize. I = lowly. P walks away—watches sun descending.

The symbol comes through imagination, emotion, and intellect.

—Marion Woodman
Dreams: Language of the Soul

Title the Essential Dream

Titles can seem wild, nonsensical, or pointless when given, but reviewing titles over a period of months can reveal quiet patterns in minutes. So they are worth giving. Mark called his dream "Amaranta Sunset." Writing out the essence and titling it provides a rich resource for later dreamwork.

Amplify

Take at least three words that jump out at you in the dream. You might not have a conscious reason for choosing them. In fact, avoid exercising conscious choice. Trust your unconscious. It knows what it's doing regarding its own dreams, even if it can lead you astray in waking life. Put the words on paper and make a spiderweb of amplifications to each. Amplification differs from free association. *Amplification* circles around and returns to the original point of conceptual departure; *free association* gallops from one word to the next, without concern for the original concept. Mark chose three words to amplify:

- *sunset*—end, beauty, Hawaii trip?, sleep, special time with Ann
- *Paula*—strong, smart, warm, broke up

- *lowly*—me at work sometimes, poor, uneducated, unacceptable, school

We don't have to understand Mark's associations. They made sense to him and stimulated his imagination, memory, and feelings. And they let him record a quick hunch about the dream's message.

Record the Hunch

Often, during the recording or amplification of the dream, we have a body-felt sense, an image, or a quiet phrase that elucidates what the dream carries. Note it, no matter how odd it seems. Mark wrote:

- *Others accept me.*
- *I don't.*
- *Don't apologize!*

These immediate and fresh comments were there for Mark to review later when he had time to reflect.

Often, a dream seems ordinary or unworthy of recording. Recording its essence usually bears fruit, however; the image can become more significant later, particularly in relationship to other images. It can become part of a larger pattern that the psyche is forming like a giant mandala. We can never estimate the exact importance of one small piece of the larger form at the time. Later, we can better appreciate it. So capturing essence is crucial. It is a thumbnail sketch of a vista from the soul.

This "spinning on" of the dream constitutes a natural process and requires an approach similar to that required by nature: patience, involvement, the right climate, a positive relationship, neither too much nor too little fertilizer, regular watering, the right distribution of light and shade.

—Kathrin Asper
In Luigi Zoja's "Beyond Freud and Jung"

ENTERING THE TIBETAN PALACE: GROUPING DIFFERENT PARTS OF SPEECH

I have learned to renounce interpreting dreams in a clear, final manner and am able to leave things open.
—Kathrin Asper
In Luigi Zoja's "Beyond Freud and Jung"

Our language divides reality into patterns, into different subdivisions, including: actions (verbs); the qualities of actions (adverbs); states of being (intransitive verbs such as *to be, to die, to sleep*); people, places, things, and concepts (nouns—subjects and objects); and qualities (adjectives). These patterns of language can reflect patterns of energy within the psyche itself—the objects that are carrying symbolic energy, the actions that the psyche is experiencing, the qualities, and so forth. Focusing on the actions in your dream can let you see the ways in which you are moving through your inner or outer worlds, ways of which you are not fully aware. Focusing on the subjects and objects can make you more aware of your personal symbolism and of the people and things carrying meaning for you at this time. Dream adjectives can indicate the present quality of your psychic energy. Each grammatical grouping of dream words can reveal a different energy pattern within you.

A quick and fruitful way to work with your dream is to group various kinds of words in the dream description. Let's see what happens to different elements within a dream when they are grouped in this way:

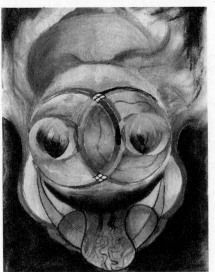

"Tibetan Monster Mask" Pastel

Entering the Tibetan Palace

I am practicing a Tibetan chant with a group of other chanters. A monk is pointing to a flag he is holding, with the chant written vertically on it. In between each chant, a bell is rung. I find myself alone and am to hold on to a thick black rope held at the other end by a second monk. I have to do the chant alone, pulling the rope between words or phrases. When I have completed it, I may climb effortlessly and powerfully up the sandy slope to the left of the monk where I may join the others. They are in a holding place in a naturally lit tunnel entrance to the pyramid. I look for the source of the wonderful singing—it's quite modern. I find the room, but inside are two more doors, both of which have Tibetan monster god masks on them. I realize this is the men's toilet and reluctantly back out. I continue on and find large, dark, lush, red rooms that are part of a museum. No one is there. Very spacious. I see signs leading to the palace that is below all the museums and realize I'd better wait for the rest of the group, so I return to the entrance.

We can hardly help feeling that the unconscious process moves spiralwise round a center, gradually getting closer, while the characteristics of the center grow more and more distinct.

—C. G. Jung
Collected Works

Grammatical Groups and Their Corresponding Energy Patterns

This dreamer's actions seem to show considerable movement. She alternates between moving forward, being still, and moving backward. Moving forward and active engagement predominate. When the dreamer noticed this, it confirmed what she was feeling in her life—lots of changes, a few times of being still, and times of returning to the starting point.

The nouns and adjectives she noticed she had used for her inner world startled her. However, she acknowledged that this was *her* dream reflecting *her* inner world; regard-

[Jung] found it essential to approach dreams with a humble attitude, because the most important dream messages are ahead of the dreamer's current knowledge and understanding.

—Mary Ann Mattoon
Applied Dream Analysis

VERBS	ADVERBS	ADJECTIVES AND NOUNS	
How am I currently moving through my inner world?	*What are the qualities of my movement in the inner/outer world?*	*What are the subjects and objects and their qualities in my inner world?*	
——	——	——	
By:		Some aspect of me evokes the feeling of:	
practicing,	I am acting:		
pointing,	effortlessly,	*Adjective*	*Noun*
holding, ringing,	powerfully,	Tibetan	monk
chanting,	reluctantly.	thick, black	rope
pulling,		sandy	slope
completing,		naturally lit	tunnel
climbing,		wonderful	chanting
joining, looking,		men's forbidden	toilet
finding,		monsterlike	masks
backing out,		—	pyramid
continuing on,		large, dark,	
seeing, waiting,		lush red, spacious	rooms
returning.		—	museum
		—	palace

less of how she felt about her inner life (which was not terrific), the dream indicated that her inner world was rich, full of contrast (light and dark), and replete with secret places.

Experiment with a dream of your own, focusing on different language (energy) patterns. As Greg Sarris pointed out, in some cultures, remembering actions in a story is more important than remembering objects; in others, remembering objects is more important. Do you connect most strongly with actions, states of being, qualities of action, subjects and objects, or qualities of subjects and objects?

What do you remember most in your own stories? How might this reflect your experience of your inner culture?

MERRILY, MERRILY, MERRILY: VIEWING LIFE EVENTS AS DREAMS

Were I to disguise and write a novel about the extraordinary people I have met and strange and miraculous tales I have heard in my office, no one would believe me. The tales are too incredible. Outcomes are perfect but so unexpected. Synchronicities—those wild, timely, acausal coincidences—abound. And then there are the crazy, lovable characters. All these would never go down in a novel!

Life *is* stranger than fiction. The fiction that best approximates life is the genre of magical realism, the tradition of Gabriel García Márquez, of Isabelle Allende. A writer friend recently published a short story in a highly regarded national magazine. She presented the story as a dream, her way of making its confluence of rare events believable. However, she and I knew that every word was true; she had lived these events.

We can better appreciate certain events in our own lives and approach them with more openness to their larger significance if we look at them as dreams. We can permit the impossible, the acausal, the out-of-time, the unexpected, the miraculous solution, the archetypal entry of dark characters.

Life situations don't even have to be extraordinary to be constructively viewed as dreams. Even puzzling, ordinary events take on a different slant when we imagine them to be dreams. Waking events that seem to respond best to

Things are not a dream, they have their own reality. Then Things themselves (since they are real participations in being) can be spiritualized— in other words the spirit they conceal can be discovered and set free by our contemplative grasping.

—Jacques Maritain
Creative Intuition in Art and Poetry

conversion into "dreams" are those that are puzzling, hurt-
ful, bizarre, synchronistic, joyful, haunting, baffling, or
repetitive. We can shift emotional, philosophical, and psychological orientation to these events by simply changing
the *genre* in which we narrate them from history to dream.
Notice the shift in your response to the following event
when it is related as a dream.

Historical Report

In June, I visited friends in Hawaii. We went over to the
ocean for the day and, after lunch, went walking around
the windy cliffs and headland overlooking the water. As
I stood on the rocks, I saw a school of dolphins playing
offshore. I watched for a while and, suddenly, one of them
leapt high in the air with its whole body suspended in the
light. Then it seemed to just dip its head down toward the
water, disappearing in a second. I watched for a while
longer but it didn't do it again. I was delighted to catch
that one leap.

Now, let's review this and rewrite it as a dream:

- Declare the genre: *dream.*
- Give it a title.
- Begin with: *I dream that . . .*
- Add: *in the dream* every so often.
- Conclude with: *And that's the end of the dream.*
- Put it in the present continuous tense.

Dream: "The Leaping Dolphin"

I dream that I am visiting friends. We are on the island and
I am walking around a windy headland. I look out to sea
and see a school of dolphins playing. Suddenly one leaps
into the air. It stays suspended out of the water a long

time. Then it disappears. I watch a while longer but it doesn't do it again. I am so delighted *in the dream* that I am there at that moment to see the dolphin. *And that's the end of the dream.*

Do you feel the import shift subtly when this life event is retold as a dream? I find I approach the image differently. I wonder and wander about the image of the dolphin suspended in air. I imaginatively consider dolphins—their intelligence, their gentleness, their sensitivity. What do dolphins symbolize for me? If this dolphin were a metaphor, what feeling or tone does it capture in its leap into space?

"Fine," you say. "Nice image! A convenient one to convert into a dream. But I don't often see dolphins! What about the banal events that just frustrate me?"

These, too, can take on new dimensions when viewed as dreams. Let's take one of those "banal events":

Report of Life Event
Yesterday, I rose early and went to the kitchen to make tea. I turned on the kitchen light and one of the bulbs blew. Then the kettle didn't heat. I tested it on another burner and it heated fine there. It was unexpectedly dark because it was about to rain. I thought I might be coming down with a cold.

Here is the event reframed as a dream:

Dream: "Nothing's Working Right"
I dream that I get up early and go to the kitchen to make tea. I turn on the light in the kitchen and a bulb blows. Then the kettle doesn't heat—I test it on another burner

and it heats fine there. I think to myself *in the dream* that the burner must be defective. *The whole dream* is pretty dark because it's about to rain. I think that I'm coming down with a cold. *Then I wake up.*

A dream tells you where you are, not what to do; or, by placing you where you are, it tells you what you are doing.

—James Hillman
The Dream and the Underworld

The import and tenor of the event deepen when I view this series of minor events as a dream. And, as a matter of fact, the "dreamer" learned something just writing this out as a dream: He realized that "the dream" could be an analogy for his body.

"I'd had minor physical ailments and I hadn't paid any attention to them. And I *knew* I'd been overusing my internal circuits—they'd been burning out or cutting out on me unexpectedly. I'd been too busy at work and coaching the team—spending more energy frustrated with those minor failures in my body than *doing* anything constructive about them. *Hmm!*"

Events that are all too familiar or repetitive also respond well to being viewed as dreams:

John's Written Report of a Repetitive Event
My supervisor called me into her office and told me that I'd been seriously considered for the promotion for which I'd applied but that, after a great deal of thought, they'd decided someone else should get the job. Pam told me that I'd been the runner-up, and that I should take this as positive rather than negative because there were so many applicants. She suggested I should position myself better and develop strategies for widening the professional experience I needed so I could reapply in a year.

John was upset. He had been with his company six years and believed he was ready for this job. He also believed this had happened to him an unfair number of times in his life:

"I've always been runner-up—the one who got second prize in competitions, the one who got stood up by my girlfriend the night before the prom for an older guy she liked better, the one who had one number off the winning lottery ticket. I was even one month too young to start school with the others my age! What *is* this?!"

John decided to rewrite this latest event as a dream:

Dream: "I'm Not Ready to Be Given the Promotion"
I dream that I am called in by my supervisor. I have applied for a position. She tells me I'm runner-up and that, with another year's experience behind me, I should be ready to take on that kind of job. She encourages me to get the experience I need to put myself in the best position for applying next year. *Then I wake up.*

John considered this "dream." If it came from within and had some constructive function, what might it be saying? He imagined that his "dream-supervisor" was a part of himself giving him a message:

"What I see is not that I'm always missing out, but that a lot of times I push for things before I'm ready. That's what the dream-supervisor seems to be telling me right now.

"I don't really know whether that's what the waking-supervisor *was* telling me—but I know when I score a point with myself. I can feel it inside. It's a scratchy feeling of anxiety, relief, and excitement all wrapped up together. I just know that this is a true statement: All my life I've been pushing to do things ahead of when I've been ready—I think it's probably an effort to keep up with Tom [an older

For most ancient civilizations, the dream meant the entrance into another world. Dream experience . . . did not pose a problem. These ancient peoples acknowledged dream experience the very way they lived it, that is, they gave it full reality. It was natural for them to interpret dream experience the way one interprets the concerns of the day world, as an encounter with beings who are real, even though, in the case of the dream, they are not embodied.

—Elie G. Humbert
"Dream Experience"

brother]. He always seems to breeze through new things whereas I can't.

"Maybe I can adjust my expectations of myself—and my timelines a bit—to my actual experience and capacities."

[Chuang-tzu] dreamed that he was a happy butterfly who was quite pleased about himself. He suddenly awoke and pondered the question of whether he was a man dreaming he was a butterfly, or a butterfly dreaming that he was a man.

—Robert L.
Van de Castle
Our Dreaming Mind

If overused or overidentified, this practice of treating waking reality as a dream can lead to our putting ourselves at the center of things too often. It can lead to an exaggerated, puffed-up belief that events are sent to us personally as "teachings." Certainly, we can learn from all events if we are "continuing-education students of life." However, we deceive ourselves if we believe that we are singled out as protagonists in all life events.

We are usually merely players in situations. When we turn a waking event into a dream event, we consciously make ourselves key players. We intentionally—and temporarily—treat the event as something from which we can learn. This "dream" perspective always differs from the waking perspective because we translate the event from a temporal context to an eternal one. The resulting "dream" is not operating like the waking event, but becomes an informative, active myth we develop for our own education. By borrowing events from waking life, we can better understand what inner patterns we bring to those outer events.

GLIMPSING THE DEER: NOTICING SYNCHRONICITIES BETWEEN DREAMS AND LIFE

One of the many gifts Carl Jung gave us was to draw conscious attention to the presence of synchronicity in our lives. At a certain point in my own life, some of my belief structures were involuntarily under demolition, and I impatiently awaited psychic financing to come through to rebuild. Operating on a different time line from my outer life, my soul was leisurely about providing this. While I waited, one of the helpful things I found I could do was attend to synchronicities. They seemed to underscore what was of possible importance during a time of confusion.

The dream world often intersects with the waking world in synchronistic ways: an unusual, repeating image of a person, place, thing, or quality (color, feel, shape, sound); an odd, repeating word; an ordinary event that bears an uncanny resemblance to an event in a dream; a dream image of a place or landscape for which a waking analogue appears within a short time; a rare but repeated phrase.

Marie, for example, was surviving a difficult time. The ways she was thinking and acting seemed to block forward movement, both inner and outer. She was working constantly at staying alert to these patterns but she found it difficult. Then she had a dream in which a deer came to her. The next day, she picked up a magazine at the dentist's office, and it fell open to a page that showed a crystal deer for sale from a mail-order house. The third day, she received a note from her sister that opened with *"Deer Marie"* corrected to *"dear."*

Marie called me, wondering what this "meant." I had to disappoint her and say I had no idea. This experience of synchronicity was hers, not mine. However, I suggested she feed the creature with the possibility of being, as Rilke suggests in his well-loved sonnet. Synchronicities don't hit one over the head with a neon-lit translation. Synchronicity is more like a boldfacing of a word in a narrative; it

The dream is also a map of possibility. In the dream state, the observer is not localized to one region of the brain. The observer is distributed throughout the brain and is picking up information from several memory locations simultaneously. The quantum wave in the brain is dependent on all of the possible locations of the observer, so that memory recall in one location is instantly correlated with other locations, giving rise to surprising and meaningful overlaps of what are usually separated memories.

Thus the dream takes on a bizarre quality as images that, normally kept apart, are blended. The dreamer has entered the unconscious mind, and there is synchronicity going on all over the place.

—Fred Alan Wolf
The Dreaming Universe

draws our attention to a theme. How we respond is our choice.

Marie liked the idea of feeding the deer with the possibility of being. What might the image of the deer offer her in her life? She spent time the following evening, reading about deer and their habits (lovable and unlovable). She took out a book of mythology from the library to see in what myths the animal appeared; she also checked out a book on symbols so she could read about what deer symbolize cross-culturally.

In dreams we catch glimpses of a life larger than our own.
—Helen Keller
In Robert L.
Van de Castle's
Our Dreaming Mind

She did not do this research to pin down the *meaning* of the deer, the message from the deer. Although she would have welcomed incontrovertible guidance, it would have been fruitless—risky—to look for a one-to-one correlation between the deer and the difficulties in her life. However, on the practical side, she discovered things about deer's behavior that seemed to have a disconcerting resemblance to her own in many situations—fearfulness, a desire to run away, distrust, hypervigilance. She began to see more clearly both helpful and unhelpful attitudes and habits that had been in her peripheral awareness. Now, this image of the deer gave her a way of recognizing these aspects of herself quickly. She remembered this image when she unconsciously moved into "deer" patterns. The deer continued to "appear" for some time.

By feeding the image, Marie trusted that her inner life would take note of her respect for its wisdom. Perhaps, in its own time, not hers, like Rilke's creature, fed with possibility, it might "put forth a horn." She valued the quiet conviction that something bigger was probably afoot than prolonged confusion. Just as radio and television waves moved through and around her in patterns, so another pattern, invisible to her lesser physical eyes, so trained to look for cause and effect, was moving. This deer emerged from a forest in which events obeyed different laws, and quietly moved across Marie's confused world.

How many times have we dreamed about someone and received a letter, phone call, fax, or visit from them soon afterward? Once again, we have to be careful. When, like Marie, we are confused, it's easy to leap on some poor, unsuspecting synchronicity and say to it: "This is *It!* You're the sign from the heavens that I need. You're here to tell me what to do! I'm supposed to go off and become a shaman in the clan of the deer!" I'd love to have clear inner direction that would send me off with a solid backpack of psychological canned food to sustain me for weeks. However, synchronicity doesn't work like that, for me, for Marie, or for anyone I know.

It is also a pity if we ignore synchronicity. If, especially during physical, mental, or emotional weariness, we look blearily at synchronicity and say, "You're just a meaningless coincidence," we close ourselves off in an equally self-important way. We assume we are fully responsible for the whole scheme—and the whole scheme is beyond redemption. If we are fiercely honest, we need to acknowledge that we are not as in charge of our lives as we would like to believe we are.

Again and again, I need to be reminded to be constructively humble about what I think I know. At a time when I was foolishly trying to take charge of a matter of heart in a step-by-step, logical fashion, a wise friend once gently said to me, "You know, you can't conquer the unconscious!" She was right. I gave up trying to win. My consolation prize was synchronicity: I could at least alert myself to unusual

Nobody likes to stumble, and the dream trips us up. Thus, directly translating the dream into daytime logic using preconceived parallels is a method that does not do justice to the discrepancy between dream reality and daytime reality and is therefore fundamentally inadequate.

—Robert Bosnak
A Little Course in Dreams

series of coincidences when they crossed my path.

In one twenty-four hour period, Ellen woke in a cold sweat from a dream about a tree falling on the roof of her house, then drove past a tree that had actually fallen in front of a neighbor's house, and then saw a house being roofed on the same block. Had Ellen not had synchronicity to underscore the dream image, she might have dismissed the dream. But now she looked at it differently. She and her husband had been having serious disagreements about important issues. Ellen had been procrastinating about addressing these. She believed that the dream tree resembled the problems threatening the house of her marriage and that this series of synchronicities emphasized her need to address the problems urgently.

The Mojave . . . concede to the dream a reality greater than that of wakefulness. The dream is a continuing revelation of the processes of creation granted by the gods to the Mojave.
—Carl W. O'Nell
Dreams, Culture, and the Individual

Sometimes, synchronicity seems to confirm our direction. When I began writing some material on spirals for this book, I was assailed by images of spirals for twenty-four hours. They weren't obvious ones that I had just failed to notice—they really jumped out of the woodwork! I dropped a book and it fell open at a design of a spiral; I dreamed of spirals; I picked up a stone with a spiral pattern; a necklace bearing a Celtic spiral fell out of a box on a top shelf. I pulled a text out of my bookshelf—Arthur Koestler's *The Act of Creation*—and it, too, bore a spiral on the cover. I realized that it was important not only to write about spirals and spiral ways of approaching dreams, but to affirm the spiral process of actually writing this book.

Keep a list of dream events, words, and images that find synchronistic parallels in your waking life. What do you notice about the pattern of these over time? Don't look for chance repetition. Look for a genuine, uncanny confluence of apparently unconnected yet meaningful events in time. Do not feed this strange creature with literality, but with the possibility it might exist in some realm between waking and sleeping; this will give it such strength that it might put forth a horn.

THE MYSTERY OF MA: LOOKING AT WHAT IS "MISSING"

In traditional Western art, artists and critics often refer to the "negative space" in a painting. "Negative" denotes the space that is *not* painted, the space around the defined object, the air around the vase of flowers. "Negative" has two other common meanings: something undesirable or unacceptable, and strips of film negative. Both of these connote "what is *not*."

By contrast, Eastern art tradition values "negative space" for what it *is*, rather than defining it by what it is *not*. It values open space in a painting, not for how it sets off what *is* painted but for its own "positive" role.

This space is sometimes referred to as *ma* in Japanese tradition. As Michihiro Matsumoto explains in *The Unspoken Way*, *ma* has endless, complex meanings, most of which defy Japanese understanding and almost all of which defy non-Japanese understanding. Yet that is the essence of *ma:* a mystery that

Ma *in Ryoanji, a Kyoto temple garden*

should be present, a potential realizing itself, an eternal moment unfolding, a deep power present in silence. It has its place in conversational pauses, in explanations left unmade in a lecture, in the Zen gardens, in the space in the painting, in the honor code ruling Japanese management practices. It is an empowering mystery, whose silence, empty time, and space is infused with the eternal present.

Ma can be felt in dreams, even in the most ordinary. Have you ever paid attention to what is *not* in your dream: to the missing link between two scenes, to the "illogical" sequence, to the dream without an end, to the dream figure without a face, to the voice without a body, to the room you entered without a door?

These apparently "negative spaces"—unfilled by sequence, location, or logic—are replete with energy. What we associate to that energy is our own to discover.

Ma can perform another important function in dreams. Where we have little tolerance for ambiguity in our waking lives, dream "spaces" can easily embrace paradox. *Ma* is one way for the dream to present the impossible—being present in two time frames, two bodies, two genders, two places, two belief systems.

Let us look at the ways we can explore the presence and functions of *ma* in David's dream.

The Open-Heart Surgeon

I'm doing open-heart surgery on some man, but I'm not a doctor. I'm doing it with someone else I can't see. I tell the other person to be careful not to cut too close. Suddenly, I'm talking with the patient in her room. She's a woman now. I tell her it was a success but that she is going to die anyway. She doesn't seem upset. Next thing, I am a teenager on the beach with friends and I see her—the patient—walking along a beach, laughing with her family.

Many places in this dream are imbued with paradoxical mystery—if we can just lift the dream narrative from the burden of causal logic. David explored the *ma* in this dream by highlighting words that opened into the mystery, to the place of worlds and unseen insights unfolding:

Our usual language for perceiving dreams is curiously imprecise. We listen *to the dream to see what it is telling us, or we* look *at what it says.*

—James Hillman
"Image Sense"

Ma in the Open-Heart Dream

I'm doing open-heart surgery on some man *but* I'm not a doctor. *It doesn't seem to bother me.* I'm doing it with someone else *I can't see.* I tell the other person to be careful not to cut too close.

Suddenly, I'm talking with the patient in her room. *She's a woman now.* I tell her it was a success *but* she is going to die anyway. She *doesn't seem upset.*

And *next thing* I am a *teenager* and I see her—the patient—walking along a beach, laughing with her family.

We can imagine all kinds of elements that could fill these mysterious spaces. However, the point is not to fill them with rationalization but to dwell in their mystery, to imagine what it might be like *in* the spaces. For example, rather than try to *explain* why he might be an unqualified doctor, David imagined how he would *feel* doing something for which he had no formal training.

Explanation leads too easily to judgment. Imagination leads to new possibilities and open-ended, new insights into what we might have been doing. Here were more directions that David explored:

A dream is not at home in our daytime consciousness. Like Mercury, the god of thieves, we have stolen the dream from its nocturnal domain. Every dream requires a switchover into a dreamlike consciousness that can follow the dream world.

—Robert Bosnak
A Little Course in Dreams

- *Feel the mystery of what happened between finishing the operation and going to the patient's room.* "I see myself floating from the operating theater to the room, dropping my theater gown behind me. . . ."

- *Imagine the patient transforming from a man to a woman. Put yourself in his/her shoes. How do you feel?* "As the patient, I feel a deep feeling of inevitability about this—as though the operation allowed me to find some deeper part of myself, the feminine part. . . ."

- *Imagine not being upset when you find out both that your operation is a success and that you are going to die. How can you hold these contradictory positions?* "Again, it's this strange sense of fate—that the operation is necessary—that something that's been hurting me has needed to be transformed, and that somehow whatever is going to die is also necessary and inevitable—maybe some old way of being?"

- *Feel the mystery of becoming a teenager again. Imagine the changes in your body, your feelings, your thinking, your perceptions.* "I feel stronger every second—more playful, less responsible, handsome, sexy. I'm flippant and don't know anything about dying. Everything is new. I think I know everything. . . ."

David rarely filled the spaces with rationales that would provide the narrative with "logical" transitions across time and space. Rather than reduce the mystery, he preserved it and respected it. When you work with your own dreams, hold the mystery with as much respect as David did. Other than avoiding rationalization and analysis, there are no set ways to explore the mysterious spaces in dreams. To explore *ma* with loving respect is simply to come away from a dream still feeling the mystery—but feeling it more richly.

CREATING *MA*: LOOKING FOR THE MYSTERY BEHIND WHAT IS VISIBLE

Ma is also inherent even in the spaces that *are* filled in a painting or narrative. A way to better appreciate elements in a painting or a dream is to remove each, one by one, and contemplate the space that it leaves. What was it that this particular brush stroke, color, shape, word, or sentence added to the whole of the painting or dream?

Patricia wrote her dream out so that each sentence contained only one major element. In this way, she could later experiment with removing them one by one:

The Ceremony

I am traveling with older Eskimo women. There are also younger men present. We have to go do a special ceremony somewhere. I am in the backseat of a car with some of them. I have a small ceremonial pot with me. I wish I had brought some herbs. We arrive and begin the ceremony using the four directions. Someone knows which way East is. Each group has a responsibility for a different direction. I think ours is West. Some of the young boys in our group are a little rebellious.

Patricia took each sentence and asked herself: How does the feeling or the mystery of the whole dream change when I remove this element? By so doing, she better appreciated the *ma* behind each element.

There are . . . other images . . . which can help us understand the basic operations through which we come to appreciate and dialogue with the timeless depths of each dream performance and its verbalized text. These are images, originally of ritual processes, which have been used since our Stone Age ancestors first began scratching linear forms on the rock walls of sacred caves and mounds. These sacred signs depict energy in motion. . . . The line is like the energy of affect force pushing through the ground of chaos to create a surface pattern. . . .

—Sylvia Brinton Perera
"Dream Design"

The dream itself is a texture woven of time and space inside which we find ourselves.

—Robert Bosnak
A Little Course in Dreams

When I omit:	*I miss a sense of:*
the American Indian women	the quiet, sacred feminine energy
the young men	unruly but good energy
traveling to do a special ceremony	sacred purpose
my place in the back seat	a sense of being led
my ceremonial pot	my unique role in the ceremony
the arrival and beginning	transition from journey to ceremony
the four directions	homage to all-encompassing Nature
one who knew where East was	a wise elder with superior knowledge
each group had a direction	specialized roles
mine was west	sunset, dusk, warm glow, letting go
rebellious boys	balance, levity

Rather than attempt to describe the contribution of an element when it is embedded in the tiles of the whole dream mosaic, ritually removing each element in turn to see what quality is lost from the whole makes us more appreciative of each element's contribution. Experiencing its absence contributes *ma* in a way we might never have anticipated.

MAKING A DREAM "ETERNAL": LOOKING AT THE ETERNAL ASPECT OF SITUATIONAL DREAMS

When I only have a few minutes to note and explore a dream, I tend to dismiss it. It suits me to view it as unimportant; I don't feel responsible for listening to myself. My hurry as I scribble in the early-morning light colors my perspective. I am more likely to view the dream's scenario as an isolated, unimportant event—often inexplicable and odd.

James Hillman suggests a simple way to shift from a temporal perspective to an eternal, from the particular to possibly wider implications of a dream in our lives. He suggests we experiment with "eternalizing" the dream:

- add *when* and *then*
- then change *when* to *whenever*

Hillman reflects that the attachment of an *-ever* suffix eternalizes a connection that might too easily be passed over. It strengthens a hidden pattern *(when/then)* by letting us imagine that a particular connection in a dream is always going on in our life, a kind of eternal mechanism operating in the psyche.

Let's see what happens if we make these simple changes in a dream Julia recorded:

Freefalling

I am watching and then become one of a group of people falling to earth from the stratosphere. . . . We are learning how to use the air currents as we freefall. We are not flying. I pull an imaginary cord on an imaginary parachute and break the fall at the last minute. . . .

Here's what can happen when we use the causal construction *when/then*:

When I watch, *then* I become one of a group of people falling to earth from the stratosphere. *When* we learn how to use the air currents, *then* we freefall. We are not flying.

All dreams are big dreams, carriers of personal and archetypal meaning that can and must be accessed for the sake of individuation . . . It is incumbent upon us to treat all of our dreams with the deepest respect, even if their meanings elude us . . . If we approach our small and large dreams with psychological faith and a little craftiness, we may well find that we understand what individuation is all about.

—Stephen A. Martin
"Smaller Than Small,
Bigger Than Big"

When I pull an imaginary cord on an imaginary parachute, *then* I break the fall at the last minute.

Adding *-ever* to the *when* produces this temporal shift in perspective:

Whenever I watch, *then* I become one of a group of people falling to earth from the stratosphere. *Whenever* we learn how to use the air currents, *then* we freefall. We are not flying. *Whenever* I pull an imaginary cord on an imaginary parachute, *then* I break the fall at the last minute.

Hillman also points out that we can reverse the images in order to play with alternative causal connections. What happened to Julia's response to this dream when she reversed *when* and *then*?

Whenever I become one of a group of people falling to earth from the stratosphere, *then* I watch. *Whenever* we freefall, *then* we learn how to use the air currents. We are not flying. *Whenever* I break the fall at the last minute, *then* I pull an imaginary cord on an imaginary parachute.

Julia responded strongly to this last series of simple word changes. As she began to play with the restatements, she reacted most intensely to *Whenever we freefall, then we learn how to use the air currents.* She thought about how often she tried to set up and control situations in her family life and her work. She wondered what it might be like to "freefall" more in her life, trusting her capacity to learn, along with those around her, how to "use the air currents."

She found further encouragement in *Whenever I pull an imaginary cord on an imaginary parachute, I break the fall.* She

[Dreams] have a superior intelligence in them: a wisdom and a guiding cleverness which leads us. They show us where we are wrong; they show us where we are unadapted; they warn us about danger; they predict some future events; they hint at the deeper meaning of our life, and they convey to us illuminating insights.
—Marie-Louise von Franz
In Fraser Boa's
The Way of the Dream

began to imagine that she could trust herself to help and protect her when the going got rough.

Over the following months, Julia worked with these two images in interpersonal situations. Before she entered a room for a meeting, she would use the threshold to remind her to freefall, to trust the air currents, to pull that imaginary cord if needed. A naturally anxious person, she learned to calm herself before stressful situations by using this image. She could also reassure herself quietly by pulling that imaginary cord, an internal symbolic act that gave her enough momentary distance from the situation to then reenter with composure and clarity. These changes in both her internal imagining and her behavior were a steady healing influence on her personal and professional lives.

This confusion between what we see and how we see is another example of the effect of ideas.

—James Hillman
Healing Fiction

THE ONLY TIME: LIMITING APPARENTLY WIDESPREAD PATTERNS IN OUR DREAMS AND LIFE

When I become self-critical, I scatter generalizations like confetti. I fling statements at myself without thinking twice about their accuracy: *I'm always running late! . . . I'm never patient enough!* When my self-criticism abates (or I throw a bucket of icy water over it), I can look with more clarity and consideration at what started the attack. I can say, *I took that extra phone call this morning. I didn't have to answer it, and answering it made me late.* Or I can say, *You were fairly patient in that situation until you got tired, and then you made one statement that might have sounded irritable.* These descriptions differ from my earlier global pronouncements. These new descriptions help me learn from what happened. I can refuse late phone calls; I can be more aware of my own weariness and leave a situation earlier so that I run less risk of being impatient with others.

Being specific can also be helpful with dreams, as James Hillman points out. He underscores the risk of always viewing our dreams so symbolically that we miss the personal point. He suggests we experiment with "singularizing" the dream by using the word *only*, as Lucy did with her dream about unknown territory:

For Philippine Negritos, the dream constitutes an equal partner with wakefulness in dealing with reality. Wakefulness and the dream exist on different planes but there is a continuity between them.
—Carl W. O'Nell
Dreams, Culture, and the Individual

Unknown Territory
I am walking or driving. It's half-dark. There are hills and valleys. It's half-known territory around a public institution or hotel with interesting entrances and alleyways, but I can't find the main entrance. One is not permitted in certain areas, certain rooms that belong to certain people. I am responsible for my mother or my daughter in the dream.

When Lucy had this dream, she was discouraged. She commented that this was typical of her: She believed that she never felt confident in any public situations. She always felt completely responsible for and inadequate in the situation. Recognizing that she was making a lot of "always" and "never" generalizations here, Lucy decided to get specific with the dream image by using the *only* approach:

- *Only* when I am walking or driving do I not know my way around.
- *Only* when it's half-dark do I not know my way around.
- *Only* public institutions or hotels seem unfamiliar.
- I have trouble entering *only* public institutions or hotels.
- *Only* when people have certain rooms am I not permitted to enter them.

- *Only* when I am responsible for my mother or daughter do I have trouble finding my way around.

This delimiting of the dream image had practical outcomes. As Lucy generated these statements, she actually identified definable circumstances that concerned her. She realized that she didn't enjoy taking both her mother and young, rambunctious daughter to new, public places at the same time. Her mother and her daughter both had difficulty walking far, and this left Lucy anxious when she was parking. She decided that, in future, when she had either her daughter or mother with her, she would phone ahead and determine where she could park that was easily accessible. Her approach to her dream had a practical outcome.

An inner result of the dream was Lucy's growing understanding of her uncertainty about taking initiative. She talked about how she had felt "at sea" in many public situations ever since she had skipped a grade in elementary school, how she had felt ever since then that she was supposed to know things she could not know. She resolved to have as much patience with herself as she did with her daughter and mother. In the future, she would not expect herself to be perfectly competent or perfectly at ease when she found herself unfamiliar with customs or protocol. She would just remind herself that she was not supposed to "know."

Becoming more specific and less general, as Lucy did, allows us to break down the apparently impossible into manageable chunks. So often, we are tempted to ask ourselves: What is the maximum I can do in this situation or for this problem? More helpful, often, is the "taming pow-

Dreams seem to challenge and deny the parallel notions of rationality and responsibility. To be responsible, one must be rational. In dreaming, the dreamer appears to be irrational, and thus the dreamer appears to himself to lose his sense of volition and responsibility.

—Fred Alan Wolf
The Dreaming Universe

er of the small," as the *I Ching* describes it, which allows us to ask: What is the *smallest* change I can make in this situation to alleviate it? Small alterations in the psyche can be as far-reaching as the butterfly's change of direction, which can be enough to alter the weather patterns on the other side of the earth.

TOUGH MESSAGES FROM THE MOTHER OF DAYS: IMAGINING A TRUSTWORTHY SOURCE OF A BAD DREAM

Bad dreams. We awake with the memory of the tooth pulled without anesthetic, our children dying in a fire we inadvertently set, the monster child born to us, the ax murderer in the unlighted house. We want to escape the image. The last thing we want is to explore the dream creatively! We turn our own images into scapegoats, boo them out of town, lock them up in forgetfulness, or run fleeing from them into the safe haven of waking reality and ordinariness.

Yet dream events are neither good nor bad. One of my meditation teachers once declared, "It is better to be good than bad but it is even better to be neither." We need to look at both sides of anything and anyone if we are to accept the wholeness of events and people. As Jungian analyst, June Matthews commented in a lecture at the C. G. Jung Institute in San Francisco, "Hell is part of the Self, too." Moreover, horrific events are not necessarily horrific from the soul's point of view. The soul has a different, timeless perspective on many aspects of life.

Some time ago, a fire rolled through the gentle hills close to my home. The sky bulged black; elderly oaks shrank to black skeletons against pockmarked hills; undulating grasses were scorched to bald ground. Driving past with a friend, I bemoaned the barren landscape. She reminded me that some environments benefit from fire. I can't believe (yet) that arsonists' fires benefit anyone or anything. However, the following spring, walking in the same hills, I was forced to acknowledge that my friend, who has more equanimity than I, was right about this fire.

Hindus perceive three aspects of divinity, each necessary for the inner and outer cycles of life to continue: creation, sustenance, and destruction. The gods and goddesses of destruction get bad press, but they do good work. They dissolve obstacles. They destroy the old to make a place for the new.

If I think about my nightmares in this way, my perspective changes. Some bad dreams cloud awareness, sear the ground of waking consciousness, burn out my ancient, cherished belief structures, and ravage my sense of who I am. At those moments, it's hard to remember that, in my inner world, grass will sprout again, birds will return, trees will green out. But I keep learning (again and again and with patient reminders) that nighttime or daytime journeys to hell are, indeed, part of my Self's way of renewing itself.

"Bad" dreams can balance out idealized versions of ourselves, others, events, and values. They can bring form to the dark side of an event, a side that is always present if we are aware of the longer wavelength of the notes of eternal time. Some dreams scream out real warning, danger. Others exaggerate, finally getting through to us like good friends shouting in our ear in a burning restaurant. Some

The best way to deal with a dream is to think of yourself as a sort of ignorant child . . . and to come to a two-million-year-old man or to the old mother of days and ask, "Now what do you think of me?"
—C. G. Jung
Collected Works

dreams indicate past experiences that need to be set to rest in heart and memory. These, too, are constructive: They alert us to places in heart and soul that are still quietly bleeding, places that need healing through forgiveness of ourselves or others, places that need new perspectives. Some nightmares warn of actual approaching dangers; others warn of subtle patterns of ill health being laid down in body or spirit; unfortunately, few of us grow skilled enough to know which dreams are prophetic until after the event. And some "bad dreams" are probably just due to bad cheese.

On rare occasions, children are born without the capacity to feel pain. They are at high risk. If they cannot feel pain, they have no idea when they are being or have been hurt. We need the wisdom of those fine-tuned pain receptors in body and psyche. Nightmares are often accurate pain receptors.

A dream is quite capable . . . of naming the most painful and disagreeable things without least regard for the feelings of the dreamer.

—C. G. Jung
Collected Works

Looking at Both the Good and Bad Associations to Images

Writing down and associating to both the light and dark sides of images, we glimpse possibilities for our hearts other than fright and misery. Andrea, a lawyer with solid, healthy relationships in her inner and outer life, awoke screaming from a nightmare, and could not fathom how she might work creatively with its content, its affect, or any inherent message in it.

I Accidentally Give Myself AIDS!

I am on an expedition to clean up the environment. We have all made a pledge to pick up garbage wherever we see it. I pick up some papers and what I think is a drinking straw, only to find that it is a hypodermic needle that accidentally punctures my lip and brings a few drops of blood. I am sure it is infected with AIDS. I am horrified. I realize I should have been wearing gloves.

I start to walk home. I know I am probably going to die a long and slow death, and that there is nothing I can do about it. I wonder how I am going to tell my husband that I was stupid enough not to wear gloves, and it might have cost me my life. I also know that I can't even get tested right away, so I have to live with the uncertainty of knowing whether I am dying.

I awake sobbing.

It rarely happens that [dreams are] either exclusively positive or exclusively negative.
—C. G. Jung
Collected Works

Not a cheerful dream for a Monday morning. Had Andrea been feeling in bad shape, we would have worked differently with this dream. But she was in good inner and outer form (at least, as good as most of us ever get). What creative possibilities could she find here? Our purpose was not to "do a Pollyanna" on the dream, to dull it into spiritual safety, or to lull our shocked senses into saying, "That wasn't horrible; that was a wonderful learning experience." It was, indeed, a horrible internal experience. Nor was our intention to interpret, although we were both open to any insights that might spontaneously emerge from walking around the dream. Andrea amplified the associations she had to AIDS. They were all bad. When I asked her if she could draw on any good associations, she found, to her surprise, one recent one:

"Someone was talking with me recently about how amazingly rewarding it was to work with a lot of her AIDS clients. She said that many often feel close to God. They have a clear sense of what is important in their lives and what is not worth worrying about. She said many patients were really committed to living fully, despite their worst fears having been lived out."

Andrea and I wondered together what it might be like for her to be willing to allow old parts of herself to die, to allow herself to be penetrated by something that might cause her suffering but that also might bring a closer sense of her own spirituality and a fuller perspective on life. Andrea retold the dream to herself using this perspective:

A Retelling of the AIDS Dream

I'm cleaning up messy bits of my life (cleaning the environment) and in doing so, am hurt by something (the needle) that might cost me my life as I currently know it. If I could get past the fear and the self-recrimination for having gotten myself into messes in the past (not wearing gloves), perhaps I could focus on things that are really important, and perhaps grow more spiritually.

Too positive, too slick? Let's take another tack.

Speaking in Riddles:
Finding the Opposite Image for the Nightmare

Andrea and I imagine that the nightmare is sent to her by a Wise Godmother who knows how to get her goddaughter's attention. Wise Godmothers can see around corners. They can see in the dark. Andrea imagines that the dream is an allegory for something in her life. What can it say?

We imagine that the Wise Godmother always speaks in riddles; she turns the dream into a trick mirror that reverses and corrects for the beliefs we live by during the day. Andrea describes the opposite of everything in her dream:

"The dream would portray a world in which nothing bad, unexpected, or unfair ever happens, in which I am

If we take the time to learn their language, we discover that every dream is a masterpiece of symbolic communication. The unconscious speaks in symbols, not to confuse us, but simply because that is its native idiom.

—Robert Johnson
Inner Work

never at risk, in which I never have to be attentive to my welfare, and where I am always assured of being rewarded for good deeds.

"That sounds pretty childlike to me. I am walking around in a sophisticated, political, and social world with my childlike trust wide open too often! I still, at heart, expect everything to turn out right if I'm a good girl! I guess it took the exaggeration of this nightmare to point out to me how overly idealistic my ideas of goodness and justice are!"

As Andrea looked at this reversal, she reflected further on what ways she was too trusting in unknown situations. She commented that her trusting nature was not always serving her with discernment. Sometimes, it put her at serious risk. While she understood that dreams often exaggerate to get their point across, Andrea was also aware that a dream like this was not to be ignored or diminished. She needed to pay attention to where her trusting nature might be putting her in dangerous situations.

Both approaches to her dream carried possibilities for Andrea. The careful and courageous attention she gave her nightmare helped her move through the world with more awareness and self-care. Like Andrea, we too can attend to the constructive function of our nightmares and dance with their skeletons until their wise energy is brought to life.

The dream world is beneficent and healing only if we have a dialogue with it, but at the same time remain in actual life. We must not forget living. . . . As soon as one begins to ignore outer life . . . the dream world becomes dangerous . . . . The dream world is only positive if it is in a living, balanced dialogue with a lived, actually lived, life.

—Marie-Louise von Franz
In Fraser Boa's *The Way of the Dream*

THE LION, THE MOUSE, AND THE LEOPARD: USING CONTRAST TO UNDERSTAND YOUR IMAGES

I awake from dreaming about a friend's swimming pool. I think about the pool. It is a pleasant rectangle surrounded by potted palms. That's about all I can remember or make of the dream. However, if I use yet another of James Hill-man's ideas—using a foil or contrast—I can glean more from this recalcitrant image. If I say, "Why Jan's pool and not Paul's or Richard's?" I use other images to contrast with the dream image.

"Well," my inner voice quickly responds, "Jan's pool is more spacious than the other two. . . . I swim more in Jan's pool than I do in the other two. . . . Paul built his for him-self. . . . Richard's came with the house. . . . Jan built hers especially to help one of her children with physical prob-lems. . . ."

Now I'm getting somewhere: I am dreaming about a spacious place that I visit frequently, created for a child to heal. Do I need a break from working so that I can just relax and restore my younger, playful, perhaps temporari-ly hampered side?

Using contrasts can be extended to any part of a dream. The trick with using contrasts is to change one thing at a time. In the next dream, the dreamer lists possible con-trasts in parentheses. There were many others she could have listed. She could, for example, have been walking up the mountain or flying. But she needed only a simple con-trast. Using one contrasting element helped her better fo-cus on the actual image her unconscious chose, rather than get distracted by the new element.

Bicycling with My Mother
I am *bicycling up* the side of a mountain. It is *cloudy* and the clouds are lying *close* to the mountain. I am with my *mother*, who is much *younger* in the dream. She is telling me about some meeting where there was a speaker

Holding the opposites means experiencing both fully. That's why when I work on dreams, I go for the contrasting emotions, intensifying them, holding the conflict. This stretches our soul. The stretching is what matters.

—Robert Bosnak
In Michael V. Adams'
"Image, Active
Imagination, and the
Imaginal Level"

who brought a *lion*. We reach the *top* of the mountain and sit down on an *orange* seat.

- *What's different about bicycling from, say, driving?* Slower, more of my own physical energy needed.
- *How does the dream change if I imagine driving down, not up?* Much more effort to ride up—have to want to do it.
- *How does the feeling of the dream change if it's sunny, not cloudy?* Less mysterious, cheerier. I like biking on cloudy days.
- *What if the clouds were in the distance? Would that change the feeling?* Less mystery. Less immersion in nature.
- *What's different about being with my mother on the side of the mountain as distinct from my father or daughter?* Most unlikely thing I could do with my mother—she's inactive.
- *How would it be different if she were the age she is in waking life, or older?* She's younger, therefore more energetic. Younger spirit. My age.
- *How would the sense shift if the speaker had brought a mouse or a leopard?* A lion is the king; a mouse is scared; a leopard can't change his spots—to be in charge of a trained lion makes the speaker very powerful—most powerful.
- *Would it feel different if we had reached a valley?* Sense of mastery and relationship with sky—king of the mountain, not coddled by the valley.
- *Would it make a difference if the seat were brown or green?* Purposeful—orange contrasts with gray sky—a really noticeable resting place.

There is no such thing as a small dream, only small dream perspective. By shifting our perspective in subtle, crafty ways, the small dream reveals not only valuable information about the dreamer's personal attitude toward life, but about his or her larger destiny as well.

—Stephen A. Martin
"Smaller Than Small, Bigger Than Big"

After you have finished exploring the contrast, you can integrate this information by restating the dream, incorporating the answers to your questions. This is how this dreamer rewrote her dream:

General Restatement

I am doing something I really like in a mysterious but pleasant environment. It involves a lot of effort but I am accompanied by an unfamiliar, young, energetic, maternal side of me, who tells me about encountering a powerful, public man who can command obedience even from the king of the jungle. When we reach our high goal, we rest in a clearly marked resting place.

After you have restated the dream, you can write a paragraph about what your current understanding of the dream might be based on that restatement. This dreamer wrote:

Current Understanding

Sounds like my professional life. I'm making a lot of effort but enjoying it. I need my energetic maternal energy for the company (better take care of myself). The powerful man sounds like our CEO. I need to respect and steer clear of his power. He doesn't like to be challenged. He is indeed a king in the software jungle. I need to take defined time to rest between bouts of working hard.

By working with contrasts in this way, we differentiate the subtle choices our creative unconscious has made, thereby enabling subtler understanding of the dream. We can appreciate how meticulous the unconscious is; it knows exactly what image will achieve the desired effect and affect.

The Senoi believe that man can see, in dreams, the images he has formed of the outside world and their potential contradictions. . . . Hostile images may, however, be harnessed to serve personality development when they are revealed in dreams and are appropriately interpreted.

—Kilton Stewart
"Dream Theory
in Malaya"

6

Myth, Tale, and Poetry

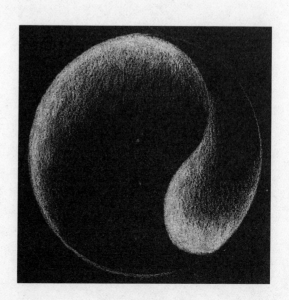

"IN THEIR NAMES ARE THEIR SOULS": NAMING THE FIGURES IN YOUR DREAMS

At various times, dream figures can be known, unknown, our personal selves, magnificent characters, or ordinary folk.

As we discussed earlier, the extent to which figures represent parts of us seems to vary. At times, dreams are founded more in memory and day residue: We replay a situation at work, rehearse a future situation based on our waking perceptions of our supervisor, our mate, our children. At other times, dreams arise from a deeper level in us: The dream figure does not behave as he or she would in waking life, or has a different personality. Sometimes, the dream figure can be someone we have not thought of for years. Some figures are completely unknown, a creative gestalt provided by our psyche—a figure in a myth, fairy tale, play, fictional story, or painting.

Regardless of the waking or dreaming origin of dream figures, we need to hold figures in a middle realm of reality. We cannot always explain them away by seeing them only as "just my aunt." My aunt is not just my aunt in my dream world. She is my *experience* of my aunt—and of myself through the form of my aunt—at that moment. This dream is *my* dream, as unique in its re-creation of the waking world as my tone of voice, my way of physical movement, my food tastes.

If I am color blind, I cannot perceive the color red. Something inside me has to carry the possibility of "red" before I can perceive it. So, too, in my inner imaginal world: I cannot perceive my aunt's grace or spirited approach to her life if I do not have an intimation of my own (realized or unrealized) grace and high spirits. Someone else will dream about my aunt differently. And I dream about my

The persons in myths . . . come with names, and Greek mythic personalities not only had each his, her, or its own name, but had a long chain of them. . . . These persons of myth were always named so as to give a particular context. . . .

One of the ways of restoring the "embracing the vision of the myth" to the persons of last evening who have entered the dream is to look at their names.

—James Hillman
The Dream and
the Underworld

aunt differently on different days. However, at this moment, my aunt's grace and spirit is what is reverberating in me.

Nor can we distance ourselves entirely from dream figures by seeing them as "unknown people in clown costumes." Diminishing them does not work. Yet neither can we turn every dream entity into a mythological being who has nothing personal to do with us but comes to offer portent of the future. Each of these possible responses does have a place at times. Fixed adherence to any one of these approaches risks diminishing or aggrandizing the figures so much that they cannot help us in that middle realm.

Many dreamers have received names for themselves or others in dreams. Some names are familiar; others, inventions of linguistic imagination. Naming these figures or paying attention to names they already have helps us hold them in that middle world in which the dream lives, moves, and has its being. It helps us preserve their roles as mediators between the realm of humans and the realm of the gods.

Figures with Names

When a figure appears with a name, explore the original form and use of the name. Imagination moves freely among visual, written, and auditory associations. Amplify the name—think of your personal associations to the name. Evoke historical and mythological associations for the name. Often names make plays on words, appearing in anagram or pun form. This might not lead anywhere initially, but at least you have paid attention.

[Boa]
Jung dreamed he was walking along a little road and came to a small chapel. He entered and was surprised that there was no statue of the virgin on the altar, nor a crucifix either, but only a beautiful flower arrangement. And then he saw on the floor in front of the altar a yogi sitting in lotus position, in deep meditation.
[von Franz]
Jung realized with a shock that this was the yogi who was imagining him, and that in his trance, a kind of active imagination, he was imagining the life of Jung, dreaming him. Jung knew that when the yogi woke up, he, Jung, would no longer exist. The ordinary Professor Jung was the dream of that great inner figure.

—Fraser Boa and
Marie-Louise
von Franz
The Way of the Dream

FIGURES WITHOUT NAMES

What about the figures in our dreams who have no names? How can we name them in a way that acknowledges and dignifies the role they play in that middle world? James Hillman suggests we capitalize the words we use to describe them. See whether you react differently to the "names" that appeared in Tony's dream when they are capitalized:

Estio's Wounds

Unspeakable horrors were inflicted on a young boy. In order just to live, he and his sister had to kill their cruel parents. Now he just has quietly snapped inside and just repeats his name, saying, "Hello Estio" every time someone walks by. He no longer knows who or what he is. He has only his politeness and sweetness left, which he keeps using automatically.

Peter gave these names to the characters:

- Young Tortured Estio
- Tortured Estio's Sister
- The Cruel Parents

When we capitalize words in English, they seem to take on a universal significance in addition to the personal. Tony had been confused about why he should dream such a thing when he had mainly good feelings about his upbringing. Yet after he gave the names to the characters, he realized that this painful dream originated more in the middle world of myth. When he capitalized *The Cruel Parents*, he could accept that all children "suffer" at the hands of their parents, no matter how good the parents are. There are times when the horror of being left as a baby, even for five minutes, is indeed unspeakable. We all carry, within us, these preverbal, archetypal experiences.

Tony was also given a name for that part of himself that had suffered and still suffered. He was an optimistic man, not inclined to look at the dark side of situations. Having a name for this vulnerable, suffering side of himself helped him make it real to himself internally. He began to include his more painful feelings in his awareness by turning within and imagining how Estio was faring in a situation and considering whether he needed help from the Sister. The actual name, *Estio,* was one to which he could not bring any associations. He finally decided that perhaps he was not meant to have any other associations; it was a unique name for a unique and hidden part of himself.

Frances had a similar dream:

I knew with my two children when I was pregnant before there was any sign . . . I saw both of my kids as well. I never had to think of a name because they already had names in the dream. Names that I never would have chosen because nobody in my family has those names.

—Isabel Allende
In Naomi Epel's
Writers Dreaming

The Persistent Urchin

I look out the window of my office. There is a dark-skinned, almost naked, thin urchin hiding in the corner of the yard. He is hungry and tired.

I am consulting with a male business client at the time. My client leans out the window and hauls the child out of my yard and over the other side of the fence by the scruff of his neck. The boy runs off. I know it was a useless gesture, because he'll just come back.

He enters by the other gate and returns to his spot. We call a child authority group, who take him to a children's shelter. I later call the shelter to see how he is doing.

Frances was a social worker. At first, she was inclined to dismiss this dream as an amalgamation of cases she had handled. However, when she named these figures, they became both more personal and more archetypal:

- The Dark-Naked-Thin-Urchin
- The Rough Male Client
- The Child Authorities
- A Children's Shelter

A great work of art is like a dream; for all its apparent obviousness, it does not explain itself and is always ambiguous.

—C. G. Jung
Collected Works

Working now at a more archetypal level, she could imagine this scene in a myth or dark fairy tale and see the weary, thin, neglected, naked, determined child as a part of all of us, herself included. She saw that this situation, apparently triggered simply by daily memory residue, had both personal as well as universal connotations. Not just a child but *The* Child. The rough male client is not just this particular man but *The* Rough One in each of us. The Child Authorities are more than just her colleagues but that part of us responsible for caring for our hungry selves as well as others.

Frances also decided to name the *I* in the dream. After all, the dreaming *I* is a related yet different *I* from our "waking" *I*. Following Hillman's suggestion, she called the personage she occupied in the dream by different names, depending on what she was doing at different points in the dream:

- Looking-I
- Consulting-I
- Knowing-I
- Calling-I

When Frances named these different parts of herself, the dream gave her a fresh view of herself. She could, indeed, see the Looking-I and the Consulting-I, those aspects of her personality most comfortable looking, staying at a distance, not only in her professional consultations but also in her personal life. She could appreciate the Knowing-I and the Calling-I, those parts she could trust to help her reach out to others. She saw how all these energies were potentiated at different times within her, toward both herself and others.

In this middle realm, the distinction between what is within and what is without really becomes irrelevant, as Ailie's dream indicates:

Killing the Spiders
There are dreadful spiders all over my yard where my children play. I go to a nursery and ask for something to kill them, but the nurseryman says I should get something to kill what the spiders live off.

Ailie gave these names to the dream figures:

- Dreadful Spiders
- Children
- Nursery
- Nurseryman
- What-the-Spiders-Live-Off

When Ailie named the spiders and the nurseryman, she responded differently to this dream. She saw Dreadful Spiders as all those things that threatened her inner connection to her heart, and she began to think of the Nursery as not just a plant nursery but a Children's Nursery. (Notice that both Tony and Ailie also capitalized important nonfigural elements such as *A Children's Shelter* and *Nursery*.) When the nurseryman became Nurseryman, he changed significance for her, evoking images of a loving paternal figure who dwelled in a childlike place in her and

In Hindu thought, there is the idea that in certain states of mind, such as dreaming, names are things in themselves. They do not represent something elsewhere embodied by the name, but are presentations of the mind to itself of its own presences. The name is then the divine logos clothed in the person of the dream.

—James Hillman
*The Dream and
the Underworld*

Dreaming is the psyche itself doing its soul-work.

—James Hillman
*The Dream and
the Underworld*

who had the discernment not only to protect her from immediate outer threats from Dreadful Spiders, but also to help her deal internally with that less-visible force feeding the threats: What-the-Spiders-Live-Off.

What's in a name? More, as these dreamer have shown us, than we think.

The Inquisitive Queen: Turning a Banal Dream into a Fairy Tale

In fairy tales, fact and fiction form the warp and woof of the finely woven fabric of story. The fairy tale is neither one nor the other exclusively. Dreams also belong in this middle realm between the imaginal and consensual reality. We recognize the fantasy element of dreams and also can be quick to dismiss it. Yet we are just as quick to dismiss "unimaginative" dreams *because* they have no fantasy elements. Both positions are extreme and exclude the middle realm. Many times, dreamers say, "Well, nothing much in my dreams this week—just some office scenes again where I was doing boring things. I must be working too hard again. . . ."

Even the most ordinary dream can open a wide window onto a field of fantasy. For example, Louisa had the ultimate banal dream: a taxation dream! It defied interest and certainly didn't fill her with uncontainable curiosity.

Looking at Private Tax Returns
I am sorting IRS tax returns in an old upstate New York house. The returns are odd. They have special contents. I come across Carol and Matthew's [the dreamer's sister and brother-in-law] and am careful not to read anything on it. I don't want to intrude on their private life.

I dreamt I was walking on the ancient rocks of Georgian Bay. The unevenness of the rock face made walking difficult. When I looked down to steady myself, I realized that I was walking on the face of Christ.

—Fraser Boa
The Way of the Dream

Begin with the exploration of the dream image as you remember it, with the exploration of memory. At a certain point, memory by itself will start producing new images.

—Robert Bosnak
In Michael V. Adams'
"Image, Active Imagination, and the Imaginal Level"

To see what else the dream might offer, Louisa turned her dream into a fairy tale. This story is reprinted as it appeared to Louisa on first writing and with no editing. It took her two minutes.

The collective unconscious influences our dreams only occasionally.
—C. G. Jung
Collected Works

The Inquisitive Queen
Once upon a time, there was a Queen. She lived in a wonderful old rambling wooden palace in the middle of the forest.

She was rather lonely there. She was always very curious about her subjects. Her subjects had always been afraid of her.

Because she had never been good at talking to them, she ordered her First Minister to bring her the records of the goods that each of her subjects had brought to the castle as payment for the land that she allowed them to farm.

Her Minister warned her that this was the one thing she was forbidden to do as Queen. However, she was very strong and thought that she was above the law of the land, as she was its Queen. She read from the large book.

As she lit a candle so she could read better in the rapidly approaching dusk, she suddenly saw that what her sister, the Princess, and her husband had given her as their annual tithing was a measure of the curse she had put on them when she banished them to a hovel in jealousy so she could be Queen.

She suddenly realized that, in ten years' time, her own curse would return to her and she would be banished.

Moral: Expect back what you put out.

What had started life as a banal dream about a tax return now suggested to Louisa that she was more envious of her sister's good fortune than she realized and, as a consequence, had emotionally withdrawn. This would never have become so quickly clear to her had she not allowed her storytelling capacity to embellish this dream. Turning this dream into a fairy tale gave Louisa more insight into her darker side and how it was actually rebounding on her.

Just as important, Louisa also saw that she had been too ready to dismiss the dream because of its lack of magic and fantasy. She had wanted to reduce the dream to her daily reality instead of meeting the dream on its own terms: meeting the imaginal *with* the imaginal.

What are some simple guidelines for transforming dreams into fairy tales?

- Begin the dream classically with *Once upon a time.*
- Give each important element—each character, animal, house—a name and capitalize it.
- Exaggerate. What is small in the dream, make very small; what is large, make exceptionally large—a book, a room, a nose, a body, a noise.
- Embellish or invent all settings.
- Make up what people look like, what they are wearing.
- Add *always* and *never* wherever you can.
- Make up dialogue.
- Use as many descriptive adjectives (using the five senses) and adverbs as possible—at least one adjective for each noun and one adverb for each verb. For example: The *tall* Queen *quickly* opened the *heavy*, *stained* book.
- Put the story in the past tense.
- Give the tale a title that would intrigue you if you were six years old.
- Add a moral.

If we cannot sufficiently appreciate the small as a doorway to the large, the mundane as a "visible reminder" of the archetypal, then we will go away disillusioned—and for all the wrong reasons.

—Stephen A. Martin "Smaller Than Small, Bigger Than Big"

Illustrating Your New Fairy Tale

If your fairy tale still holds interest and mystery after you have written it, explore it further by illustrating it. I just heard you laughing and saying, "Oh, of course! What a breeze! After all, I'm an accomplished illustrator!" I'm not suggesting (unless you happen to be an illustrator) that you attempt formal illustration. Rather, there are delightfully quick and easy ways we can bring visual richness to stories without needing artistic training or talent.

The Senoi advise continuing pleasant dreams for as long as a climax of some kind is reached. In addition, it is important for the dreamer to be left with a beautiful or useful memory of good dream experiences, such as a poem heard from the loved one, which can be shared with other members of the community on waking.

—Kilton Stewart "Dream Theory in Malaya"

- Write the dream on one or more different colored pieces of paper. (You can find cheap, colored construction paper at arts-and-crafts outlets.)
- Before you write on them, cut the pieces into simple shapes. If shapes appear in your dream, cut out those shapes—the bowl, glass, star, circle, square, egg, path, tree. Make them simple. Make each sheet the same or different, as you prefer.
- Use several colored marking pens, crayons, or pencils to write the dream.
- Substitute stick figures or simple line drawings (in a different color) for objects you can draw. A person can become a stick figure; a face can be a circle with a happy smile or sad smile; a tree can become a green triangle divided by a brown line. Imagine you don't have words for things in the dream. How would you illustrate them if you belonged to a society that recorded story through image? You would draw a rectangle for a box, an open square with a line on top for a chair, a rectangle with a triangle on top for a house. As you write out the story, substitute childlike drawings for words wherever possible.
- Clip scenes, faces, or objects from newspapers or maga-

zines, images that capture aspects of the dream. Glue them onto the construction paper. Write your dream around them. It's easy to find pictures of houses, nature, animals, faces, and figures. If you appear in your dream, photocopy photographs of your face. You can even use your face for the other characters in the dream.

- When you have finished your illustration, make a simple title page and another page that says, *The End, To be continued,* or *This story has no end,* or make up your own.
- Staple the pages together. Put the fairy tale and its illustration away for a while.

Keep your fairy tale private. Share it only with your dream group or therapist. It is not a production. It is food for the soul. If you leave the food well protected, the soul will come and dine. You are possibly too close to your tale to

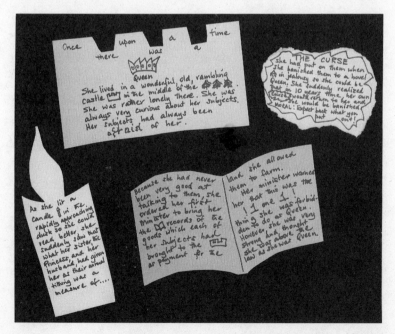

"The Inquisitive Queen"

work with it yet. Later, you can turn the pages and wonder who made it up. When the tale no longer seems to "belong" to you, you will be better prepared to approach the its mystery and wisdom.

The dream always takes place on that bridge between worlds. To ask it to walk the rest of the way into waking interpretation is to diminish it. To suspend conscious connection to the dream is to lose ourselves in the realm of night. But with practices such as fairy-tale writing, we can meet in the middle of the bridge.

If a person doesn't believe in his dreams, he might say, "It's only a dream, it's not real; the gods aren't really talking to me." Little by little everything will become less clear. . . .

—Huichol Shaman
In Harry T. Hunt's
The Multiplicity of Dreams

THE ONLY DREAM THERE IS: WORKING WITH A PASSING DREAM AS IF IT WERE YOUR LIFE MYTH

When we identify in waking consciousness with who we are or what happens in our dreams, we delude ourselves. (Edward Edinger, Jungian analyst and theorist, describes this as falling prey to the concretist fallacy.) We can take our dreams too literally: "This dream about making love to someone other than my spouse is telling me I need to have an affair." Going out and having the affair, we translate the content and rules of the dream world directly into the waking world.

We are equally at risk of self-delusion if we reduce the dream's importance, saying, "It's only a dream. This powerful woman who makes love to me and encourages me to return to my art work is just a product of my overactive mind after watching the movie last night." We keep the dream from taking up psychic residence in the body. (Edinger calls this falling prey to the reductive fallacy.)

To avoid these extremes, imagine, for a moment, that the thin ribbon of a dream you had this morning (say, about solving a problem with your child or coworker) were the *only* dream you have ever had or ever shall have. What would it mean to you that *every* morning of your life you woke up remembering solving a problem with your child or coworker?

Treating your dream as eternally true—an exercise James Hillman suggests—turns your dream into a myth, your life myth. It keeps the dream symbolic (clearly you do other things in your life besides solving problems with children and co-workers). It also ensures that you don't dismiss the dream, so it provides you with a third way to look at the dream. By treating the dream as myth, you can have what Edinger calls a "conscious dialogue" with the image or symbol, a dialogue that allows the symbol "to perform its proper function as re-leaser and transformer of psychic energy with full participa-tion of conscious understanding." The following is a simple way to apply this approach:

The value of a small dream depends greatly on the dreamer's ability to be aware of it.

—Stephen A. Martin
"Smaller Than Small, Bigger Than Big"

- Title the dream: *My Life Myth.*
- Open your first sentence with: *Every morning I awake having dreamed that . . .*
- Add *always* and *never* where you can.
- End your write-up with some statement such as *and I am destined to dream this for the rest of my life.*

Rebecca used this approach with a simple dream:

Getting Off the Roof

I am on a roof that is being repaired. I want to get off the way I got on, but I get nervous. I know I need to wait a minute, so I calm myself before I get off. However, the man who is repairing the roof starts to push me in an attempt to get me going again. I yell at him to stop but he won't. He keeps pushing. I am baffled and enraged and scared. Finally, I spot an open window and crawl through into my mother's bedroom.

My Life Myth: Getting off the Roof When I Am Ready, Not When I Am Pushed

Every morning I awake having dreamed that I am on a roof that is being repaired. I want to get off the way I got on but I *always* get nervous. I know I need to wait a minute, so I *always* calm myself before I get off. However, the man repairing the roof *always* starts to push me in an attempt to get me going again. I *always* yell at him to stop but he *never* will. He *always* keeps pushing. I am *always* baffled and enraged and scared. However, I *always* spot an open window and crawl through into my mother's bedroom. *And I am destined to dream this for the rest of my life.*

Rebecca was fascinated with the result of her exercise. She began to recall many incidents in her life where she felt that she had either capitulated or almost capitulated to some outer authority's timing or agenda that had nothing to do with her inner timing or body's readiness. She had even acquiesced to having a second child when still debilitated from complications from a difficult first birth and postpartum depression. Her husband had wanted two children close together, and both of them had ignored her compromised health. Rebecca recalled accepting jobs she hadn't really wanted because of pressure from a professional job search company. She also remembered the false bravery she had adopted, having grown up with two adored older brothers for whom she dared anything in return for their company.

We cannot take in the meaning of a dream when we have it. . . . The images in the dreams are trying to point us in directions that we can't imagine for ourselves. . . . We get glimpses of this image of ourselves, but sometimes we find ourselves walking into the image of a dream we had years ago and we think, "Here it is! Sure enough!"

—Marion Woodman
Dreams: Language of the Soul

Rebecca also saw that, if she were, indeed, destined to dream—and live—this for the rest of her life, she would be very, very tired before she reached middle age! She realized that she needed to move more into the realm of her mother (a quieter, more reserved, and slow-moving woman), where she could escape both the fear of doing something against her own will and the struggle to maintain her position against inner forces that pushed her ever onward.

This practice takes only half a minute longer than merely writing up the dream but, as Rebecca's work shows, it allows the dream to be viewed through a different, timeless window.

Touching Jupiter and the Guarneri Quartet: Unearthing the Natural Poetry in Your Dream

When people walk along the stone path, open my Western version of a torii gate, and walk through the Japanese garden to my office, their dreams accompany them. I can almost see the air around them change when, in that quiet, interim garden space, they allow the images from their night worlds to resurface.

They often carry notebooks. I have always invited people to tell rather than read me their dreams, although some, for good reasons, prefer to read. I rarely just read the written words. Initially, I suspected myself of laziness. I wondered if I were unwilling to struggle with handwriting (forgivable, given the sleepy hand in which most dreams are written). Later, I realized that my request originated not in concerns about legibility but in my desire to *hear* the

In narrational reading, the sense emerges at the end, whereas in imagistic [poetic] reading there is sense throughout. Most poetry (not the heroic epic, of course) is printed on the page in a form that forces the eye to slow itself to the cadence of the images.

—James Hillman
The Dream and the Underworld

images (note the synæsthesia here). We bring a feeling tone to our dreams when we read them or tell them. Often, forgotten dream images return even as we speak.

When people tell their dreams, their cadence is often poetic. The dream evokes a different rhythm of speech because its logic is soul logic: a pause as a powerful image permeates the imagination and body again; a rise in inflection as the image expands the heart, catches the breath, carries feeling to an unexpected place.

Many dreams are natural poems. Others are pure story. Some are both. The following dreamers wrote out their dreams in linear narrative form and then broke them into free verse lines "to force the eye to slow itself to the cadence of the images," as Hillman says. They weren't trying to write *good poetry*—an ambiguous term in the finest critical circles. While it is debatable what good poetry is, "good" poetry writing leans heavily on the poet's capacity to release images from inner worlds so that they can incarnate in bodies of word. This needs courage, honesty, integrity, and connection to a source of inner cohesion: the soul. Skillful use of poetic devices is not needed for dreamwork.

These two dream poems capture unfettered, metaphoric truths that sprang from these dreamers' souls. This first is what I call, for want of an official term, a big dream. The dreamer, Claire, was profoundly moved by it. It permeated her awareness for days. Eventually, she painted it and rearranged its narrative into poetry. She could find no other way to express its ineffability. This first version appears as she wrote it on waking.

The more transcendent is the inner revelation—ineffable in itself, contained in the poetic intuition, within the creative night of the poet's soul—which a work of words has to express through signs and symbols, in irritating the senses and seducing reason— the more exacting and, as it were, crucifying is the task imposed on the virtue of art. No one is expected to do the impossible; that is what the poet is required to do.

—Jacques Maritain
Creative Intuition in Art and Poetry

Touching Jupiter (Narrative Version)

I am dressed in a large black cloak. R. picks me up and carries me. It is night. There is no other scenery. I collect the edges of my cloak so they don't drag in the water on the ground. I am full of delight. We stand and look up at Jupiter. It is the largest, most luminous and beautiful planet I have ever seen. It has other planets and stars spinning around it, making rings because they are spinning so fast. It is an entire universe! I am overwhelmed with the sight and with its beauty.

Then suddenly the whole universe around Jupiter and Jupiter itself move across the night sky with rapidity.

Then, just as quickly, it moves away from this new position and shoots down to earth and lands at our feet, appearing as a luminescent, incandescent, blue ball of light about two feet in diameter. I cannot take my eyes off it. It wants me to touch it.

I am overcome with awe and terror and only with the greatest difficulty and with the sense of R.'s support as he stands behind me do I utter, "Yes." The effort of saying yes is so strong that it wakes me.

People who go illegitimately mooning after the infinite often have absurdly banal dreams, which endeavor to damp down their ebullience.

—C. G. Jung
Collected Works

Several days later, Claire took this first version, underlined what she wanted to keep (indicated below with italics), put slash lines where she wanted to break it, and then played with moving the images around.

Touching Jupiter (Intermediate Version)

I am dressed *in a* large *black cloak.* / *R.* picks me up and *carries me.* / It is *night.* / There is no other scenery. *I collect the edges of my cloak so they don't drag in the water* on the ground. / I am full of *delight.* / *We* stand and *look up* at Jupiter. / It is the *largest,* most luminous and beautiful planet I have ever seen. It has *other planets and stars* spinning around it *making rings* / because they are *spinning* so fast. It is an entire *universe!* I am overwhelmed with the sight and with its beauty.

Then suddenly the whole *universe around* Jupiter *and Jupiter itself* / *move upwards across the night sky* / with rapidity.

Then just as quickly, it moves away from this new position and *shoots* down *to earth* and *lands* / *at our feet,* / appearing as a luminescent, incandescent, *blue ball of light* / about two feet in diameter. I cannot take my eyes off it. *It wants me to touch it.* /

I am *overcome with awe and terror* / and only with the greatest difficulty and with the sense of R.'s support as he stands behind me do *I utter,* "*Yes.*" / The effort of saying yes is so strong that it wakes me.

Now here is Claire's free-verse version developed from her underlining. Be open to your own response. How does this version affect you?

Touching Jupiter (Poetry Version)
Night.
He carries me.
I gather the edges of my black cloak
away from the water.

Delight.
We look up.
Jupiter.
Planets and stars
spin rings of light,
a universe.

The universe and Jupiter
move swiftly across the sky,
land at our feet,
now a blue ball of light.

Jupiter silently says:
"Touch me."
With awe and terror
I utter, "Yes."

"Touching Jupiter"
Chalk

"Fine," you say. "But that *was* a big dream! How often do
we have those? I dream about the office and fixing my kids'
breakfast and balancing the checking account. Make poetry out of *that!*"

It's your dream to explore as you wish. If you don't
want to make poetry out of your dream, don't. But if you're

By confusing our usual sense language, images and dreams are also retraining our senses themselves. They are being freed from the conceptual constraints which decide how they must perform and what their proper objects are. So, a dream is indeed a derangement of the senses.

—James Hillman
"Image Sense"

not sure whether your own emotional response to your dream might change by seeing it in a new form, work as Alan did with this dream he had one year after separating from his partner of many years. It was a painful separation, and Alan had been feeling heavily despondent about his failure to keep the relationship together. He believed there had to have been something extra he could have done. His dream gave him this gift:

Trying to Please Bob (Narrative Version)

I fix dinner for Bob and also arrange for the Guarneri Quartet to play. Bob is most unappreciative. He wants to know if they are going to play something he has already heard them play, and doesn't wait for me to sit down to join him to eat but finishes immediately. When I am pushed to mildly protest that he didn't wait for me to eat, he indicates that he thought he was doing me a favor by coming to dinner so I wouldn't be lonely. I am furious and say that, on the contrary, Chris [Alan's oldest friend] and I had given up a perfectly good party to do this for him.

Alan believed that this dream was giving him a gilt-edged message on a sterling platter. It was laying to rest his anxiety about whether there was anything else he could or should have done. He saw that, no matter how he might have tried, his partner would never have been satisfied. He paid homage to this dream that extinguished the embers of self-doubt by rearranging it into verse form:

The Guarneri Quartet (Poetry Version)

I fix dinner for you,
arrange for the Guarneri Quartet.
You want to know

if they are going to play
something you have already heard.
You don't wait for me
to join you
but eat quickly.

When I mildly protest
that you didn't wait,
you tell me
you were doing me a favor
by coming—
so I wouldn't be lonely.
Even the Guarneri is not enough!

*Contemplate your
dream and let it
contemplate you.*
—Harry Aron Wilmer
Practical Jung

Now that you've experienced the essential poetry that
Claire and Alan found in their dreams, let's review the
guidelines they followed to brush away the verbal dust to
reveal the jewel underneath:

- Omit detail that carries less subjective force.
- Omit words that are approximate, redundant,
  ineffectively repetitive, vague.
- Use short lines.
- Keep sense descriptions (tactile, visual, auditory . . .)
  where possible.
- Change the tense if it's awkward—from present to past,
  or past to present.
- Change the form from third person (*he/she/it*) to second
  person (*you*) if there is one other dream character involved. As Alan's poem shows, this can add immediacy by bringing a conversational voice to the poem.
- Break the lines of the narrative either by: phrasing; meaning units; a change in imagery, time, place, direction, or
  intent; or breathing point.

- Convert paragraph breaks into new verses.
- Leave out explanations. (*She looked like my sister, but she was my boss in the dream* can become *My sister, my boss.*)
- Remove the uncertainty (*The room looked a bit like a cave.*). Pretend to be certain (*This cave of a room,* or *This room is/was a cave,* or *This cave*).
- Omit such modifying words as *very, almost, quite, somewhat, most, really, highly,* and *extremely.* Be absolute! It's your dream. Feel free to exaggerate or be flatfooted.
- Omit qualifying words that are judgments and/or abstractions, such as *beautiful, ugly, wonderful, terrible,* and *meaningful.* Keep only those that unequivocally add to the charge of the poem. Where an image from the dream can convey the same feeling as the judgment word, leave out the latter. The words Claire left out about the moon, for example, were redundant.
- Stop when the poem *feels* complete, which might not necessarily be where the dream stopped. Poems know when they are whole. You are not bound to be historically faithful to the dream. In fact, the poem might dream the dream onward, take over unexpectedly. Don't fight this. It is a gift from your imagination, another way of allowing your inner explorations to evolve.
- Leave out parts if you think they don't belong, not because they make bad poetry. Leave them out if you feel that they are not salient to the images you are developing.

Dreams are analogous to forms reflected in water.

—Aristotle
Parva Naturalia

The poetic form of a dream simplifies, clarifies, and reaches for essence, creating something psychologically strong. The very act of putting the dream in poetic form allows for slowed-down, quiet, nonreactive meditation on the images. Dreams are often poems, and poems are often waking dreams. Let one form nourish the other.

THE TAMED BEAR KILLS: CONTAINING A NIGHTMARE THROUGH POETRY

Nightmares overwhelm us. They bleed into every part of life and temporarily disarm our personalities with foreign, untamed energy. Containment is essential if we are to perceive the nightmare without too many defenses but with enough to enable us to receive its message. Ways for working with nightmares are in each chapter, but here we focus on poetic forms.

Finding the essential words in a nightmare brings containment to the dark images. Write out your nightmare as quickly as possible without attending to punctuation or spelling. Using only about half of the words you have written and only in the order in which they already appear, build a five- to eight-line, free-form poem. Containing the terrifying image within a fixed form restores perspective and proportion.

The poetic form respects and contains the intuitive, nonlinear structure of the wild, overwhelming affect of the nightmare. The intensity of a poem respects the enormity of the affect, while corralling its images; the density of a poem gathers in the runaway energies that threaten to stampede consciousness.

Here is Stuart's nightmare in its original form:

The Tamed Bear Kills (Nightmare—Narrative Form)
There is a bear—a very large bear. It has been befriended and tamed and lives across the street in a pretty house. But

A useful message for the interpreter of dreams is to be careful neither to "fly with archetypes" (and hence "spiritual" interpretations) nor to reduce the psyche to biological urges alone.

—Mary Ann Mattoon
Applied Dream Analysis

things go wrong. A baby starts to cry. It races over to protect the child but when it starts to pick it up, it mauls the child with its claws, and the child emits a piercing scream. We rush to protect the child, getting the bear off. The bear loses a paw with claws that fall through the floorboards. We realize we have created a monster by befriending it. Then we see someone else killed or someone tries to kill the bear. Shots ring out and someone is killed. We race over.

Stuart set about finding the essential words in this narrative. He was determined to use only the minimum needed to capture this terrifying scene.

The Tamed Bear Kills (Nightmare—Intermediate Form)
There is a bear—a very *large bear*. It has been *befriended* and tamed and *lives across the street in a pretty house*. But *things go wrong*. A *baby* starts to *cry*. It *races* over *to protect* the child but when it starts to pick it up, it *mauls* the child *with* its *claws* and *the child* emits a *piercing scream*. We *rush to protect* the child, getting the bear off. The *bear loses a paw* with *claws* that *fall through the floorboards*. We realize we have *created a monster* by befriending it. Then we see *someone else killed* or someone tries to kill the bear. *Shots ring out* and someone is killed. We race over.

The Bear and the Child (Poetry Form)
Befriended,
the large bear lives
in a pretty house
across my street.

Things go wrong.
A child cries.

The bear tries to protect her
but mauls.
A child's piercing scream.

We rush
to get the bear away.
He loses a paw.
Claws fall through the floor.
Shots ring out.
Someone, perhaps the bear,
is killed.

We have made a monster
by befriending it.

Both aesthetics and psychology have tried to deal with the confusion of the . . . senses in terms of "synæsthesia" and the relation between poetry and painting. . . . Synæsthesia— confusion, interpenetration of one sense with another—goes on all the time in our common speech when we talk imaginatively, or of imagining. Evidently, synæsthesia is how imagination imagines.

*—James Hillman
"Image Sense"*

After Stuart wrote out the nightmare in this form, he observed subtle shifts. Because each image was contained on a separate line, he didn't have to deal with them all at once. He could take in one at a time. This allowed him to be more receptive to each image, to see it discretely without severing it from the whole of which it was inextricably a part.

The poetic form also allowed Stuart to see each image as not only personal and specific but also archetypal and universal. A larger process was being portrayed here. Certainly, it described aspects of Stuart's development, but it also portrayed larger truths about maintaining a healthy respect for the wild part of all nature, especially our own natures. Stuart had been reining in various parts of his personality that seemed to overwhelm others. After this dream, he realized that he needed to distinguish between times when his fierceness was actually hurting him by being overprotective and times when fierceness was appropriate. He realized that he would always have a wild and fierce part, no matter how he tried to domesticate it. However, he could begin to channel that energy into more appropriate contexts where it could wander undisturbed.

The attempt to make prose sense of a dream subjects the dream to a grammatical logic that may be alien to the symbolic logic of the dreaming state, which is closer to poetry than prose.

—Marion Woodman
The Pregnant Virgin

BRUISED IRIS: WRITING DREAMS HAIKU STYLE

Most haiku carry the essence and passion of a simple action or event and place it within a specific, yet timeless, context. A woman's hand, trembling as she holds a cup of tea, is juxtaposed against an autumn tree. She weeps. There are no explanations, no causes, no expanded stories. We do not know why she weeps; we know *that* she weeps. We do not know why she trembles; we know *that* she trembles. Does she tremble because she is cold? We know it is autumn. Does she weep because it is autumn? Because her lover is not there?

The woman's tears remain forever a mystery in exactly the same way our dream images remain mysteries—mysteries that carry the charge of the known act or image and the mystery of the unknown history behind the act or image. They carry *ma*.

The haiku style is uniquely suited to many dreams. It is one of the loveliest, least intrusive ways to record a dream image—either appearing alone or as part of a bigger dream. It is particularly suited to short dream images that we might dismiss because they are too short to really be a "story." The following was such dream. The dreamer was almost ready to dismiss it because it seemed to her that she had lost too much of the larger dream and was left with only this single image. Once she altered her viewpoint, however, and realized that she could look at what she had saved rather than at what she had lost, the haiku emerged.

Javanese Dancers (Narrative Form)

This was part of a much larger dream. All I remember about it now was that somehow we were all down at the harbor. There's lots of noise. I look out to sea and see these dancers—they seem to be dancing on the sea or on a low boat I can't see. They're way out. They're like those Javanese puppets who portray mythological stories. And they're dressed in black and white.

Javanese Dancers (Haiku Version)

Two Javanese dancers in black and white
dance the gods
where sky meets sea.

In this next dream, the dreamer has selected one part on which to focus in haiku style.

Iris Dream (Narrative Form)

I am in some kind of department store. I am too hot, so I walk out the back door past some sort of store security guard. I find myself in this really beautiful setting. It's early morning and I'm in a clearing in the forest. There are lots of irises blooming all over the grove. They are a

"Bruised Iris"
Watercolor

sort of purple-blue, like a bruise color. The air is really still.

Bruised Iris (Haiku Style)
Dawn. In the dry grove,
irises are still,
mauve as eyelids
bruised with dreams.

It is not to be bemoaned that imagination has no conventional language of its own (except the word-play of image), for imagination seems to turn this weakness into an amazing grace.
—James Hillman
"Image Sense"

A traditional haiku follows rules: It arranges seventeen Japanese syllables in three lines of five, seven, and five syllables. Some translators keep to seventeen; others do not. It is not important that you abide by this rule. You are not entering into a haiku-writing contest; you are entering into the essence of an image. You can, however, abide by the *spirit* of haiku by keeping to around three short and simple lines. Here is another dreamer's original narrative and resultant haiku-style poem:

Looking out over the Valley Dream
M. and I have been on some sort of expedition with some other people. I don't remember who is there, but there are other couples. My kids aren't there, but I have a feeling they are okay. While the others set up camp, we climb to the top of the hill beside the camp. There's the most beautiful view from there, a really green, rainy valley below us. I am so happy to be there with him—that we are together—and I put my head on his shoulder and place my hand on his heart area.

Looking at the Valley Together (Haiku Version)
We gaze at the wet, green valley.
I lay my head on your shoulder,
my hand on your heart.

Haiku focuses on sense detail, locating a feeling in a minimalistic, strongly etched image. It is a parenthesis in eternity. The poem often indicates season by the mention of a plant, flower, or weather condition. You do not need to do this, but staying with one or two natural images can gently sustain the feeling embedded in the dream, the essence of which you bring to this poem. Here is yet another dream narrative and its haiku form:

A dream that is not understood remains a mere occurrence; understood it becomes an experience.

—C. G. Jung
Collected Works

Night Ceremony Dream
We are at some kind of ceremony. I don't know who "we" is, but there is a feeling of peace and harmony as though we have all been together a long time. It's a beautiful night. There's a moon—and lots of clouds. It's pretty warm, so I think it's spring or early summer. This beautiful woman is standing off to one side. She looks over at me and we know we are supposed to go through something together. To mark this somehow, she lights a candle and walks slowly over to me. I wake up before I find out what we are supposed to do, but I have this sense of a beginning.

Night Ceremony (Haiku Version)
The moon rises through blue clouds
in spring. Lighting a candle,
you move toward me, smiling.

Like dreams, haiku taps into essence, into the candlelit place where the temporal and the eternal meet for one brief, exquisite moment.

I Am a Railway Station: Making a "List" Poem

Most of us relate strongly to objects. And we have been taught to attribute metaphor and symbolism to objects in stories. We need to avoid either falling into the trap of immediately seeking symbolic meaning (thereby missing the shimmering energy of the image itself) or overidentifying with the image (for example, "becoming" the image in Gestalt approaches). We can do this by acknowledging a paradox: We are separate from and one with the dream image. When I say, "I am a round, white table," there is also an "I" that is acknowledging my identification; something is still observing the identification.

A "list poem" allows you to explore this paradox. It is a quick practice, too—one that you can do easily with limited time:

- Make a poem that consists of a list of six to ten nouns and their accompanying adjectives, selected from one or more dreams. Don't worry about which words to select. Trust the deeper order that emerges when you let normal logic go.
- List the words in whatever order your nonrational mind decides.
- Title the list *I Am*.
- Add the words *I am* at the beginning of some or all of the lines.

Naomi had the following dream and then used this exercise to explore her response to the images:

The Traveler, the Dunes, and the Snakes
I am picking up an older woman—my sister?—from a railway station to take her to her other home. She has

Rimbaud said: "I is another." In poetic intuition, objective reality and subjectivity, the world, and the whole of the soul coexist inseparably. At that moment, sense and sensation are brought back to the heart, blood to the spirit, passion to intuition.

—Jacques Maritain
Creative Intuition in Art and Poetry

clothes in both places, so she has no luggage.

We are walking up a beach. I comment on how good this is. It is easier to walk in the sand than I would expect.

We arrive at strange conformations and patterns of mineral sands striated between the white sand. They have formed crystalline patterns that resemble the center of a flower—a small circle surrounded by a larger set of circles. I wonder how the minerals form into this pattern. It must be by weight. There are hundreds of these circles all over the sand dunes.

I also see hundreds of small and large snakes. They are writhing and moving all over the dunes. My companion seems unconcerned about them. Another woman walks amongst them, apparently unconcerned. They don't appear dangerous but they do rear up their hind bodies when threatened. Some are tiny. Some are large. They are all around me and even touching me.

Circumambulation makes possible looking at the image from all sides, and describes a metaphoric circle, the content of which suggests the meaning of that image.

—Mary Ann Mattoon
Applied Dream Analysis

Naomi allowed her nonrational self to include certain images from this dream in a poem. She might well have chosen other images on another day. Her selection was "true" for that day and that inner experience. Read the poem aloud with as much feeling for each phrase as you can; you'll have a lived experience of the dreamer's (and your own) relationship to these metaphors.

I am
A railway station
An older woman
I am black and white sand dunes
Crystalline patterns
The center of a flower
I am small and large circles
I am small and large snakes.

After Naomi read this aloud several times, she drew the images that came to her inner vision and through her body from speaking each image out loud. Finally, she enacted the poem as though she were signing it for a deaf audience, finding gestures for each image. This allowed her to embody the images.

Much of what we see when we close our eyes at night depends upon the attitude with whivh we go to sleep. And much of what we do by day may be affected by the attitude we bring to our dreams.

—June Singer
Boundaries of the Soul

Later, she began to note outer situations in which she felt like each of these images. She noticed, for example, that she often felt like "a railway station" around her large family who came and went, expecting her, as mother, to keep the whole show going. She also noticed that the image of the center of the flower came back to her when she meditated late in the evening after the children had gone out or to bed.

When we play out one side of ourselves with no memory of the others, we blanch out our subtler shadings. When we allow ourselves to fully embody each aspect, remembering quietly that each belongs to a subtle whole, we remain anchored in our true selves, in the silent harbor of the heart. By symbolically living out all of these images in these varied ways, we fully embody yet do not overidentify with each. We can sustain and celebrate their paradox.

7

Painting, Collage, and Sculpture

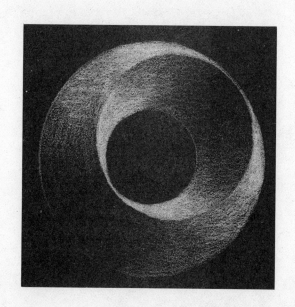

THE BODY'S CALLIGRAPHY: TRANSLATING THE FEELING OF THE DREAM INTO ENERGY PAINTINGS

The dream seems to reside in a fourth dimension, free of time and space limitations. When the dream enters into memory and into body sensations, it moves into a time- and space-bound world. Just as a photograph translates the three-dimensional world into two on the developing paper, so we translate the experience of the dream. Our memories, emotions, and bodies translate the dream into three dimensions, and then hands and arms translate those sensations into two dimensions on paper.

In essence, through the vehicle of the body, we translate the energy of the dream into personal calligraphy that emerges in line and color. Energy translations usually take less time to *do* than to read here *how* to do them. They require no talent and few materials. You need only a few minutes to yourself (rise early), a blank page, and cheap oil pastels, colored markers, or crayons. Keep a set of colors beside the bed, together with a pencil and a small block of blank paper or spiral-bound, blank book. Write the main dream elements on one page and then draw on the opposite.

The body response to a dream is so immediate and so true. You can think that you know what a dream's about but once you get going with the emotions in a dream, all of a sudden something else totally explodes.

—Marion Woodman
Dreams: Language of the Soul

Translating the dream's energy

- After you write down the essence of the dream, close your eyes and replay the dream in imagination, allowing the feelings, ambience, and atmosphere to permeate your body. Dreams engender feeling and emotion, connectedness and disconnectedness, elation, despondency—every shade of affective response.
- When you can re-experience the feelings in your body, half open your eyes, let your nondominant hand choose

a color from the set, and use your breath to breathe the energy you are feeling in your body down through your arm, hand, and crayon and onto the page. Use your nondominant hand or both hands at the one time to choose colors and draw.

- Keep your meditative focus on the feeling of the dream in the body and the images of the dream in your heart. Focus on your exhalations, using each to direct inner sensations through your nondominant arm and hand. Continue this until you sense that all the energy the dream has generated in your body has been breathed out through your arm, hand, and colors. Then stop.

- Look rarely at and don't be concerned about what goes on the page—maintain just enough focus to keep yourself from running off the edges. Sometimes your hand will reach for another color if the dream has a change of feeling or direction. You might even turn the page and start a new sheet for a shift in feeling or direction. Don't decide this beforehand. This practice replays the dream through the instrument of your body: Let your creative unconscious make these spontaneous decisions.

- When you have finished the energy translation, date it, name it (often the same name you have given the dream), and set aside the colors.

- Briefly meditate on the page(s).

- Don't interpret your paintings (for example, "Aha! a black *X!* I must be angry!". . ."Hmm—look at that spiral. Am I evolving here?"). And don't judge them. Free yourself from secret (and confining) hopes that your unconscious has produced a Kandinsky or Picasso out of the inspired content of your dreams. If I were to *critique* from an artistic standpoint the energy paintings I

Close your physical eye, in order first to see your picture with the eye of the spirit. Then make what you have seen in your night rise to daylight, in order for your action to be exercised in turn on other beings, from the outside toward the inside.

—Caspar-David Friedrich
In Jacques Maritain's
Creative Intuition in Art and Poetry

have done over the years, I would call them *Mess I, Mess II,* and so on. I can't make a contract with my creative unconscious to produce something impressive. I can only step aside so that the "embodied dream" can express itself in two dimensions.

"Night in the Forest"
Oil pastels and watercolors

Translating the Painting Back into the Body

A rich way to meditate on your energy painting is to translate it back into the body through movement, feeling, and sound.

Place your fingertips on the painting and let them follow the lines as though you were expert at reading the Braille of your own calligraphy. Imagine that your fingers can translate color and line into sound, let that vibration move up your arms and into your throat area, and then let out that sound freely through your throat. You are "sounding" the painting. Different syllables will come—you might find yourself making high-pitched sounds for high, thin lines and swooping down into low, guttural sounds for thick lines low on the page, or making staccato sounds for jagged lines.

Your visual consciousness will follow a split second after finger and sound movements. Your eyes are not the medium of translation. By using your fingertips to completely take the energy back inside, you can bring the experience of the dream, which was projected onto the page, back into the body for safekeeping and for cellular memory and transformation.

Both dream and painting show in their very fabric the work of an abstract-symbolic intelligence.
—Harry T. Hunt
The Multiplicity of Dreams

Allowing the Form to Evolve

Many dreamers who have experimented with this translation practice have noticed that, at times, their unconscious wants to move on. They might start with a dream but, as they allow the energy of the dream to paint itself, other emotions, other memories, arise. Some dreamers choose to return to the original dream image like a meditation practice, to focus on that energy to generate the painting. Other dreamers like to follow the associative energy. Essentially, these two positions are a pictorial analogue of the difference between amplification and free association. We can choose to allow all our associations to derive from the original image, or we can allow one image to lead to the next and the next, often moving far away from the originating image.

Both amplification and free association practices have their place, particularly in this genre of painting. Be alert to the inner impulse and stay conscious of the origin of that impulse. For example, if your energy painting is expressing a painful dream, your impulse to move away from the originating image might be a way to avoid staying with something that needs to be carefully tended and moved through. However, if you start with a puzzling image and find your unconscious beginning to move you visually through a series of quick sketches, you might find that it is resolving issues. There are no guidelines for deciding which way to go. Experiment with both ways and allow for the possibility of both during any one session.

SCRATCHINGS ON THE WALL OF THE CAVE: USING ENERGY PAINTINGS WITH BAD DREAMS

Mixing strong energies from the realm of the dark gods with the human energies and needs of the day is challenging and demanding on the psyche. When you are working with nightmares (or images whose charge feels almost too much to handle), it's wise to approach energy translations slightly differently.

Set a Time and a Time Limit

Energy paintings are most effectively done immediately upon waking. However, when the translation is from a nightmare, there are other things to consider. A translation of a nightmare is better done quickly, within a time limit (ten minutes at most), and when followed by a scheduled, nonstressful event such as exercise. Don't do one just before you drive the children to school or have an important meeting. Allow recovery time, doing something repetitive and easy after you work with a nightmare—do a load of laundry, walk the dog, weed a flower bed, pay the phone bill. Avoid doing energy translations of nightmares before sleeping; they usually raise adrenaline.

The advantage of active imagination is that you return to the dream image, and by precisely reimagining it you get to the subtle feeling tones inside the image.

—Robert Bosnak
In Michael V. Adams'
"Image, Active Imagination, and the Imaginal Level"

Choose Your Paper Carefully

Choose a piece of paper that seems too big to fill. If you don't have big pieces, use newspaper or tape several pieces of newsprint together. Alternatively, you might prefer to choose a piece of paper that is tiny—three-by-five inches feels right for many people. (I keep spiral-bound, three-by-five books of cheap painting paper around.) If you want to get an idea of how "big" a tiny painting can seem, look at Alice Miller's book, *Pictures of a Childhood*. These are big images—painful ones—yet they are done on postcard-sized paper.

Make a Container

Once you've chosen your size of paper, draw a visual container for the dream on the page. Usually, a thick lined, strongly colored "frame" suffices. However, if this doesn't

"They're After Me Again!"
oil pastel

seem strong enough, think of something that *would* be—a metal safe, a thick pot, a bottle, a box.

Monitor Yourself While Doing the Translation

Make the energy translation within the boundaries of the container you have drawn. As you are doing it, if you feel that the container is not strong enough to hold the energy of the image, reinforce the boundary.

If you feel too much energy building up as you are doing the transfer, jump up and down a few times and bellow out some energy. If you can't do this because your house companions or neighbors might throttle you for disturbing the peace, walk briskly around the block, swinging your arms, and then return to the painting.

When you have finished, give it a name, date it, take a few long, deep breaths, and go off and forget it. Don't even think about it. There's no virtue in working on the dream any more that day. You have listened well to it. Allow it to be quietly reabsorbed into your psyche in its new form.

YOUR OWN LANGUAGE: "RE-MEMBERING" THE IMAGE THROUGH SIMPLE PAINTINGS

Sometimes I want to do more than translate the embodied energy of the dream onto the page as a series of abstracted gestures. Sometimes I actually want to "re-member" the image through a more representational drawing or painting. When I do this, I don't want to feel influenced by my capacity or incapacity to draw. I still have trouble unprying the talons of my judging mind; they instinctively rip at the soft underbelly of my self-acceptance and creativity.

My nightmares are very precise. I have only two nightmares. They recur all the time. I know what they mean and I know perfectly well why I have them. In the longest nightmare, which has been with me all my life, I dream of a very disorganized and messy house. I know that the house is me. . . .

Very often I wake up very anxious with a terrible headache. The headache lasts until I can identify what is bothering me the most. Many things bother me in the messy house but often it's one thing in my real life that I've not been able to solve and am postponing.

—Isabel Allende
In Naomi Epel's
Writers Dreaming

One way I loose their grip is to use my nondominant hand or both hands. Then I can't even begin to try to paint or draw "well."

When you want to render particular images, follow the same ritual you do for energy paintings—with some differences. When you close your eyes and go within, allow the dream to replay until you find one part that draws your energy and attention more than any other. This image might not seem to be the most important or meaningful. Work with it anyway. You are attracted most strongly to this image for a reason you probably won't discern for days, months, or years.

If you stay with the image and really feel yourself into the color, then it begins to release metaphor. Any rote method is counterproductive.
—Robert Bosnak
In Michael V. Adams'
"Image, Active
Imagination, and the
Imaginal Level"

When that single image coalesces in your imagination, pick up a color and express the essence of that image with deliberate, childlike simplicity. Bodies become stick figures, ovals, or crosses; faces become round circles or eggs with dots for eyes; houses become boxes with triangles on the top. Everything will look as though it has been drawn by a six year old.

Perspective in dreams is usually fluid, so ignore perspective when you draw. How, for example, can I be leaning on someone's shoulder at the same time as I am holding their opposite hand without lifting up my shoulder? In dreams, we do these things effortlessly. There is no limitation on time and space in dreams, so don't

"African Priests Bless Me"
Poster paint

limit your painting. If a figure *feels* big in the dream, make it big on the page, even if it ends up bigger than the house it occupies. That's the way your dream felt and your hand moved. Sometimes, I even have the same figure appear twice on the page because he or she appears at different times or places in the dream.

Painting Dream Animals

Our ancestors have drawn the spirits of animals important to them in innumerable ways—from the Lascaux cave drawings to the stylized, abstracted figures found amongst Native American art, from the abstracted dot forms of certain Australian aboriginal tribes to the elongated carved figures of certain West Irian and African groups.

Dream animals carry so much energy that presenting their qualities and forms in two dimensions and color is important. You are sure that you can't draw an ant or an eagle any better than you can draw a person or a building. It doesn't matter. As with our ancestors and contemporary tribal groups, the spirit in which you approach the painting is more important than the rendering.

If you really want to make an accurate representation of the animal, don't draw freehand. Go to the library, borrow a book on animals, and photocopy or trace the animal. However, if you want to express the feeling of the animal, its spirit, rely on the wisdom of your nonartist's hand—the nondominant—to express its essential quality. You will probably end up with something that your inner critic will think is childish and humorous. Tell the critic that its assessment is irrelevant. What is important to you is the directness, honesty, and unapologetic intensity of your childlike response to this animal.

The painter must paint not only what he sees before himself, but also what he sees within himself.

—Caspar-David Friedrich
In Jacques Maritain's
Creative Intuition in Art and Poetry

Upset your overtrained mind. Draw the animal from the top looking down. Draw the animal from the back or from underneath. Draw the animal's eye or tooth. Draw whatever part of the animal captures its essence for you. Don't try to draw a profile of the animal with all the proportions correct! Color it all in if you like, the way a child fills in all the spaces contained by lines. Make up patterns that fit into the different body parts—torso, head, legs, tails, wings. Draw your primitive, uncensored response to the appearance of this animal.

The dream is exact in the image that it chooses.

—Marion Woodman
Dreams: Language of the Soul

When you feel finished, hang the painting where you can see it (and no one else can—at least, no one nosy). See how your response to the painting changes over time. There is an invisible cord of energy that pulses between me and a newly finished painting for hours, days, sometimes weeks. (I usually keep the painting up until I sense that this pulsing cord has withered. Then I know that the inner, unspoken work I was doing around those images is complete—for now—and I take the painting down.) Alternatively, meditate on the painting with a fixed, unblinking gaze. Do this for ten minutes a day for a week and then take it down. Or, keep the painting up until the next is completed and takes its place. Find your own way of knowing when your preliminary work with the painting is finished.

These paintings do not *represent* dreams but *present* dreams. They constitute your personal visual language, which is evolving over time.

WHERE THE SUN AND THE MOON ARE ONE: MAKING A MASK OF A CREATURE'S ESSENCE

Maskmaking has as ancient and honorable a history in cultures' spiritual and psychological development, often appearing as pictographs and petroglyphs do. Mask making is a universal, cross-cultural practice. This experience of making one usually takes on as powerful a sacred, meditative quality as the experience of wearing it.

To make a mask of your own face as it appears in a dream or to make a mask of another figure or animal is to deepen your connection to that figure significantly. This kind of maskmaking resembles the energy translation practice. You do not have to know how to draw a face in order to make such a mask. You are presenting the essential energy of the figure or animal; you are not representing the actual figure or animal. To wear such a mask is to tap into the archetypal patterns and sources of that figure. Approach this work with respect, containment, and privacy.

There are many excellent guides on mask work, including sections in Renée Emunah's *Acting for Real*, Keith Johnstone's *Impro*, and the forthcoming book by Woodman, Hamilton, and Skinner. If you find maskmaking a powerful tool, read these and other excellent books on cross-cultural use of masks.

Let's take a short dream that Leo explored through maskmaking:

Where the Sun and the Moon Are One

I dream that I am wading out in the lake. I look up into the sky and see the sun shining brightly. I swim a bit. Then I look up and it's the moon looking down. I look at the reflection of the light in the water and can't tell whether

Ajutap [ancient warrior souls] dreams have two parts; an initial vision of a terrifying beast or comet-like blast of light that the dreamer must confront and touch, followed by a second dream . . . in which the ajutap *presents himself to the dreamer in human form and tells him of his future victory in battle. A man who receives such a vision is called "owner of a dream" or "one who has had a vision."*

—Harry T. Hunt
The Multiplicity of Dreams

it's sun- or moonlight, but it seems to be both somehow. I'm really intrigued by this and can feel this odd, hot-cool light on my body and face when I stand up in the water. I feel as though this Sun–Moon is a real being, somehow.

Rare are those who can handle [structure] by letting it come, instead of hunting for it or hunting it down, filling it with their own marks and markings so as to consign it to the meaningful and lay claim to it.

—Trinh Minh-ha
Woman Native Other

Let's review the guidelines that Leo followed and note how he applied them:

- Listen to music that helps you grow quiet—drum music, ocean music, bird calls, classical music—whatever focuses energy and lowers self-consciousness and self-criticism. Leo listened to sitar music that he had purchased at a hatha yoga class. Later, he remembered that the Sanskrit word *hatha* combined the words for sun and moon and that *yoga* meant harnessing or union. His choice of music was unintentionally synergistic.

- Take a heavy sheet of white or colored paper that absorbs water-based paints, such as poster or acrylic, without wrinkling or dissolving. Leo used cheap watercolor paper. It was all he had around.

- Cut or tear the paper into a simple shape that represents the shape of the figure's face. If you are confused about how to do this, think about what geometric forms the figure's face resembles *in your imagination*. Leo cut the paper into a simple circle. It looked like both the sun and the moon.

- Cut out places for eyes. Don't worry about the *actual* shape of the eyes. If they *feel* big to you, make them big; if they *feel* almond shaped, make them that. Leo cut out one eye to look like a sun with spiky rays and cut out the other to look like a new moon.

- Do you want the figure's mouth or beak to be open or closed? Don't think about it; look at the inner image of the figure or feel it standing in front of you. Ask your-self, Is the mouth open or closed? You'll know. If it's open, cut out a hole for the mouth.

Leo meditated for a moment and saw in his imagination this sun-moon figure. The mouth seemed to be open, like the "man in the moon's" mouth. So he cut out a circle for the mouth.

Don't plan how you are going to paint or collage the mask. Focus on the spirit of the figure as it came in the dream. If it was quiet and still, you might choose restful colors unlike the color of the real figure. Focus on the figure's spirit. Let it move through your arms and into the colors, pieces of glitter, torn collage images, or other elements you paint or glue on the surface.

Leo knew immediately that he wanted the right half of the mask with the moon-eye to be blue and the left half with the sun-eye, bright yellow. He used poster paint to color each side. He found himself drawing curly clouds on the moon side—on the figure's cheek—with marking pens. On the sun side, he found himself using different crayons to draw simple flowers and a tree.

- Let your body and the mask's spirit tell you when you have finished. Don't assess this by artistic criteria, which only obstruct. Leo kept drawing until he suddenly felt his energy drop. He felt as if he had lost interest in the project. But he knew this was not true; only a minute before, he had been concentrating and interested. This was merely his body's way of telling him that no more needed to be done.

- When you have finished, title the mask on the back, date it, and write down the words that first occur to you when you look at this image. Leo titled his mask *Sun-Moon*

The persons with whom I had dinner and who return in my dream embody . . . my traits and actions and divine traits and actions. . . .

Because these friends embody both, they cannot be resolved by a one-sided interpretation, by a personalistic reduction into me or by an archetypal reversion . . . to spirits, without losing the in-between world of soul.

—James Hillman
The Dream and the Underworld

Spirit and wrote "cool, watery, calm, woman, my better half, something I'm afraid of, watches over me" on the back of the moon side. Then he wrote "fiery, angry, out there, growth, enlightenment, strong" on the back of the sun side. Right in the middle, he suddenly found himself writing: "peace."

• Now hold up the mask and look in the mirror. Leo put the mask on in front of the mirror and then looked at each side in turn. When he could see only the moon, he felt "calm, cool, withdrawn." When he could see only the sun, he felt "warm, assertive, active." When he looked at both, he felt "almost dizzy—as though the mask could do something I can't do yet—put two sides of me together."

• Have a trusted friend or dream group member take a photograph of you wearing the mask. Sit quietly with the photo and allow it to speak to you. Write down carefully what it says (and don't take it literally).

Leo mounted the mask on a piece of thick cardboard, poked a couple of holes in the side, and used string to tie it on. Then he had his son photograph him in the mask. After he had it developed, he sat down with the photograph—and with the mask (which he had hung beside his computer in the family room)—and let it speak to him. It began like this:

I'm where you're headed. No more division. No more either/or stuff. I'm you all put together with all the bits operating at once. You need me—not just the pieces of me but the whole me. Keep looking at that place where the blue and the yellow meet. They make green. There's growth there in bringing us together. . . .

Like omens and oracles, masks rarely bother about the daily exigencies of life. Occasionally, they offer practical wisdom (slow down; be more attentive; open your heart; sleep more). Simmer advice or wisdom offered to you by inner figures in the pot of everyday living for a while before you eat it. Masks are concerned with impersonal energies, with archetypal energies, both bright and dark; and their messages need to filter into our lesser consciousness slowly so that we can tolerate and absorb their greater scope.

Dreams call from the imagination to the imagination and can be answered only by the imagination.

—James Hillman
The Dream and the Underworld

AFTER THE RAIN: USING COLLAGE TO EXPRESS COLOR, SHAPE, AND THEME

Dream images can open to transformation through the quiet invitations and firmer demands of the collage process. Collage, like clay, is an assertive medium. It influences us as much as we influence it. This is particularly noticeable when we make a collage for a dream. Collage comes already half made. It meets the maker halfway across the bridge of creativity, bearing colors, forms, and texture that we only need to shape and combine. This can be freeing and helpful when we have less time and even less creativity.

Two-dimensional collage plays with five basic factors: color, shape, theme or content, texture, and composition. The first three are most relevant to dream art. As dreamworkers, most of us don't have the time or luxury of making images accurate. We don't keep many magazines and, even if we do, we would have trouble finding images that well represented places, things, and people in our dreams. Moreover, there's no advantage in making a collage piece

I take a dream to be a psychic organism, in spatial form. One cannot remove an organ from a human being without altering the entire body, and the same is true of a dream image. All the constituent elements of a dream image belong to the identity of the dream. Each part is necessary for the existence of that specific dream image.
—Robert Bosnak
A Little Course in Dreams

that "looks like" your dream. Rather, let the different dream elements play out impressionistically through collage. Finding a picture of an angry gorilla might be faithful to the dream image, but you don't need the gorilla picture to successfully express the feeling of anger in the dream through the collage. So forget content and composition until you have finished.

Consider color and shape. As children show and art instructors remind, colors and shapes carry feeling, and their relationships to each other carry the relationships among the feelings (and often carry the composition). Colors traditionally carry connotations and symbolism. The traditional associations, however, do not necessarily reflect the feeling *you* might have about a certain color in a dream. Black can feel mysterious in one dream, depressive in another, full of depth and the night sky in another, and a reminder of a friend's skin tone in another. After you let your own feelings about colors arise, you might then—and only then—wish to research archetypal and traditional meanings for these colors. Be careful of literality and overgeneralization. Symbols are not signs. They do not equal anything, do not denote one thing. They connote many. Be aware of what this color evokes in your *personal* realm of image and symbol at this time.

Color

Some dreams are drenched with colors. Others are drenched with feelings. Look at a magazine picture and let yourself imagine that the shiny, blood-red lipstick advertisement can be cut up and recycled to evoke a mood of anger. Let the deep turquoise of a picture of Hawaii become the twilight sky or feeling of peace in your dream.

Let the yellow in the fashion advertisement express the happiness you felt. Find an image that evokes rather than represents. And allow it to infuse your body with its feeling tone.

Patricia dreamed recently that she was looking out over a verdant landscape. The color of the hills reminded her of Europe. She didn't understand the dream, but let the feeling of that green perspective suffuse her. She took a small piece of thick paper about four by six inches (at least 60-pound weight), school glue, and a few magazines. (She doesn't have time to do large pieces often.) She ripped out pages that showed different greens, then tore up the pieces until they resembled rolling hills, and glued them. She cleaned up the edges of the collage with scissors and glued it onto a larger, white framing page in her portfolio. After she glued it on the larger page, she gave it the same title as the dream: *After the Storm*. She had no logical explanation for why she titled it that. It's what came. She dated it and clipped in the dream, opposite.

She realized as she worked with the green how restful the color felt. Despite the view of the deep greens of the hills, she longed to be out *in* green more often. Making and meditating on the collage made her aware—at the cellular, optical level—of how healing it was for her to walk in the hills. It put her back in touch with her body and its longings. She resolved to walk more often, accompanied, alone.

Shape

The mood of the dream determines the shapes you cut or tear. (So does the time you have available. Complicated shapes take time.) Jagged edges evoke jagged feelings;

The overall content of a dream or novel may determine which of its multiple possible meanings predominates, but the richness of such material often depends on the fact that the context evokes more than one such signification. It is just this multiple evocation and open spontaneous intentionality that we appreciate in the arts, and that artists strive to achieve.

—Harry T. Hunt
The Multiplicity of Dreams

ragged edges, ragged feelings; rounded edges, smoother feelings; square edges, orderly feelings. Don't plan shapes. Let the scissors be an extension of your hand, which is an extension of your arm, which is an extension of your body—which is the container of the dream. You can feel this uninterrupted flow easily if you keep the feeling of the dream in the body and in the breath. Sometimes, you won't want to use scissors. They can feel too removed from the energy of the dream as it spreads through the body. At other times, you can appreciate the graceful skill of scissors.

Shapes often work themselves into dream collages in two ways. A shape in the dream itself—the oblong swimming pool, the square room, the spiral staircase, the broken glass—can appear in the shape of the collage pieces. Often, you won't even realize until you begin the collage that there is a repeated shape in the dream. Just let the shape appear. Reflect on possible indications later.

Shapes also work themselves into the collage through feelings. If you want to express a formal mood in a dream, you might find yourself cutting long, rectangular shapes and placing them vertically on the page. If you are in a peaceful mood, you might find yourself using undulating shapes and placing them horizontally. If you have a dream chaotic in content and mood, many shapes might appear, some only partially realized. Don't plan—follow. Reflect only in retrospect on your patterns.

Recurring Themes and Content

If you want to mark the recurrence of a figure or object in a dream series, you might actually focus on content (see also Chapter 9). This takes time. Even when you choose to work with a particular image, however, don't get caught in making images exact. A torn piece of paper can express an image well if you let your imagination flow.

One woman dreamed repeatedly about infant girls. Over weeks, she collected pictures of infants from magazines and then combined them in a collage. She also included color copies of herself as a baby. One man dreamed of wild animals. He eventually collected enough *National Wildlife* magazines to make a collage zoo. Another dreamer had recurring dreams of beautiful women laughing in cathedrals; he bought a couple of glossy fashion magazines and a couple of travel magazines and combined images. Another woman had a recurring experience of flying. She decided to represent it by painting a blue background and adding pictures of wings onto which she pasted photocopies of her own face.

If you are fascinated by the actual characteristics of a dream animal or familiar figure, collage photocopies of the animal or figure in various poses and aspects. Animals are easily photocopied from library books and children's books, and familiar figures can be copied from albums or other sources. When you photocopy pictures, use the highest-quality copier available so that gray areas show. Make at least two and preferably four copies

Not all dreams have such depth. Many come from the personal unconscious with metaphoric images of psychological dynamics. . . . But others plumb the profundities of the dreamer's existence and require knowledge of collective unconscious dimensions gained from familiarity with the mythological storehouse of humankind.

—Sylvia Brinton Perera "Dream Design"

"Moon Mother" Collage

of each image so that you can play with cutting up images and making patterns. If you can afford it, make color copies.

A word on composition: Feel free to make either a free-form collage on which you place the pieces purely according to where hand and eye put them (use rubber cement so you can move them later if you wish). Or you can make a more formal, ritual collage that forms patterns—a mandala form, a circle (with or without "pie piece" divisions), a spiral, a mobile, a square, a Styrofoam ball covered in images, a cardboard box covered in images outside, inside, or both.

Don't analyze why you include certain images or why you place them where you do. Attend to your intuition and feeling for selection and placement. Notice your body's response once you have selected and placed them. Surprise yourself.

Working with the Collage

After you have finished the collage, spend time contemplating it and writing about your experience of making it. This is now the time to quietly observe its texture and composition.

When you consider texture, ask yourself such questions as:

- Are the edges smooth or torn? Are they a combination? How does this smooth/torn texture of the collage affect me? Does it enhance my experience of the dream in some unexpected way?
- Have I included differently textured pieces? If I were to describe those textures, what adjectives would I use?

How do these adjectives reflect my inner state at present in relation to this dream or my life in general?

When you consider composition, you might reflect on these questions:

- Do my collage pieces each have their own space or do they overlap?
- Which pieces are closely connected to others literally or visually? What do I associate to those connections?
- Have I overlapped the edges of the board or paper on which I made the collage, or was it important for me to stay within the edges of the paper? What is my reaction to that intuitive choice now?
- Is there a particular collage piece around which all the others seem to fall into place? What is its shape and color? What draws me about this piece? Is its shape and color and dominance a metaphor for something about the dream or me?
- Can I see an overall, unifying principle to the collage? What adjectives would I use to describe that principle (for example, *circular, spiral, jagged, bilateral, dark, elegant, heavy, undulating, spacious*)? Do those adjectives reflect my inner state in some way?
- To where does my eye return in this collage? What associations do I have to this place?

[Dreams are] the commonest and universally accessible source for the investigation of man's symbolizing faculty, apart from the contents of psychoses, neuroses, myths, and the products of the various arts.

—C. G. Jung
Collected Works

After you have considered questions that intrigue you, place your collage just below eye level and meditate on it with unblinking eyes for as long as is safe and possible. Doing this allows you to reabsorb the color, feeling, and shape into body and memory in a way that allows them to evolve silently and invisibly toward the next image.

Last, pay attention to the dream you have the night after making the collage, and see what commentary your unconscious might have on your experience. Notice whether colors, shapes, themes, or textures that revealed themselves through your collage reappear or evolve. Each art nourishes the other, and your collage will have nourished your dream life in unexpected ways.

Take collage work in your own direction. For those dreams overflowing with feeling—anger, frustration, love, excitement—find ways to create your own pieces, to reexperience the emotions and responses that arise both during and after their creation, to gain insights, and to make promises to yourself. Sometimes, a collage that begins with a dream image takes a direction of its own, departing from the original. This is a wonderful experience, not something to be controlled. You are giving expression to your dream not to preserve it but to pay homage to it, to nourish it, and to allow the images and symbols to evolve. Remember, you are not doing this for a class but for your soul.

FINDING MY WAY HOME: DRAWING MANDALAS AFTER DREAMS, AFTER NIGHTMARES

Yesterday, I spent a pleasant afternoon at a local arts-and-crafts fair, where a fine beadwork artist was making jewelry. I spent a warm evening with friends and, as conversations do late at night, ours jumped all over, from sports and good fiction to diamond earrings! Still later in the evening, I spoke about my challenges writing this book. Especially trying to decide on the clearest organization of the material. I went to bed, reflecting on these threads of conversation and wishing that I could have a dream that would tell me how to organize this work!

I awoke with two images. The first was a small, round piece of beadwork for an earring with a wheel design. The second was a page of writing, whose every letter was formed from tiny, cut diamonds. Viewed together, the diamonds spelled out a message.

I was ready to dismiss these images until, as I was feeding my impatient dog, I realized that they were both gifts that drew their inspiration from the images of the day before. Both dream images contained mandalas: the beaded wheel and the diamonds.

I still didn't have my organizing principle, but I did have help. In beadwork, each small part is vital to a whole circular rather than linear pattern. I also associate the earring with hearing. The diamonds (from the conversation the previous evening) are also associated with the ear and hearing. Once again, each constitutes a small part of the whole message.

Perhaps each of these sections I am writing resembles one facet or one bead that, together with other facets or beads, slowly builds a whole circular message. Each facet is a necessary part of the whole. My dream images—partial at best—have given me a gestalt of the solution. I must see whether I can translate this understanding into practical form.

Mandala images provide a gestalt of a wholeness that comes straight from the center of our Selves and our deepest understanding. Unconscious mandala forms (sacred circular patterns intentionally drawn as a spiritual practice in the East) are often organically embedded in dream images. If you review your dreams, you can probably find

Relearning to perceive the spiral process—to discover the clustered facets around an energy core or theme— trains us to work patiently and imaginatively with dreams and their associations and amplifications.

—Sylvia Brinton Perera
"Dream Design"

mandala forms, particularly if you look at a dream image from a different angle. For example, people dream about circular buildings, cities with roads radiating from the center, cut gemstones, patterns of shadows on the ground, clothes that have patterns that radiate from centers, flowers, actions that move in mandala forms. Mandala images from dreamers show wide variation:

- My friend has made a beautiful ceramic pot that has crisscross designs all around it.
- I'm dancing with my husband, and we're making complicated patterns as we dance. We're on a circular dance floor.
- I get my diploma for my degree, and its background is decorated with some kind of round cake design.
- Round stones on the beach, each patterned differently.
- A child's top spinning.
- I have lost my engagement ring. In the dream, it's a cut sapphire.
- Something about the wheel of my car is really important. I keep looking at it every time I get to a stop sign.

Some of these examples are complete dreams; others have been taken from larger dreams. Each contains a mandala.

A Western sense of individuality arises from a linear awareness; the believer must establish a linear or triangular rather than a circular relationship with God. [The] Japanese insist that God, nature, and man are one and the same, embracing a flowing rather than a fixed, definitive form of religion—by no means triangular. To the Japanese, an individual life is an interrelationship of body, mind, and spirit: the circle.

—Michihiro Matsumoto
The Unspoken Way

Drawing Mandalas

Drawing mandalas, whose conscious practice in the West we owe to Jung, allows us to pay homage, in external form, to images of wholeness, completeness, Self, that take us home to our inner core. Mandalas don't have to be complicated. In fact, simple mandalas are often even more powerful than complicated ones.

Here are some initial suggestions for creating mandalas:

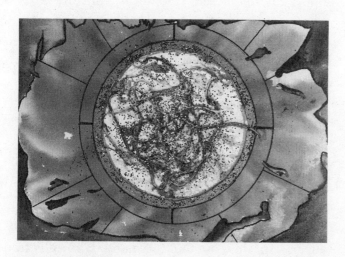

"Sun Mandala"
Collage with paint, string, and glitter

- Use a small piece of square paper (white or black) and black or white pencil.
- Draw a containing circle with something circular, such as a cup.
- Play with drawing curving lines or geometric shapes within the circle.
- Draw equilateral triangles and squares within the larger circles. Use a ruler or the straight side of whatever is close by.
- Connect the corners of those lines with other corners.
- Make circles inside the triangles or other squares.
- Alternatively, draw free-form within the containing circles.
- Color the contained areas if you wish with whatever medium you prefer. Don't attempt to make your mandalas perfect. I used to try; now, my greater challenge is to let them be imperfect. I'm not deliberately careless or

sloppy; I do them with care, focus, curiosity—and the expectation of imperfection. When you're anxious or bothered, do geometric, symmetrical designs. When you're more relaxed or focused, make freestyle, asymmetrical, or flowing designs within the circles.

Each dream image . . . can be seen as manifesting and taking its focus from . . . a gravitational, energic center.

—Sylvia Brinton Perera "Dream Design"

Sounding the Mandala

When you have finished, imagine that the mandala lines are raised like Braille. Let your fingertips slide over the lines slowly, slowly, with your eyes half open. Let your body take in the small form of the mandala and magnify it with your breath. Imagine that the mandala form is translating itself into a three-dimensional form in your body, a form that takes up residence in some protected corner where it is needed. Let your voice "sound" the mandala by letting your voice go up and down and around and in and out with the movement of your hands.

Materials as a Meditative Choice

If you start with white paper, use a soft-lead pencil to color. Soft pencils take me back to childhood. If you use black

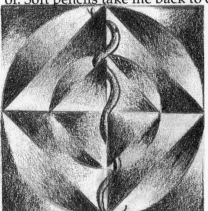

paper, start with white lines and color in with graded shades of white. Add color if you have inclination and time. As a child, I was required to draw maps at school. I would spend hours shad-

Mandala
Pencil

ing mountain ranges of Australia or places I could only imagine: the Rockies, the Apennines, the French Alps, the Swiss Alps (they always took the longest). There's a quietness and a pointlessness about doing this that is a delightful balance to goal orientation. If you are strongly drawn to abstracted shapes and want to enrich your imaginative understanding of them, read Angeles Arrien's *Signs of Life.*

Drawing Mandalas for Important Dreams

Now that you have some basic ways to construct mandalas, you can work with very powerful dreams by drawing a mandala as you contemplate the images, story line, symbols, or feeling tone of the dream.

- Draw a containing circle.
- Divide your circle into four quarters.
- Draw a line gesture in one quarter, a gesture that expresses the energy or feeling you have when you contemplate a special aspect of the dream (What is the *feeling* of compassion? the *feeling* of overflowing love? the *feeling* of unalloyed freedom?).
- Repeat the mirror image of this gesture in the other three quarters, making a four-way mirror pattern.
- Alternatively, let the dream re-experience itself in conscious awareness while you doodle inside a containing circle.
- Color the enclosed spaces in the pattern in ways that please and inspire you.
- If you prefer, shade away from each line edge with a pencil by coloring heavily and evenly near the line and lightening pressure as you move away from the line. If you like shading, read Judith Cornell's book, *Mandalas,* for a more detailed description.

Writing the Short Dream as a Mandala

Short, important dreams can actually be written in mandala form. The mandala provides a fresh way of "holding" and "containing" the energy of the dream.

Often sailors even spent nights in the temple of the sea god, Poseidon, before setting sail, in order to have prophetic dreams about their voyage and possible dangers awaiting them (Hill, 1972).

—Kalle Achte and Taina Schakir "Dreams in Different Cultures"

- Take a short dream that feels important, even numinous (filled with an ineffable sense of deep import).
- Write it in a mandala form such as a single circle or concentric circles or four quarters within a circle.
- Use different colors for each section, and color each section afterward.

Making Paper Cutout Mandalas

Another easy way to create a dream mandala is to make paper cutouts with folded paper. Hans Christian Andersen made many, and they are as vivid portrayals of mystery and myth as his tales.

- Take a thin, square piece of paper, fold it in half and then in half again.
- Draw a simple outline of a symbol or image from a dream onto the folded square.
- Cut out the form through all four folds of paper.
- Unfold the paper and place it against a contrasting, colored background.
- Meditate with soft, half-open eyes on this mandala version of the dream symbol or image.

A Collage Mandala

The collage form provides one of the most easily made mandalas of all. Follow these basic guidelines as you contemplate a dream.

- Draw a containing circle on a piece of paper. Put a set of abstract collage cutouts of different colors into the circle, keeping roughly within its bounds.
- Alternatively, fold each piece of collage paper into quarters and cut four pieces out of these layers that are all the same shape.
- Place each piece in one of the quadrants of the circle.
- Because the edges get messy, lay another piece of paper with a slightly smaller circle cutout over the now-messy collage circle.
- When energy begins to leave you for doing the collage, turn it over and name it the first thing that comes. Be suspicious of profundities (I'm not good at being profound and don't find it of much use to me later).
- List all the descriptive words (not in sentence form) that might describe this collage mandala to a trusted friend who is talking with you on the phone or who is blind.

Dreams always point to the inner center. They are like hundreds of forms all pointing to the inner center. Every dream is an attempt of nature to center us, to relate us again back to our innermost center, to stabilize our personality.

—Marie-Louise
von Franz
In Fraser Boa's
The Way of the Dream

Mandalas for Nightmares

Sometimes you don't feel like working with dreams. You especially don't feel like exploring last night's nightmare. It's tax season, you have a cold, you owe letters and phone calls, you need to spend time with a family member in the spare moments you do have today—and you don't want to look at the bad dream that deprived you (and possibly another) of an extra hour's sleep.

But the nightmare won't blow away. It hangs in the air like cooking oil in a small restaurant. It hangs in hair, nose, and clothes and subtly flavors your day (often to the detriment of others).

Give in. Do a mandala. You can color in books of pre-drawn mandalas while you wait on endless voice-mail systems for a real person. You can do them while idly watching television (not the "correct" approach to mandala making, but it actually works anyway). If you have more energy, quietly go to another room while you color one.

If you have more energy, draw your own. When you're distressed by a dream (waking or sleeping), make a mandala in which each half or each quarter mirrors the other half or quarters. There's comfort in repetition, rhythm, and mirror image-making (less invention, too). Don't think about the nightmare. Doodle in the circle until you forget that you need to forget your nightmare or until your body settles into itself like a tired child succumbing to sleep. You don't always need to understand the nightmare to bring yourself back to yourself. After the terror of the journey, sometimes you just need to know the way home.

Memory and learning seem safer topics for North American psychologists than imagination and creative thinking, and so the temptation arises to see the latter in terms of the former—if they are seen at all.
—Harry T. Hunt
The Multiplicity of Dreams

WATER-WIND-BREATH: USING CLAY TO EXPRESS FEELING, MOVEMENT, AND FIGURE

The first time I worked with clay, my heart caught its breath and soared. I found myself making love with space, with the unknown. In every second, I saw my unconscious express itself through a different hand movement, through an unrepeatable gesture. The clay started to direct me, to take charge of the dance, to capture my attention, to teach me receptivity, to evade my control. It taught me to be messy, sensual, and childlike; to sacrifice one idea for another; to have courage to occupy physical space with my visions.

Friends who are potters in Pueblo Indian villages in New Mexico speak about the spirit of the clay, about their needing to attend to its desires. Something similar usually happens to me when I paint and write poetry. And in this first experience with the clay, I found myself being led, not by something invisible but by something apparently inert yet tangible. This didn't feel like part of me to which I was responding; rather, I was responding to the *clay it-self*. I stopped "working" the clay and started being led. In the space between two moments, the clay started breathing me. It was clear about what it wanted, although my lack of expertise often redirected its movements. My awareness was suspended between breath, body, and clay as I watched my hands move in response to its subtle direction.

That first piece I made is still in the garage. It reminds me of yet another day I fell in love. No one else said much about the odd, abstract piece I made (or that made me) that day. Actually, I preferred that they did not comment. My piece felt exposed, like a photograph of an embrace. Soon after I made this, I dreamed about passionate male potters forming fine-lipped, elegant pots.

These days, when I want to bring important dreams, feelings, or body experiences into form, I often invoke the spirit of the clay. Clay is one of the most responsive media in which to explore dreams. Clay work takes longer than other dream practices, so you might not do it as often. When you do, however, it will richly repay you. Keep malleable, cheap clay available. Keep it cut (with string) into pieces about six by six by two inches—easily carried and usable. Because clay depends on water for life, keep the plastic bag sealed so that it doesn't harden. Keep a few "tools" handy—old kitchen utensils washed and in a separate plastic bag.

Breath and Body

When you are ready to explore a dream with clay, warm up with slow, full-body movement, sometimes accompanied by contemplative (but not sentimental) music. Some days, you won't like music at all; you will feel too receptive to the mood changes it creates. At those times, listen to trees or birds (or traffic) or your breath.

The body is the unconscious in its most immediate and continuous form; the dream is also the unconscious, though as a body of images it lacks the immediacy and continuity of the physical body.
—Marion Woodman
Addiction to Perfection

Work with your breath. Rhythmically align each body movement with your in-breath and out-breath. Let the breath decide how it wants to move your body. Let your body follow. When you have truly given up directing the movement, you can notice that awareness of where your body is moving follows a split second after the body has moved. Unless you are in a large, protected space or have a friend around to protect you from falling, keep your eyes half open.

When your body is rhythmically and easily responding to your breath, move quietly to where you have two pieces of clay laid out on newspaper and plastic—one about the size you can grab with one hand, the other about three times that size. Work the clay with the whole body, not just the hands. Move around all sides. Make whatever position you are working in easy on your back and neck.

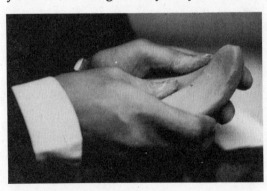

Breathing into the clay

Breathing into the Clay

Close your eyes. Place your hands on the clay—both hands—and invoke the dream. Breathe in, and then breathe out. Allow each in-breath to fill your body with the dream's images and energy. Then, breathe *out* the dream experience into the clay by making a *single*, two-handed movement. You might find your hands twisting, pummeling, squeezing, or bisecting. Whatever body and hands decide to do, put your whole breath into that single movement.

Open your eyes and look at the small piece. Turn it around until you find a part that surprises or intrigues you. Whether it looks like something in the dream or not is unimportant, because your focus is only on which shape holds your visual or emotional attention.

Using the larger piece you have set aside, begin to build a larger version of the section that appeals to you. Don't replicate the smaller piece. Use it as an imaginal departure point for the larger. Hold the dream in your imagination and body as you form the piece, even though, at this point, the shape it is taking has no logical connection with the dream. The logic has shifted to the kinesthetic realm. Keep holding that dream image and continually breathe it into the clay as you let this larger piece build and change itself. Just as the breath enters and leaves, creating a place for the fresh breath to enter in, let the clay form and reform itself, each time letting go of old shapes to make a place for new. Let go of all expectations except the constancy of the dream image.

Sometimes even the dream image itself changes, dreams itself onward. Don't resist this. Welcome it as you welcome new breath and new shapes in the clay. You have been re-

The body is the unconscious in its most immediate and continuous form; the dream is also the unconscious, though as a body of images it lacks the immediacy and continuity of the physical body.

—Marion Woodman
Addiction to Perfection

ceptive to the dream image and it is now free to reveal more of itself.

You probably won't want to use music while doing this. The dream carries its own silent music, and your breath can be the steady rhythm that accompanies the syncopated slaps and thuds of the clay as it moves your hands.

Keep your muscles flexible and loose. It's easy to become so absorbed into the flow of the image, the breath, and the clay that the body can slip out of awareness until something begins to hurt. There is no need to pay for a clay session with discomfort. Keep your whole body present, actively receptive to the image and to the feelings breathed out. Stretch. Stand. Move from one side of the clay to the other. Walk around the house or garden. Shake your body out in the kitchen.

Feeling

Relive the dream until your body is filled with the feeling the dream evokes. When you are overflowing with the feeling, let the out-breath carry the feeling down your arms and into your hands. Allow the overall feeling of the dream to permeate every cell of your body and then breathe that feeling into the first gesture in the clay. If you feel confined in the dream, find a body posture that amplifies that sense of confinement and then breathe it into the clay. If you are feeling elated, let the elation expand your cells and explode down your arms into the clay. Make a long sound as you expel the breath, and allow the feeling down your arms. Squeeze the clay until the breath is completely expired and all the affect expressed down through your arms.

Movement

Some dreams contain a repeated movement. When you warm up for clay work, let that dream movement repeat itself in waking time. Do it slowly. Do it fast. Do it jerkily. Do it smoothly. Explore its every nuance. When you know that dream movement from the inside out, go to the clay and, still moving, pick up a small piece and watch what your hands do with it. Then amplify the small piece into a larger piece.

Embodying the movement from the dream allows insight into its quality. Meg told me that she dreamed about hundreds of tiny, harmless snakes who were raising up their tails. After everyone else was asleep, she stayed up and moved around her kitchen like a snake. Then she went to the kitchen table and, still slithering around in her old jeans, looking nothing like a snake but feeling like one, she picked up a small piece of clay and elongated it into a most unremarkable coil. The clay wouldn't hold itself up the way the snakes could in the dream but, in making it larger, Meg found she could support it with a water glass long enough for her to take a photograph of it. The whole activity took her about twenty minutes. She learned how strong and well supported a snake needed to be to go stand up against gravity. She went to bed pondering where in her life she might use unexpected strengths, support herself in new movements, in her tail (tale?).

Figures

If you want to make a clay piece for an important figure in your dreams, first tell yourself that this is a reminder, not a replica. Don't think about "making a figure." Instead, express its essence. The clay piece is your personal, three-dimensional hieroglyph, your dream image taking its own peculiar and nonrepresentational shape. Actually, I'm not sure I would want to replicate even a magical, numinous, or healing figure from a dream. What I want is to express its essence or the quality the figure carries for or evokes in me.

Mohammed believed the dream to be a conversation between man and Allah.
—Carl W. O'Nell
Dreams, Culture, and the Individual

- *Behold the figure.* Remember all through your body what it felt like to encounter the figure in the dream. How was it to see your beloved grandfather again? How did it feel to embrace that new baby who could talk? What was it like to feel that stringy-haired murderer pursuing you? Hold the image of the figure in your imagination and then allow the feeling to suffuse you as you touch the clay.
- *Become the figure.* If you are feeling strong, "become" the figure. Become your grandfather standing on a windy hill smiling. Become that miraculous baby speaking poetry to her mother. Become that gentle, loving face

"Elephant Woman"
Clay

that is being touched with wonder by your dream-self. What a different feeling! Sometimes, allowing that figure to move in you can be enough, and you might not want to work with clay as well. At other times, you might want to also express that figure's energy by breathing it into the clay.

- *Express a figure's life force.* Imagine that you are making a secret symbol that stands for the dream figure's life force. It might have arms and legs and even a face, but it might not. If the figure is exceptionally kind, for example, you might find yourself making a small, curved thing with gentle, rounded edges that capture the essence of kindness for you. If you are expressing the life force of a wise figure, it might become a simple pyramid that seems still and quiet to you. It won't look like the figure, but it will remind you of its energy.

Sculpting an Animal Figure

Most of the approach to figures also applies to animals. Rather than replicate an animal, express its spirit. To bypass self-criticism, make a child's version of the animal or of a part of it that captures its feeling or attitude. You make the piece in clay that can be fired in a kitchen oven or air-dried and then painted. Check with a crafts store about the type of paint to use.

Clay allows us to dwell with dream images at a nonrational level, at an embodied level, at a meditative level, so that they feed the soul. Clay allows us to pay homage to the forms that appear in and for the soul.

THE DARK HAG RETURNS:
WORKING WITH NIGHTMARES IN CLAY

Clay is an excellent medium for working with nightmares. It immediately directs the nightmare's flyaway energy through the breath, through the body, and into the clay. The clay brings visual focus and tactile form to the fear, rage, terror, grief.

Using clay for nightmares requires small but important variations, best understood by seeing how Joanna worked with her nightmare in clay:

The Dark Hag Returns

I am walking through my maternal grandmother's home with my son. I wonder where my grandmother is. I can't find her. Finally my son says, as though he knew all along, "She's in the bedroom." I find the bedroom, which is in a different part of the house in the dream from where it was in real life.

Instead of my grandmother, there is a revolting old witch—hag—sitting in the chair by the window. I can smell her from the doorway, and her clothes are filthy. I see her face in the light of the window. It's all caved in and hawky. Somehow, I know that she has killed my grandmother and that she is planning to kill my son and eat him. I can't seem to find the way out. I start screaming at my son to run. He won't pay attention to me. He seems more curious than afraid. I scream louder and wake myself up, screaming and crying. I was so frightened I went into his room to make sure he was breathing.

Let's review the guidelines and see how Joanna applied these to her Hag dream.

- *Set a time limit.* There are no medals for bravery in facing the inner world. No one is going to set limits but you (and family members and friends who won't put up with your preoccupation). Your self-care while doing inner work is your responsibility, particularly when you are exploring big, apparently dark dream energies. Limit the time and energy you invest in these explorations, unless you are on retreat. Twenty minutes to an hour is the most helpful length of time to explore a nightmare with clay.

  Joanna decided to spend fifteen minutes doing clay work around the hag dream that same day. She asked her partner to take her son to school early so she could work with the clay briefly before she had to leave for work.

- *Warm up and cool off.* Usually the energy infusing a nightmare is high and difficult to focus. First, walk around, jump up and down, stomp, run, swing your arms. Take a large piece of clay and pummel it. Poke, pull, jab, karate-chop it until your body tires a little.

  Choosing to work off some of this energy when she did her aerobic exercise earlier, Joanna just loosened up her shoulders that were tense from hurrying and reliving the dream.

- *Set aside beforehand the amount of clay you are going to use.* Just as you draw a frame or a container for an energy painting, so decide on the amount of space your clay piece will occupy. Work with a piece that you can either fit into the palm of one hand, or that is too big for both hands to encompass. If you are afraid of the image and want to lessen the energy of the dream, work with a

Yolmo dream images . . . help to disclose the private reaches of the self. They are a vehicle for social understanding, for they communicate the dark fires of the heart, and are an education into self-experience, for they chart domains of body and soul which the dreamer would not otherwise have access to.

—Robert R. Desjarlais "Dreams, Divination, and Yolmo Ways of Knowing" small piece. If you want to express and exorcise the dream, work with a large piece.

Not wanting to take either the time or the courage it would require to make a large piece, Joanna chose a single handful of clay.

• *Drink fluids and take breaks.* Excitement and fear usually heighten adrenaline responses. We get dry-mouthed. We forget to breathe, or breathe shallowly. As you are working with the clay, keep breathing the energy of the dream into the clay. Take breaks and take slow, rhythmic, deep breaths. Then return to the piece.

Forming the basic head came quickly for Joanna. She made an egg shape, stuck a nose on, put the clay down, and took some deep breaths. So far, so good. Now she was getting to the part she didn't like—the horrible face. She needed more energy and breath to approach this.

• *Keep releasing the body.* Negative responses also tend to tighten the body. Muscles prepare for fight or flight, or freeze like a panicked animal. There's little point in working creatively with a nightmare if you just come out feeling as though someone has thrown you down a well. Release jaw, neck, and shoulders at regular intervals. Breathe that tightness out into the clay or stand and shake yourself out frequently.

While Joanna made the features, she kept breathing out her fear into the clay, as though she were putting all the dark spirit of the hag into the very clay itself. She noted later that her anxiety about the figure gradually abated as she began to form the facial features and breathe the darkness out.

• *Photograph the piece.* Photograph it from all four sides and from the top. Often, hidden, positive aspects of a nightmare can become clearer to us if we photograph the piece. Black-and-whites are usually more effective than color. If you use quick-dry or home-fired clays, you might want to paint the piece later and photograph it in color.

- Joanna chose not to paint her piece. She wanted to keep it raw and earthy. It also seemed easier to cope with, somehow. She knew that, were she to paint it, the color would be ugly, and she had faced enough of this figure for the moment. Instead, she decided to take a black-and-white photograph of the piece, dimly lit. This made it look dark and threatening. When she had the photographs of all four sides developed, she was surprised. One of the side views was not threatening at all. In fact, it reminded her of her godmother whom she had known and loved. She had been focusing so much on making the face ugly that she had forgotten to make it ugly from all sides. This apparently unintentional "omission" was not lost on Joanna. She named the piece *The Hag and the Loving Godmother* to acknowledge the two qualities that had unexpectedly emerged in the clay.

The dream was significant . . . to the ancient Chinese. . . . Inasmuch as human experience was perceived to be unitary, the dream was interpreted to be an integral part of total human experience.

—Carl W. O'Nell
Dreams, Culture, and the Individual

Many people have noticed an odd phenomenon: No matter how fierce they try to make a piece to portray the dream intensity and ugliness, the painting or figure turns out

"The Hag and the Loving Godmother," Clay

to have a comical or ridiculous side to it. Don't oppose this phenomenon. It seems to be inherent in some processes, and has something to reveal to us about the trickster nature of some dark images.

In the Pueblo communities of the southwestern United States, the community priests often dress as clowns. This custom is also found cross-culturally: The divine makes its appearance clothed as its opposite—the fool, the child, the court jester, the clown, the joker. Clothed in this way, it can disarm our defenses, break down boundaries between the physical and mystical realms, and, by maintaining a paradoxical balance of divine and comedic, pierce our awareness with new insight into ourselves or our worlds. This is often what can happen with an art piece created from a nightmare. It takes a form that holds both terror and humor. We cannot make this happen; we can only marvel at its appearance after the fact.

• *Consider sacrificing the piece at a later date.* Certain images and experiences carry dark power for us only at certain times. Later, we wonder what was so fearsome about them, or find ourselves ready to let them go. When I was a child, I used to walk to school past a nature reserve where I was certain a witch lived. I always scuttled past that area, uttering magic words so the witch wouldn't emerge from the wild, purple undergrowth and grab me. When I drive past that spot now, I feel the distant echo of that fear in my body, but wonder how such a pleasant area could have held such fascination and terror. The energy has released from the image.

We cannot force a release. Ritual that forces release of energy from a charged inner situation can be ill timed and destructive. If the dark image preoccupies us to the detriment of our daily life and sense of proportion about ordinary living, it's wise to consult an experienced and well-trained consultant.

However, there are times when we are ready to just move on, or when we notice that the fearful image has transmogrified in imagination or feeling. This can be a good time to ritually sacrifice art that has embodied that image. You might decide to smash it, drop it in a lake, take it to the beach and consign it to the ocean, burn it, tear it up, or recycle it. Whatever you decide, do it with respect, attention, care, and gratitude for its place in your life. Disposing of a piece can evoke feelings that deserve your calm and loving attention.

Several months after making her piece, Joanna had a second dream about this figure. In it, the Godmother side of the figure predominated. Joanna had an inner conversation with both the Hag and the Godmother to learn more about how she unconsciously evoked these energies in her parenting and work. The more she took responsibility for the destructive and loving aspects of her own personality, the less she found she was interested in her clay figure. One day, she quietly buried it in the backyard and planted a geranium over it.

By working with the nightmare and its clay form in these ways, you can pay homage to the dark wisdom of the soul and the ways it finds to walk us safely through a small part of our own interior hell, helping us catch glimpses of archetypal terrors in a way that does not compromise our daily orientation to waking life. The nightmare can transform itself. We can assist by bringing it, through the strength and containment of the body

When we dream, we are programming ourselves for survival by meaningful experience, or we are eliminating scenarios that do not satisfy those purposes. Dreams are therefore important to us, even if we forget them. But, they are more important to us if we choose to make the effort to remember them.

—Fred Alan Wolf
The Dreaming Universe

and through the steadiness and fidelity of the breath, into clay form. In this way, rather than rot within from neglect, the dark image can weave itself into the whole cloth of our individuation.

8

Movement, Drama, and Ritual

HAND IN HAND:
MOVING DREAM FIGURES ON THE INNER STAGE

Working with drama brings yet another kind of emotional involvement in and perspective to dream images, especially to dreams that might have previously been seen as too brief or understated to retain.

One way that we can bring dramatic life to a scene is to imagine that we are directing it for a stage play or a movie. If, as many theorists say, the dream is like a play happening on our inner stage, we can explore dreams as though our soul is a mysterious writer who has left us the play to direct (and enact). We need to determine how best to present the play so that it touches the core of the playwright's theme.

This morning, for example, I woke too early in my country of origin, Australia. Jet-lagged, I had difficulty catching my dream. I struggled to go back to sleep (it was four A.M. and the kookaburras hadn't even started to cackle in the eucalyptus). However, a single image flashed across my inner eye: two young women—one a little older—running together companionably, with the younger woman slightly ahead and looking back over her shoulder. Oh well, another dream lost, I reflected, as I attempted to sleep again.

However, my body knew it was late morning and I was not destined to sleep again. So I picked up the pencil beside my bed, drew a rectangle representing a stage, and sleepily drew the movement the young women made as though I were plotting their movements as stage directions.

What I had done with the dream so far was neither exciting nor enlightening. Then I wondered if a dramatic variation on active imagination might help. I decided to

[A dream is] a theater in which the dreamer is himself the scene, the player, the prompter, the producer, the author, the public, and the critic.

—C. G. Jung
Collected Works

"talk" to two imaginary actresses standing on a stage in my mind's eye.

"Stella [the younger woman], begin to move stage right. Let there be a slight pull as you draw Jane along—but no sense of stress. Look back at her, trusting that she'll be able to keep up with you as you move across the stage. Show her by your facial expression that you won't go too fast for her. Don't stop your movement at all. Keep in the straight line of forward movement.

"Jane, lag just a little behind but don't drag on Stella's movement. Give just a hint that she is giving you direction and energy, but show that you acknowledge what you bring to this friendship—your presence is giving Stella's forward movement more purpose and pleasure."

Whether a dream should be taken on the objective or subjective level is seldom unambiguously indicated by the dream itself. The decision is much more a question of feeling on the part of the dreamer or his consultant. Hence dream interpretation is also an ethical matter, not simply an intellectual procedure.

—Marie-Louise von Franz In Fraser Boa's The Way of the Dream

Now the dream image took on life and direction. The dream could be viewed many ways, but right now, in my disoriented state, these women feel like parts of myself I am encountering this morning: spirit and body. My spirit feels like the young woman: energetic and excited to be here. My jet-lagged body feels more like the older woman: less energetic and lagging slightly behind.

When I imagine the figures in this way and let them interact with my awareness, I realize that I can better harness these different energies. I can accept the natural tension between wishes and capacities, ensure that there is not too much of a gap between them. I can be more patient with my body, which has crossed so many time zones.

So much for one simple dream image that I thought held little. By giving it these few minutes' attention, I feel better able to address activities today.

In a similar way, imagine that you are giving stage

directions to figures from a dream. Speak them out loud. Demonstrate to the mythical actors how you want them to move and look. Note down new insights you gain from their interaction or your perspective as stage manager.

Each action in a dream is absolutely correct contextually for the dream. There is a reason why the figure moves the way she does, has the hair color he does, coughs as he does, limps as it does. By taking on the imaginary responsibility of staging a repeat performance of this play, we come a little closer to the unknown playwright's intent. Although we shall never know exactly what the writer had in mind, we can plumb more of the rich depths of the play itself.

PIERCING THE HEART: REENACTING AND MIMING MOVEMENTS IN YOUR DREAMS

When some people tell their dreams, they cannot stop using their hands. They unintentionally mime—they relive and unconsciously embody each figure or entity in the dream through gesture. Their faces, hands, and bodies express different qualities.

Wanting to show body gestures or movements of a figure or entity—a waterfall, a falling rock—they begin to embody the energy of the dream, to allow it into cellular consciousness. The body is often able to express what words cannot, so it can be helpful to set aside analysis and words at times, and intentionally mime the dream from beginning to end.

Miming bypasses noisy minds and directly taps into dream feelings and movements. Miming also allows access to unfamiliar ways of moving—literal moving. Often,

A dream of . . . a Malaysian Senoi, accelerated democratically a social change by breaking down the strongest barriers created by clothing and dietary habits between his group and the neighboring Chinese and Mohanedan colonies. The dream was about a ritual dance in which the participants were required to alter their ways of dressing and eating.

—Kalle Achte and Taina Schakir "Dreams in Different Cultures" these ways are not part of the body's active vocabulary of movement during waking life. We don't swing back and forth slowly like an old oak tree in our daily lives. We don't often move like a waterfall or rainbow. These are unfamiliar body gestures, and their wisdom can often stay unfamiliar to us unless we physically embody our symbolic capacity in this physical way.

Dreams are a "drama taking place on one's own interior stage."
—C. G. Jung
Letters
Vol. 1, 1906–1950

When we can free ourselves from the burden of verbalizing, we can have different consciousness: we can experience an oak tree, a waterfall, a rainbow. When we do this, we need to quietly and nonjudgmentally observe our miming. Embodying a dream entity can sometimes result in our becoming unhelpfully overidentified, and we can lose our imaginative way.

Something inside chooses, without our conscious consultation, which of the many people and entities we know (or which of the many composite characters we don't know personally) to put into our dreams. It is even more intriguing when the figure is someone we do not like or who is strongly alien. Although we might not know now, there is probably a reason this figure, as opposed to any other, appears in the dream.

When we can let some part of a dream character's behavior or gestures reenact itself through our bodies, we can bypass overactive intellects and have an larger intuitive picture of the situation. By miming the character's expression or behavior, we can more closely kinesthetically intuit what is motivating the figure. This practice is related to the Gestalt therapy technique of becoming a dream figure or object.

Patricia worked as a successful, powerful executive, but longed for more balance in her life. She wanted to nourish an artistic side that had been subsumed under the great demands of graduate school, and she longed for an intellectual peer and life partner. She suspected herself of obstructing her efforts at balance, although she couldn't see how.

As an executive, Patricia believed that time and money were closely interrelated. She usually arrived at therapy sessions with a list so that she could feel she was maximizing our effectiveness. She was understandably dubious about letting a session run in directions that lacked definable outcomes.

Patricia remembered few dreams, let alone ones of the magnitude she brought in one morning. She was distressed by its alien quality and dark content, and wanted to excise it from consciousness as soon as possible.

The Ritual Death

I am watching a ritual death. A foreign man is condemned to die by his own hands. Two men stand behind him on guard. The man makes two vertical shallow incisions on each side of the heart. He does not close his eyes but looks a little below and straight ahead. Then he takes two steel pins and presses them through the incision points into the two sides of his heart.

I know this will kill him because it will pierce the heart and stop the blood flow through the chambers. I identify with his action so strongly that I wake myself up, crying out on a long breath.

Patricia wanted to explore the dream, but asked that we limit the time because she had "other, more important things to talk about." Patricia trusted and relied on her reasoning powers to make uneasy situations more

Whenever people are too rational and too materialistic, the dreams point to something completely supernatural. I remember the dream of a woman who dreamt that she saw a little mechanical animal. It was made of diamonds, but it was alive and walked around on the floor. She consulted Jung about the dream, and he said to her, "That is to prove to you that the impossible is possible. You are still too rational. You think that such a thing cannot happen. You are not open to miracles, and there are miracles. In the realm of the psyche, miracles can happen."

—Marie-Louise
von Franz
In Fraser Boa's
The Way of the Dream

Children [in the Senoi tribe] are guided . . . to dream correctly. In dreams of falling, for instance, they are advised to relax, to fall without fear and find out where the fall leads them. With time, the social prompting, advice, instructions, and criticism achieve transformation of the falling dreams into the supreme joy of flying.

—Kilton Stewart
"Dream Theory in Malaya"

immediately tolerable, and we had both agreed previously that her intellect sometimes ran roughshod over her emotions during verbal exercises. So we decided to work from another, less rational perspective.

She was still too baffled by the figure to begin to speak from his point of view. Instead, I asked her if she could either physically replicate the position of the man in the dream or whether she was willing to close her eyes and imagine being in that posture. A private person, Patricia preferred to imagine. I sat quietly. This would be a difficult exercise for her, but we trusted our history together and her commitment to doing whatever she could to help regain better balance in her life.

The effect of Patricia's doing this was powerful for both of us. I, too, imagined how it might be to go through this ritual as I metaphorically held Patricia quietly in my conscious awareness so that she could feel a protective presence during her inner reflection. Patricia wrote later:

I imagined myself kneeling. I *felt* those two guards behind me—but I realized suddenly that they were actually quiet and loving, not fierce—there to help me do this thing, not to force me or punish me.

I imagined making those small incisions and didn't feel much—they just went skin deep. They weren't really painful—somehow just a prelude.

But then I picked up that steel pin and put the first one in. When I imagined it piercing my heart, I really *felt* what this dream was about! I understood it in my body! I knew that this was about my making the sacrifices I need to make to let my heart be pierced by my own feelings again. Then I *wanted* to pick up the other pin so that I could pierce the other side!

When I imagined myself into the gestures of the dream, it wasn't a bad dream at all. It just looked that way from the outside. I could see that I've been too shut down to let my connections with important people go more than *skin* deep! But I have to do it! I can see now that it won't happen unless I sacrifice my present habits and attitude toward life.

I have to turn that warriorlike energy I have at work toward my own well-being. I can't wait for someone to come along or for the business to ease up. I need to make some sacrifices—keeping up the perfect image, time, some new projects, perhaps even this promotion with all its travel. It's going to take me more courage to open up my heart than it does to wheel and deal! I could feel my hand making tight fists holding those steel pins; it took courage and the sort of determination I use at work. Except now I'm going to use the same energy to make time for my own heart—for my creative outlets and for relationship.

I will tell you some-thing about stories . . . they aren't just entertainment. Don't be fooled. They are all we have, you see, all we have to fight off illness and death.

You don't have anything if you don't have the stories.

—Leslie Marmon Silko
Ceremony

Through enacting one simple series of physical gestures from her dream, Patricia became aware of what she need-ed to do to change her priorities to fit her values. We didn't have to discuss or analyze. She could feel it in her body and in her heart. She could feel the necessity of the sacri-fices more keenly and quickly after this one imaginary ex-perience than after hours of well-worded conversation.

Dream gestures and physical movements contain vast reservoirs of energy and wisdom if they are explored and lived out symbolically within a protected environment such as a therapy office, bedroom, or garden. Choose one of your dreams and work with it in similar ways to the way Patricia worked.

- Mime your dream-self in a particular dream. If you are lying down in the dream, lie down. If you are stroking a tree, put out your hand and feel yourself stroking that tree. If you are running, run.

It is important to let the dream speak without allowing the dreamer to look at the written text.
—Robert Bosnak
A Little Course in Dreams

- After you have mimed your own movements, mime the movements or gestures of other entities in the dream: the unknown person pursuing you, the old school friend using the telephone booth while you wait. Mime the tree creaking in the dusk wind, and imagine its trunk being stroked by your dream-self. Take each entity in turn.

- Now mime your entire dream. Put the whole sequence together. Reenact it without words. Imagine that you are communicating the dream to a friend who doesn't speak your native language.

- After you have mimed the dream in natural time, mime the dream again very, very slowly as though the film were running in slow motion.

- Close your eyes. Focus on the facial, hand, and body gestures that carry a special charge or interest. Repeat those gestures until they resemble a ritual dance. What do you feel in your body? What emotions fill you or play at the corners of consciousness? What spontaneous images intersect with the already vivid ones of the dream?

- As an alternative to physically miming the dream (which is sometimes socially or logistically impossible), close your eyes and work as Patricia worked: reenact the gestures of the dream in imagination and find important gestures.

- After you have finished, briefly note responses or insights. It's quicker and closer to the nonlinear nature of dreaming to note them in nongrammatical form; don't write them in sentences.

Embodying the Spirit of a Dream Animal Through Mime and Movement

Just as it is possible to work with dream figures and objects by miming their movements, so it is even easier to explore the movements of dream animals. They are particularly receptive to embodiment.

- Take five minutes to warm up your body and free up your movements from the censorship of your critical mind.

- Invite the spirit of the animal to enter into your body through the rhythmic intake of the breath.

- Use music or a nature tape to enhance the experience, if you wish. You don't need it, however. You can just listen to what your animal ears hear.

- With each breath, feel the body's shape and size change, the muscle masses reforming, strengthening, lengthening; the skin growing scales, hairs, fur; the eyes widening or becoming multifaceted; the ears growing larger, flatter, longer; the hands and feet changing into paws, claws, wings.

- Follow the change. Don't make it. Let your awareness follow a moment after the change. Explore your new size and shape and gravitational relationship to earth and sky.

- Take your time. Do this exercise when you have at least fifteen minutes. Explore slowly. Let your animal form do the things it might do during the day or night. Imagine soaring, crawling, pouncing, creeping, sliding, devouring, diving, hovering.

In Japan the highest compliment to an artist is to say he paints with his soul, his brush following the dictates of his spirit . . . The Japanese artist is taught that even to the placing of a dot in the eyeball of a tiger he must first feel the savage, cruel, feline character of the beast, and only under such influence should he apply the brush.

—Henry P. Bowie
On the Laws of Japanese Painting

*The dreamer moves
into the inner space
of the dream to the
extent that the images
can be recalled. In this
remembered dream
space, the dream
events reoccur . . .
Fresh dreams that are
retained as spatial
dream images and
survive as real events,
not just as a story,
must be approached
as much as possible
through their spatial
details.*

—Robert Bosnak
*A Little Course in
Dreams*

- Let sounds come. Don't attempt to sound exactly like the animal. You are not a perfect mimic. Embody the spirit of the animal. Let yourself laugh if an odd sound comes out. The spirit of sacred improvisation almost always involves both gravity and humor. Take your experiment seriously, but don't take yourself too seriously.

- Stop before you get tired. Set a time limit on the exercise. It's sometimes easy to enter into a slightly altered state, but to be inattentive and careless (for ourselves as well as others) about leaving that state.

- Allow time to reenter your human body just as attentively and patiently as you entered the essence of the animal.

- Draw, make notes, or dictate your experience. What feels unforgettable at the time is often lost in the press of getting the brakes fixed, the child to the game, the report in, the garbage out. Each of these activities is as important as the animal movements you made, and needs to be completed with as much attention and awareness. There is no hierarchy of experience; there are just repeated opportunities to bring loving attention to each experience.

Exploring Miming and Movement with Groups

Groups work well with mime. Whereas the verbalized dream might seem too revealing to share, we can often tell the most penetrating, personal, or private dreams in a group through the grace of mime. Ask that group members simply empty their minds and open their hearts. It is not the time for group members to interpret or judge. Nor is it the time for members to admire others for how well they can mime, or for comparing themselves with the person currently miming. Focus loving attention on the mime in a way that seals off the outside world and makes a safe, invisible container in which the group and individual performer can explore without fear of betrayal, nonreceptivity, or interpretation.

Developing a Ritual Sequence

Over a period of time, build up a reservoir of the significant ritual movements you have discovered for yourself alone or in your group. Imagine that these are a sequence in a ritual dance. Experiment with moving from one ritual gesture to the next, until the sequence feels complete and flowing. This sequence constitutes yet another alternative narrative structure, a series of personal hieroglyphs narrating the history of your soul.

In Matters Controversial: Telling the Dream from the Viewpoint of Opposing or Threatening Figures

In my last year of graduate studies in English, one of my literature professors called out to me down the marble stairwell one day. His keen, dry wit always delighted me and, though I have a poor memory for quotations, his words stuck. We had been batting around some literary interpretation earlier, and he decided to have the final word (it wasn't hard). With a grin crinkling his sharp, sun-faded, blue eyes, he quipped: "In matters controversial, my perception's rather fine. I always see both points of view: the one that's wrong and mine."

Although I don't usually see points of view in dreams

There's a phrase in West Africa called "deep talk." When a person is informed about a situation, an older person will often use a parable, an axiom, and then add to the end of the axiom, "Take that as deep talk." Meaning that you will never find the answer. You can continue to go down deeper and deeper. Dreams may be deep talk.

—Maya Angelou
In Naomi Epel's
Writers Dreaming

as right or wrong, I notice that I tend to dream from one perspective, though I occasionally have a dream in which I am both watching and participating. I have even occasionally encountered figures I knew to be myself. I've also known what someone else was thinking in a dream, too, but have rarely been more than one person at a time.

Dreams already encourage us to have a different perspective—sometimes many. Several dream theorists (including Carl Jung and Fritz Perls) postulate that dreams use familiar or unfamiliar players from our lives to play roles with which we are less familiar than the role we, ourselves, play in the dream. Whereas Perls' Gestalt approach suggests that we *become* the glass of water we drink in a dream, James Hillman has reservations about this stance, believing that there is a reason we are in a certain position in the dream, that becoming the glass of water is not as helpful as exploring the experience of drinking.

While there are drawbacks to playing out other roles in a dream, it can also be helpful if we don't take it to melodramatic and overidentified extremes. If becoming an element in the dream lightens our burdens in a substantial, coherent way and helps us move in our inner or outer lives with more independence, mutuality, clarity, acceptance, energy, ethicality, and grace, we are using the practice well. If acting out every part of a dream just provides for a florid show without integration of the drama, it is a waste of our psychic and emotional energy.

Let's look at Paul's dream which, in its conflictual stance, seems to indicate that part of Paul is opposing his own well-being:

I am training in the army, doing physical moves with a partner. We each have guns. I forget my move and say so

The self, in all its efforts at self realization, reaches out beyond the ego-personality on all sides; because of its all-encompassing nature it is brighter and darker than the ego, and accordingly confronts it with problems it would like to avoid. . . . The experience of the self is always a defeat for the ego.

—C. G. Jung
Collected Works

without embarrassment. The instructor ridicules me. He demands to know when and where I was born, and comments that I must have been rejected really early—he says this with derision. I am livid. I tell him he has no right to say these things to me. I walk out.

The instructor collapses and starts crying in a way to gain the attention of the other people in the class, who help him into bed. Clearly he is not used to being confronted. I know this is going to present problems for me in the rest of the course, not only with him, but also with other instructors. However, I don't care.

Although Paul was encountering opposition at work when he had this dream, he sensed that the dream had more to say than that he felt beleaguered by his boss and needed to stand up to him. In fact, he was doing an excellent job of negotiating a difficult political situation. Paul explored what it would be like for him to narrate the dream from the point of view of the army instructor. Here's his journal write-up of what "the instructor" said:

"I've been an instructor in the army for a lot of years. I've got a new bunch of trainees in. One's a bit slow on the uptake. I like the guy, but I'm afraid that he's going to blow it now that we're training with guns. He makes some pretty bad mistakes, but doesn't seem to care. He could kill his training partner!

"I blast him out of the water to teach him a lesson he won't forget. Instead of listening to me, he just gets angry and acts as if he's above the other guys.

"I am so angry that I get a heart attack and have to be helped into bed by some of the trainees. I'm frightened and humiliated."

Only when I have been able to move into the other-as-other as deeply as I can, I take a step out of the dream world and understand the feeling that now pervades me as an unconscious emotion of my own as well. Then I return to the imaginal reality. In this way, I weave back and forth, constantly aware of the paradoxical nature of my experience.

—Robert Bosnak
In Michael V. Adams'
"Image, Active
Imagination, and the
Imaginal Level"

Insights and break-throughs often come during periods of pause or refreshment after great labors . . . Not doing can sometimes be more productive than doing.

—Stephen
Nachmanovitch
Free Play

What became clear to Paul as he retold the dream as the instructor was that he had to come to terms with two parts of himself: one that was careless and irresponsible and one that was wise but rough. He had an internal self-monitor who was more like a tough army instructor than a kindly coach. He realized that, if he could tone down his internal instructor's ways of talking to him, his irresponsible side might really learn something. He also realized that his anger at himself was similar to the paternal wrath he experienced from his impatient father, a loving but unbending disciplinarian.

Paul saw that he was right to defend himself, but that he needed to negotiate with this inner instructor. He also realized that he was afraid that his pattern of underperformance followed by overwork was possibly putting his health at risk. It was no accident that his imagination came up with a heart attack in the second version: Paul had several male relatives who had died early of heart disease. This dream became the subject of some long-term behavioral change that Paul effected in his life, and some internal renegotiations with his rebellion and idealism.

What about the other possibilities for the dream? What if it were not about this issue at all? Wrong questions. There is no "right" interpretation, as we have agreed. Did Paul nourish the dream? And did he find a way to let it nudge him along? Right questions.

Retelling the dream from another dream character's point of view, particularly if that character is anathema to us in some way, can bring unexpected riches. Often, an unfamiliar character can metaphorically encapsulate sealed-off energy we need to either express or rein in. The personifications of these energies in dream figures provide fine entry points into that never-ending cycle of bringing ourselves home to ourselves.

THE SHY MOUNTAIN LIONS: CONVERSING WITH DREAM ENTITIES

It's a sign of a rich encounter with inner figures in a dream when what they do or say surprises us. As Jungian theory suggests, it can be even more surprising and fruitful if we allow the dream to dream itself onward in waking life by engaging in active dialogue with the dream entity. By keeping our controlling mind out of the picture, we let imagination reign over everything—except our sense of ourselves as ordinary humans. This is one of the most commonly applied uses of active imagination, described earlier. This form of dialogue differs from the last two practices, in which only one imaginary figure is speaking: either the dream-self or another figure. In this practice, your waking self has the opportunity to actively engage and converse with a dream entity, allowing the dream to move onward into another scene that might or might not be related to the original dream.

Anna, for example, recently had this dream:

The Shy Mountain Lions

I am staying at some sort of resort with an old school friend. We wake up in the morning and are supposed to go down to a communal dining hall for breakfast. But my friend says we can't, because there's a storm coming.

Just then, I look out the window. The sky is really blue—no sign of a storm—but I see two shadows on the wooden veranda. They look like wild animals. I yell at C. to hide because I know they are going to come in. We hide

There are two kinds of active imagination. One kind entails a reconstitution of the dream image. You get your memory to give you back the image. . . . The other kind of active imagination lets new images emerge.

—Robert Bosnak
In Michael V. Adams'
"Image, Active
Imagination, and the
Imaginal Level"

under the beds. My heart is pounding. We hear the breakfast gong.

Then I see this huge paw beside the bed. I lift the bedspread a bit and suddenly am eye-to-eye with a mountain lion. Another one—it looks old and moth-eaten—is standing beside him. They don't look fierce at all.

I am just about to talk to them when my alarm goes off.

When Anna had an imaginary inner conversation with these two fellows, she followed Jung's suggestions for active imagination. She grew quiet, closed her eyes, and re-entered the dream. When she could see the mountain lions, she asked them some questions. Anna stayed herself—her ordinary, waking personality—while she spoke with them. She didn't allow the mountain lions to persuade her to do anything that she would not do in waking life. She didn't give up her own personality. If she didn't understand something they said, she told them; if she couldn't do what they asked, she told them. Here is some of what she wrote about this encounter:

I went back to the point in the dream where I was looking in the first mountain lion's eyes. We just stared at each other for a while. I thought nothing was going to happen, and I might as well give up on the active imagination.

But then suddenly it winked at me! At first I thought I must have mistaken what happened. It was too silly. It must have just blinked. So I looked again. After a while, it winked again—just one eye so that I really knew it was a wink!

"Can I trust you not to hurt me if I come out?"

"Do I look like someone who is going to hurt you?" he answered.

"How about your friend over there?" I asked, checking out the tufty looking one pacing around the room.

"Her? She's deaf and old and just wants some milk."

I climbed out and went and got her some milk. She got it all over her beard but kept on slurping while I talked to the first one.

"What's your name?"

"Nothing you don't know."

"What's *that* supposed to mean?!" I was getting impatient.

"Well," said he, in the manner of a patient teacher, "if you can't remember, I suppose I have to tell you *again*— 'Braveheart.'"

"Are you brave?"

"Not particularly. But I'm the part of you that's really courageous when it comes to taking risks with your feelings. I thump and thump my tail (you hear it as your heart) when I'm scared. But I go ahead anyway. But I've come to tell you something."

"What?"

"Stop putting me on that damned leash when you go off in the mornings! I'm tired of sitting around in the garden all day snoozing. I want to go with you when you go to work and meet people and have adventures. I'm bored and I'm insulted. And I'm getting bad tempered from being cooped up so much!"

"People will be terrified if I take you with me! They'll take one look at you and run screaming in the other direction!"

The mountain lion sighed and looked at his old friend who was licking the milk off her great lips. "You are so literal! Do you think I'd be dumb enough to turn up looking like this?! I have the power to get smaller or larger without losing my strength. So you can put me in a special place inside your body, where I can see everything but not be seen unless you want me to come out. Then I can get as big or as small as you need. OK?"

"Well," I said, pretty dubious. "I'll try it out . . . By the way, who's your friend over there? Another part of me I'm supposed to know?"

"Too soon for you to talk to her," he replied, knowingly and breezily. "You'll need her after you get used to walking around with me."

Then suddenly he seemed to fade and I was aware of being thirsty. So I went to the kitchen and poured myself—yes, a glass of milk!

The Greeks, the Romans, and later the early Christians sometimes resorted to induced dreams for diagnostic and curative purposes. Dreams were induced in the temples of the Greek god Asklepios, symbolized by a serpent. Harmless serpents were housed in the temple rooms occupied by dream petitioners. Various rites were performed by the petitioners to put themselves into proper dispositions to have dreams and be cured.

—Carl W. O'Nell
Dreams, Culture, and the Individual

Anna continued to work imaginatively with these two mountain lions for some weeks. They taught her things about her inner life, her fear of taking risks, her need to stay on her own soul's side when she had close connections with others. The images never left. These two figures became like totem animals for Anna.

This kind of dialogue can be used with many different kinds of dream entities, but most frequently with figures and animals who appear to be unfamiliar to us and whose role in our inner lives is one that we would like to appreciate more.

WRITTEN IN STONE: PAYING RITUAL HOMAGE TO THE WISDOM OF THE IMAGE

Our ancestors carved and painted images and symbols of their dreaming and waking lives in caves and on rocks. These petroglyphs and pictographs survive the ravages of time and the waxing and waning of individual lives. They remain silent, eloquent, mysterious testimonials to the lived experience of inner and outer lives, and to the universal desire to record experience in image, ritual, and tale.

Stone messages. When I visited Uluru (Ayer's Rock) in central Australia, we walked around part of its huge perimeter, which is several miles, and looked up at the pictographs on the blood-red overhangs and caves, shimmering in midday heat. There were pictographs of hands and figures, of images I did not understand. We walked over to an aboriginal camp, where I purchased from a male elder a "Snake Dreaming" painting laboriously done in pointillist style.

At sunset, I sat with my companions and silently watched Uluru turn into flames. I had my paints with me, and found myself picking up some of the blood-red silky earth on which I was sitting to complete a small watercolor. I could not paint on the sacred monolith, but I could scoop up some of its earth—the finest and softest I have ever sat or walked upon—and paint with it. I still have

Cairn, Norway

that small painting. The earth in it still evokes the mystery of those ancient markings.

Stone messages. Under a similar shimmering midday sun, a friend from a northern Pueblo Indian village took me to visit ancestral pictographs and petroglyphs. The symbols and figures reached across generations on this silent, cloudless New Mexico day, reached across the cultural ignorance I brought to this land. I did not understand their visual language, but felt their import as I do when I travel and hear conversations in a foreign tongue. I wanted to touch them, to feel in my fingertips what my friend's ancestors felt as they worked on these stones.

Stone messages. On a chill day in midsummer in Norway, we crossed the highest pass—a forbidding, plantless landscape shrouded in severe folds of snow, broken only by the lake's edge, stained peacock blue by submerged ice. In this barren land, there was one sign of life: cairns of stone left by climbers. Explorers leave cairns like this all over the world to mark their passage, to leave a message for others, to acknowledge that they have traversed this foreign territory and survived to tell the tale.

Stone messages. Carl Jung, at a difficult time in his own inner journey into unknown territory, stayed by the Zurichsee and gathered stones from the edge of the lake with which to build. He also carved symbols and words into stone in the house and in the garden. He spent a long time building and carving. It renewed him so that he could travel farther into the realm of the individual and collective psyche. A quietness comes when one walks around this part of Jung's home, an instinctive respect for the courage, despair, trust, patience, love, and faith that must have gone into those stones.

We, too, can build a cairn to mark our passage through new lands. We, too, can record wisdom from the land of dreams on our own stones. Not every dream. Not every piece of wisdom. But the life dreams, the big dreams. We can gather stones from the beach, the hills, or the valleys— smooth stones to write on. We can even go to a gardening-supply store and thoughtfully choose smooth, large, river pebbles from the piles, keeping the stones small enough to be able to carry but large enough on which to write or paint a symbol or a few words.

We can buy paint—perhaps earth colored—paint that will survive rough weather. And we can paint these symbols on the stones to remind us of the Snake Dream, the Tidal Wave Dream, the Spirit Guide Dream, the Voice on the Wind Dream. We can record their wisdom in word or symbol or simplified line image, and place the stones in a small cairn in our garden, or in a special place in our room or apartment—perhaps even in a tray of sand that we can smooth and design like a Zen garden.

At some Japanese shrines, often tucked away in a small, shaded, forested corner of the garden, visitors come upon a *jizo*, a small, tubby stone god with barely the hint of a face. It is the guardian spirit of children whose lives ended early, either because the mother could not carry to term, or because the infant died. Parents visit these stone gods and ladle water from the pool beneath them over their heads. Enough ladles, and the stone gods grow mossy hair on their oval heads. Most of them have moss. The ongoing care for and love of the child and the care for and love of the statue seems to be embodied in this silent, single gesture of ladling water over stone.

If you wish, keep a wooden ladle and special container for spring water, and occasionally pour water over your dream stones. It will remind you that wisdom—both joyful and painful—not only is eternal but must be remembered and allowed to flow in the waters of our daily lives as well.

A cairn or a stone garden of dream wisdom pays visual homage to the eternality of our dream world, to its refusal to accommodate our daily needs, to its faithful marking of the passage of our souls through unknown lands. We need not talk about these stones or show them to others unless they understand what it is to walk softly in this land. We never need explain the symbols or words. They can speak for themselves. They can reach out across the eons of our own night into the day and speak secrets to us as do the pictographs on Uluru, in Pueblo country, in the high country in Norway, in Jung's garden.

You can say that each ladle full of the water of life is a dream. That's what a dream is. Every night, we get . . . a sip of the water of life, and, if we understand the dream, we are vivified. We feel in contact with our psychic depth and with our own living substance, and then we subjectively feel that life is flowing, we are alive.

—Marie-Louise
von Franz
In Fraser Boa's
The Way of the Dream

A PAPER TREE OF DARK DREAMS: OFFERING UP DARK DREAMS TO NATURE

It is a misty, chill morning in Kyoto. As I walk along Philosopher's Walk under ice-pink blossoms floating in the sky and in the water beside me, I reflect on the night's dream. Jet lag leaves the gate between night and day worlds wider open. Even though I am surrounded by the promise of spring, and feel the delicacy of fine rain dusting my skin, I am still pervaded by the darkness of the dream. I had not thought to dream such a black dream on my first day in this exquisite city of temples.

So many temples and temple gardens! I prefer the smaller. Fewer people. Older priests. Less noise. I wander into a side street and enter the temple grounds.

The pine tree is covered in white. It looks like snow but it is not snow on its limbs. It is covered in paper fortunes, each tied to a small branch. These are bad fortunes that recipients have now consigned to return to the gods, to the chill spring air. If the fortune is good, you keep it.

I think about my dream. I realize there is much to contemplate in it, much of my own darkness to absorb me as an inevitable bad-fortune part of my inner world. Yet some part of this dream needs releasing. I stand in front of the tree and imagine the morning's dream written like a bad fortune on a piece of thin paper, the dream images drawn with a sumi brush. Trees absorb pain like rain, judge neither our words nor lack of words, nor signs of love we leave on them.

I imagine sitting quietly and writing my dream, and then coming to this temple to silently release the spell of those dream words by tying them to this dark, forgiving, elegant, gray-green pine. I take a deep breath and feel the dream entering a larger dimension than my poor jet-lagged mind, which has a limited approach to the wisdom of my dreams.

We do not need to live in Japan and have a temple close by in order to come to more peace with the dark mystery

Bad Fortunes left at temple in Kyoto

Yolmo dream images . . . help to disclose the private reaches of the self. They are a vehicle for social understanding, for they communicate the dark fires of the heart, and are an education into self-experience, for they chart domains of body and soul which the dreamer would not otherwise have access to.

—Robert R. Desjarlais "Dreams, Divination, and Yolmo Ways of Knowing"

of some dreams. Yet this blessing and releasing of dark dreams beyond our immediate understanding is a ritual we can enact in our own garden or in our own ways. We, too, can call upon the greater patterns and wisdom of nature to contain what feels too big for us to contain.

We can write dream images or tales on thin paper (even bathroom tissue), tie them to a tree in the garden, and watch them slowly become absorbed by the elements. We can find bark from a tree and, like the Australian aborigines who use smooth bark on which to paint their dreamtime stories, we can write on it and place it in the ocean, up in a tree, in the ground. We can make a paper boat of dark dream stories or wrap the words or images from our dark dreams around a stone. Then we can bless them and consign them to the larger elements: to the sea, to the lake, to the earth, to the air, to fire.

In winter, we can write our nightmares in snow and watch them be covered over or melt. We can write or paint them, and then consign them to the next evening's fire—not in order to destroy them, but to symbolically acknowledge that the image needs to transform into something less immediately fearful, more invisibly assimilated into a larger rhythm and flow of life we might not understand but trust and accept.

When we do not give form to dark energies, they ricochet endlessly around in the chambers of the heart and soul. They repeat and replay, often just out of awareness, leading us into obsession. When we do give symbolic form to dark energies, we transform repetition into conscious ritual, thus helping their integration into the larger life of heart and soul.

DRUMMING THE BIG DREAM: MARKING THE PASSAGE OF DREAMS WITH A DRUM OR MUSICAL MARKER

Finding a way to pay homage to "big dreams" is crucial. These dreams often contain unknown figures in strange, numinous environments and situations, and a clearly felt atmosphere of significance. These are archetypal dreams, dreams that touch into deeper layers of the psyche and have a natural mythological quality.

Dramatic and musical reenactments are ways to allow us to enter into and frame both conventional and unconventional narratives for big dreams. Let's see what Alex did with a big dream with an unconventional narrative:

> *By manipulating and massaging form, we perform a sympathetic magic on the spiritual insides of our work; we evolve shapes and structures and live by them.*
>
> —Stephen Nachmanovitch
> *Free Play*

Encounter with Two Cougars

When the dream opens, I am heading into unknown territory. I am heading away from trustworthy streets, into run-down neighborhoods, and to the edge of the bushes.

I hear noises and decide that it is unsafe to be walking around here at dusk. I turn around. But at a hut are two cougars or jaguars. I stop in the hopes that they won't view me as hostile.

One of them comes up and starts to snarl at me. It grasps my red shawl in its teeth and starts to tug fiercely at it. I tussle back. I figure that I might as well keep its attention focused on the shawl and off my body. I begin to really take it on.

At one point, we are eye-to-eye. I somehow feel at that moment that even if it kills me, it will have been an honorable battle. It finally walks away and leaves me alone—almost as if I have become one of them, almost as if it might protect me now.

I leave, walk down the hill. I reach the bottom. Various

people live in these huts. They all know each other or make themselves known to each other.

I realize that I have left my shoes with the cougars and deliberate whether or not I want to go back. I need those sandals. I find myself walking barefoot in the city edges, angrily noting that it is more dangerous to walk barefoot here because of all the broken glass than it was in the jungle.

Then, somehow, I have my shoes on again.

First, Alex freed her narrative from words she had added to explain space, perspective, time, and emotional shift, including:

when the dream opens	I realize
almost as if	then
but	because
I find myself	somehow
suddenly	
I somehow feel	
and	

Then, wherever possible, Alex followed these guidelines:

- Add repetition.
- Replace passive verbs with action verbs.
- Make sentences short.
- Repeat nouns and names rather than substituting *it* or *he/she/they*.
- Simplify sentences as much as possible.
- Delete as many *the*'s as possible.
- Break the narrative into dramatic units according to the shifts in the dream.

Now that Alex had prepared the dream for a dramatic reading, she was ready to add sound. She could have chosen a cymbal, a gong, a Tibetan bowl, a drum, a favorite tape that seemed to fit the atmosphere of the dream, a cheap bamboo flute to play a single note. What she chose was less important than the fact that she wasn't trying to make music; rather, she was adding sound to mark shifts and amplify the feeling:

> *Improvisation, composition, writing, painting, theater, invention, all creative acts are forms of play, the starting place of creativity in the human growth cycle, and one of the great primal life functions.*
>
> —Stephen Nachmanovitch
> *Free Play*

[Drum]

I head into unknown territory. I head away from trustworthy streets into run-down neighborhoods.

[Drum]

I go to the edge of the bushes. I hear noises. It is unsafe to walk around here at dusk. I turn around.

[Drum]

At a hut are two cougars. I stop. Will the cougars see me as hostile? One cougar approaches. The cougar snarls at me. The cougar grasps my red shawl in its teeth. The cougar tugs fiercely at the shawl. I tug back. I keep its attention on the shawl. I draw its attention away from my body. I take the cougar on. We are eye-to-eye. If it kills me, the battle is honorable.

[Long drum]

The cougar walks away and leaves me. I am alone. I have become one of the cougars. The cougars might protect me now.

[Drum]

I leave, walk down the hill. I reach the bottom. People live in these huts. The people all know or make themselves known to each other.

[Drum]

My sandals are with the cougars. I don't want to go back. I need those sandals. I walk barefoot in the city edges. I walk barefoot through broken glass. I am angry. It is more dangerous to walk barefoot in the city than it was in the jungle.

[Drum]

I have my sandals again.

[Drum]

This dramatic, musical reading of an unconventional big dream allows us to hear the deeper beat of the soul's imagery, symbolism, and innate structure. It calls to us in a different way.

Choose dreams carefully for this practice. Overdoing it results in your taking yourself too seriously and inflating the importance of your dream and yourself. Provide this kind of musical environment only when the dream demands it, when the dream feels anticlimactic if merely retold in an ordinary, "I went to work and came home" way. This practice works well with dream arts groups— and just as successfully at home, where you become your own receptive audience.

Working with big dreams using musical markers frames the dream in the ancient tradition of native ceremony and mythological re-enactment. The import of the dream is both respected and carried nonverbally by the music, allowing feelings to expand into, yet also be held by, sound: an essential paradox of music.

9

Tracing Dream Patterns

Embracing the Dragon: Following a Series of Dreams

Dream series are amazing threads in the soul's tapestry. A series can be developmental, repetitious, increasingly archetypal, or increasingly threatening (until the dreamer pays attention). It can also present variations or different perspectives on a theme.

A dream series that chooses the same topic, theme, or symbol is easy to trace over a period of time if you keep records. (Some dreamers use the "Find" function in their word processing programs to locate the recurrence of dream themes.) When you have time, review your dreams for clear, repeated entities, themes, symbols, or images.

Just as it is vital with an individual dream not to kill it by fixed interpretation, so it is crucial not to get lost in interpretative possibilities for repeated themes or symbols in a series. There are many ways other than interpretation to be sensitive to topics, themes, and symbols, and to use creative intuition in understanding their role in your psychic life.

Ever since she was a young woman, Robin had dreamed of dragons. They felt important, and came at times when she was undergoing major internal transformation. The first dream she remembered having about dragons was brief:

Golden Dragon Eggs

I am lying in my bed asleep. I wake up to find that a dragon has laid a pile of glistening green eggs beside my right ear.

Much has been written about the importance of dragons in dreams, about the dragon's symbolic significance in

If you miss the message one night, it will come in a different light another night. If you hang in there, it will speak to you.

—Harry Aron Wilmer
Practical Jung

Each recurring dream image becomes a "word" in a kind of "private language" for the dreamer, and its meaning becomes clearer as it is used more often.

—Mary Ann Mattoon
Applied Dream Analysis

different cultures. Robin, an anthropologist, was aware of these connotations and found Jung's archetypal approaches to dreaming both consonant with her values as an anthropologist and helpful in appreciating the relevance of her dreams to her inner life. She sensed that this long series of dreams was a deep message from her own underworld culture, a message whose bearer came and went in unaccountable fashion, like a wandering monk.

In her dreams, Robin's dragons appeared in many forms and sizes. Some were lethal; others were not. Once, when traveling in Alaska, she dreamed she was kissed on the lips by a dragon. In another, the dragon undulated in space, teaching her how to move in air. All these dreams felt like big dreams. But none compared to this one that subtly yet profoundly altered her attitude toward her life:

Embracing the Dragon

I am standing. A great red dragon is roaring in front of me. It is almost my height. It looks ready to strike.

I hear myself saying out loud in my mind—in the dream!—"Well, I know it will definitely breathe fire over me if it smells fear on me, so I'd better not be afraid. And if it isn't going to strike me, there's no need to be afraid. And if it *is* going to strike me, there's nothing I can do, so there's no point in being afraid, and I might as well embrace it." I reach up and put my hands around its neck, and it purrs like a kitten.

In her day world, Robin had no particular attraction or aversion to reptiles. She had more than average familiarity with them, having traveled to several South American countries with her parents. Beyond having a healthy respect for lethal reptiles, however, she had no personal associations to the mythological creature. Yet her dreams had given her this totem beast.

Each dream felt complete. But Robin also believed there was value in seeing the relationship among the dreams. She didn't attempt to make a classic narrative—a story with a beginning, middle and end—out of all the dreams together. She did not approach them as chapters in a book. Rather, she explored the theme and its images through a variety of practices. She explored these recurring images through various media. Over the years, she did simple drawings in oil pastels (again and again until she felt the image capturing something of the feeling of the dream); she made a dragon out of clay; she bought a small dragon carved out of stone; she had active imaginary conversations with some of the dragon figures. She made dragons out of clay, and also bought herself several small carvings on her travels.

How Robin approached her dragon series reminds me of a show by Nathan Oliveira that a friend and I attended at Stanford University. I looked at the first painting. It was a delicate, impressionistic watercolor of a kestrel with subtly colored wings (I nearly wrote *winds*; that is how they seemed to me), a celebration of the kestrel. Then I looked around. There were many paintings: some, about six inches square, in oils or watercolors; others, oils as long as the gallery wall, as high as the ceiling, and layered on, in striking and evocative pentimento. Every painting was of a kestrel.

My friend and I resolved to return when no one was around and dance silently in the space to the accompaniment of these magnificent paintings: essence and heart of kestrel. Each evoked a different experience of and

Dreaming of snakes in Chile means money. I have had that dream twice and I'm not a gambler. I hate gambling. . . . I had this dream that nineteen snakes were crawling up my brother-in-law's legs. So the next day I said, "You should go to the casino and gamble, because you will get a lot of money playing nineteen.". . . [He] played nineteen and won! We were so surprised and so appalled at the same time that we started yelling and screaming.
—Isabel Allende
In Naomi Epel's
Writers Dreaming

appreciation of the airborne power of the kestrel.

How did this series begin for Oliveira? A student brought him a stuffed kestrel, which he painted about seventy-five times. Then, nine years later, as he was moving his studio, he found a dead kestrel at the front door. He brought his imagination and love to those birds! He let them fly. Had he "figured out" what the kestrel meant to him, "why" it had appeared on his doorstep, he might not have had the gift of these magnificent paintings. Instead, he sought, in this series of paintings over many years, to keep the spirit of his connection with the kestrel, to preserve its mystery. As I looked at his paintings, I felt as though I were dwelling not only in the heart of the kestrel and soaring with it, but in the heart of the painter.

This is how Robin approached her dragon dreams. Certainly, she researched the mythological, religious, and cultural history of dragons. But she did not do this to pin her dream images down. Rather than attempt to pin down each dream like a dead kestrel, she allowed her imagination to roam over her amplifications around the dragons, allowed her soul to be fed by the numinousness of their appearances without getting swelled-headed or terrified at such magnificent appearances. She treated the dream series the way she would have treated the unexpected but frequent arrival of a mysterious, eminent guest who always seemed to leave the house richer, wiser.

It is the cumulative numinousity and mystery, the ritual repetition of an image, that gives a dream series its power. No matter what you create, treat your dream series with as much respect as Oliveira showed the kestrel in all its aspects—whether dead on the doorstep, stuffed on a stand, or soaring above the Stanford hills, forever mysterious, powerful, and free.

Our dream images, even if we don't remember them, invade our waking awareness as patterns. By these patterns we live. By not recognizing them, we live unconsciously.

—Fred Alan Wolf
The Dreaming Universe

Black and White, Left to Right: Exploring the Repeating and Evolving Patterns in Dream Series

Across time, dreams can reveal inherent patterns, repetitions, or coherent variations on a certain figure, perspective, color, place, season, feeling, structure, or theme. One woman dreams about her childhood home all the time. It doesn't matter what's taking place in the dream or whether her husband and children or old loves are there; she is somewhere nearby or in that house. Another dreams of submerged rooms; another dreams again and again of tidal waves. Another dreams regularly of dark streets in an unfamiliar town, with shadowy figures chasing him. Another dreams of shy encounters with smooth-talking, seductive men.

When we are totally faithful to our own individuality, we are actually following a very intricate design . . . We carry around the rules inherent in our organism. As living, patterned human beings, we are incapable of producing anything at random.
—Stephen Nachmanovitch
Free Play

We can imagine many reasons why certain images repeat. Some theorists see these repetitions as symbolic attempts to resolve unresolved issues; some see them as constellations of psychic stars endlessly circling around some benevolent or malevolent sun in our personal or collective experience. No matter what the reason, *if* we pay attention to the evolution of the series, recurrent themes and images leave us a little more conscious after each visit.

Once you have used the following guidelines to bring to light some of the repeated or evolving images, you can use the same practices to work with them as you do with other dream images. Certain practices, however, work particularly well with repeated or evolving images.

Visiting an Art Gallery of Repeated Dream Images

Read through your dream journal. Each time you come to a particular recurring theme, create a title, capitalize it, list it, and date it on a separate piece of paper. Put these in sequential order. Here is one dreamer's list of titles:

Tidal Wave over the Office Block
My Sisters Are Caught by a Tidal Wave
Night Tidal Wave
I Ignore the Tidal Wave
Tigers in the Tidal Wave
Tidal Wave Breaking Against Our Beachhouse Window
Surfing the Tidal Wave

After you have titled, dated, and listed all the dreams around a particular theme, put the list in front of you and imagine that this is your gallery guide and that these are titles of art pieces. In your imagination, walk around the gallery and look at each of these in turn. Imagine that these images are rendered in many different media. Some are large, some small, some in vivid relief, some in sculpted form, some in watercolor, some in oils. What is your response to the images?

Take time looking around. What kind of a place is it? What kind of people are currently looking at this show? Eavesdrop.

Listen to how they respond to the power of these images.

What do you see or feel about your theme after viewing it in this way?

"Tidal Wave"
Watercolor

Amplifying Associations to a Repeated Image, Dream by Dream

A simple way to enrich your associations to a repeating symbol is to notice what happens to each dream if that image is removed. Notice the *ma* created by the symbol's absence and, therefore, by its presence. Note what it was that the image contributed to each dream in turn. By doing this with a series, you can develop a cumulative sense over time of the function of that image, metaphor, or symbol within your inner world. The Tidal Wave dreamer took the image of high seas and skimmed through her dreams to see what the image contributed to each. Here's an excerpt from her list:

Dream 1: tossed about, powerful, strong
Dream 2: threatening, without care for those drowning
Dream 3: sailing on—making it, but only just . . .
Dream 7: setting out on high seas; using winds and waves to make forward motion—feel the surging power moving boat forward . . .
Dream 11: surfing big waves—dumped but go right back again— waves helping me do what I want—serious playfulness

The image of the high seas shifted for this dreamer over time—from something threatening to something she could use, once she learned how. She had not seen this development until she wrote out the contributions of the image to each dream.

The dream state is representative of superpositions of brain-generated quantum waves or quantum states. These states, although present in the waking state, are masked by the input of waking data much as sunlight masks the starlight during the day.

—Fred Alan Wolf
The Dreaming Universe

Visiting the Rogues' Gallery

It is only natural that our wonderfully plagiaristic inner dream artists would use the same figures over and over at times—especially friends, family, and colleagues. What becomes especially intriguing is noting how a particular figure appears across time in a series. One dreamer discovered that her younger sister always appeared in dreams about pregnancy; another, that her mother was always about to say something the dreamer could never quite catch. Another dreamer saw that over several years, the dreams about her mother did, indeed, seem to be evolving from her being a distant, fierce figure to being loving and physically vulnerable; another dreamer saw how his early dreams of his family always portrayed an ideal situation but that, over time and as he grew stronger in himself, later dreams revealed the human frailties of his family.

In addition to the appearance of people who have played or are playing important roles in our lives, odd folk appear: an old school friend—sometimes not even friends, but neutral people who happened to be in the same class, or some passing acquaintance met only once or twice and whose name is recalled only in the dream. Appearing once, these figures bring their own curious flavor to a dream: they contribute something that no one else could have contributed.

What walks through my dreams is not actual, other persons or even their soul traits mirrored in me . . . but the deep, subjective psyche in its personified guises. A dream presents "me," subjected to "my" subjectivity. I am merely one subject among several in a dream. In sleep, I am thoroughly immersed in the dream. Only on waking do I reverse this fact and believe the dream is in me. At night the dream has me, but in the morning I say, I had a dream. . . .

—James Hillman
The Dream and the Underworld

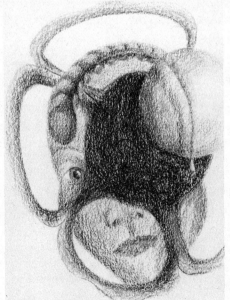

"My Dream Sister"
Photocopy and colored pencil

Appearing many times, they take on more import. What does Jenny Pimblett keep doing in my dreams? Well, she's always accompanying me on some kind of journey. Sam Mack, that rotten little boy from elementary school who stole my ball-point, always turns up as a rescuing type. They are mysterious figures in a subplot. They are like a recurring leitmotif, a painting gesture, a design on a pot.

Brainstorm your associations to the figure:

- What function(s) does the figure perform in each dream?
- How does each dream change if that figure is left out?
- What does the figure contribute to each dream?
- What are five positive and five negative adjectives I would use to describe this figure?

If you are still intrigued by the figure's appearance, you might make a collage of photocopied photographs of this person. Meditate on it for five minutes a day for a week and see what else the image evokes. The image could well reflect back something of yourself.

Looking for Perspective

Perspective is a repeated element frequently missed. Sometimes, dreamers notice that they have multiple perspectives in the one dream, or even in the same moment in a dream. At other times, they notice that they are often on the outside looking in, or they are always looking down from a great height, or they are both looking at events and participating in them, or they are always seeing things from a great distance.

Noticing the repetition or development of perspective

within a dream series can alert us to an unconscious way in which we might be viewing our lives. For example, the young woman who was always on the outside looking in realized that this was exactly her experience of family life when she was growing up. She was the fifth of six children, and the only quiet child in a group of outgoing siblings. She realized that this outsider feeling was one she didn't necessarily have to bring to all situations, now that she had her own family and community. Here's what another dreamer noticed:

Close Vision

The thing in my dreams that keeps repeating itself is close vision—I see everything really close up—I rarely see the whole of anything—a face, a hand, a toy, a piece of paper, a computer screen. . . . There's no commonality in the things and I don't see much personal symbolism in them for me (unless there's some big universal something I'm missing). But I'm really wondering about what it says that I'm always seeing just part of things and never the whole. . . .

It didn't take a degree in symbology for this dreamer to soon realize that she might need to step back from certain situations to be more effective in them!

Working with Repeated or Developing Gestures and Actions

One action rarely makes a ritual unless it is done with great consciousness. More often, ritual involves the conscious repetition of actions that are imbued with symbolic significance.

The distinction between metaphor (connections based on imagistic and spatial similarities that ultimately transcend syntax and language) and metonymy (connections based on linear linguistic combinations) . . . is a major clue to cognitive processes involved in different types of dream formation. Indeed it will help to distinguish between the dreams and dream theories of Jung and Freud.

—Harry T. Hunt
The Multiplicity of Dreams

Repeated activities are common in our dreams. Again and again we fly, walk on the beach, fight with dark forces in alleys, give a speech, run late for class, lose our lover in the crowd, have sex with a stranger, defend ourselves with knives, get on trains for fabulous destinations, leave our wallets at home. It is easy, however, to focus on the *content* of what we are doing more than on the *action* connected to the content: We focus on the wallet, the destination, the knife, rather than the forgetting, the traveling, the defending.

What links the dreams is the *act* of forgetting, traveling, or defending. You might find that you are always looking: looking for, looking around, looking up, at, to, from. There is something about this "looking" energy for you.

Dreams show a remarkable flexibility about moving back and forth between language or imagery. At times, a theme can appear in the imagery itself; at others, it can appear in words that describe the dreams—word play, puns, names, symbols. Different modes of repetition are evident in these dreamers' findings:

Piercing

Something gets pierced—over and over. I'm a little girl getting my ears pierced again. I describe a cry as piercing, a sunset as piercingly beautiful. In several dreams I am pierced by something but it doesn't hurt. One dream, I'm having a bone stuck in my side by a tribal member and I know he is putting a hex on me; in another, I'm a Japanese warrior committing suicide with a long knife—except I don't die. In others, I'm watching my wife prick her finger with a needle as she sews.

Sometimes in my dreams [my grandmother] is writing and I read what she's writing over her shoulder. She's always young in the dreams, although I never knew her when she was young. . . .

I don't remember the word she is writing in these dreams. Sometimes I remember that she's writing with colored ink or she's writing in a notebook or at the bottom of a photograph. . . . It's a very soothing dream. When she comes in the dreams it's because I'm really doing well. I'm writing. I'm happy. She always represents, for me, protection.

—Isabel Allende
In Naomi Epel's
Writers Dreaming

Digging

I couldn't believe how many digging ideas turned up over two years. Dogs were digging up bones in the garden. I was "digging up dirt" on someone. My daughter was making digs at me. On and on. I've no idea yet what it might be trying to tell me—if anything—but it's really a theme!

Review your dreams to see whether you are being or acting in repeated ways in different contexts. Imagine that these activities are repeated in groups of paintings in a gallery. What seems to want to make itself known to you through these different groups of dream paintings? One dreamer imagined walking around and standing quietly in front of the first group of paintings that portrayed his images of fighting; then he looked at the group in the second room, focused on running; in the third room, there was a group on waiting.

Alternatively, you can mime the repeated or evolving actions and see what emerges for you, what emotional reactions you have, what is evoked in your body, what images come. Or you can do an energy painting by holding the image within and breathing it out, down the hand, and onto the paper, letting it hold all the subtle shifts in function of these images across all the dreams in one paradoxical whole.

Exploring Repeated Seasons and Times of Day

Many dreamers notice that their dreams seem to take place in the same kind of light—deep gloom, an unearthly pale light, dim natural light, midnight. Others also have observed that a particular season reappears in their dreams—they are

The most important thing I've noticed [about working with dreams from people from different technological cultures] is similarity. People everywhere seem to dream about walking, sitting, breathing, streets, landscapes, cars, technology, and so on. They all believe they are awake when in a dream state. So, as long as I work entirely on a non-interpretive level, I can work with dreams of people whose cultures I don't understand. I just ask questions: "What does that look like?" "How does that feel?"

—Robert Bosnak
In Michael V. Adams'
"Image, Active
Imagination, and the
Imaginal Level"

looking out the window to the flowering trees of spring, walking through autumn leaves, driving through snow. Something about that season or time of day carries special importance.

Night

It's often night in my dreams. In fact, when I went back over a lot of dreams, I either didn't know what time of day it was or saw that it was night. Moons, stars, candles, dark paths, dark streets, talking in dark, dark forests.

"Moon, Stars, Talking in the Dark" Collage

There is . . . an Australian aboriginal tribe which has a festival, Kunapipi, which lasts thirty years, a whole generation. Every year only a part of the festival is performed. At the end of each part of the festival, they assemble the tribe and ask for dreams about the ceremony. The dreams are then discussed, and if there are proposals in the dreams to change the ritual, it is changed. So that the ritual always corresponds to their inner dream life, or their inner dream life always has a say in their religious ritual.

—Marie-Louise
von Franz
In Fraser Boa's
The Way of the Dream

Snow

I have endless dreams about being in snow. I always know what time of year it is in these dreams—whether it's the beginning of winter or the end.

The "snow" dreamer worked with his associations across the dream series and saw that they had a double connotation for him: He thought of snow essentially as clean, beautiful, and untouched; he also thought of snow as covering up and freezing things. Both themes seemed to touch on certain of his values and actions that distressed him: He saw his inability to feel warm and spontaneous in situations; he was always looking for the perfect response and feeling "frozen" if he could not construct it.

Seasons and times of day are particularly receptive to collage work. It's always easy to find photographs in magazines. Follow the earlier guidelines for collage expressions, spending time afterward contemplating your piece briefly, and noting any words that come to you about the importance of this time of day.

Exploring Repeated Colors

Wander through your dream journal and notice whether colors repeat themselves in varied forms. Colors can sometimes repeat themselves in words as well as in image, as these dreamers illustrate:

Blue

Feeling blue, seeing blue rooms, buildings, clothes, blue ice, ocean, turning blue with cold . . .

Black and white

I didn't see it before. People are in white shirts; I am reading the newspaper; white walls, white snow, black night, a black dog, a black-and-white tiled floor; someone's in a black mood; I'm in the war and there's a blackout. White sheets on the bed. I have to wonder whether I'm a black-and-white kind of person!

How does the repeated color contribute to each dream? How do those individual contributions accumulate into an overall feeling about the color? Work with your amplifications. Make a collage or energy painting that features the color. When you have finished the collage or painting, list on the back all the associations you bring to the color in each dream.

Mapping Directions

Directions are less obvious in dreams unless we begin to look at a series and see what visual movements and *words* associated with directions seem to reappear across time:

Left

Left—going left, being left, turning left, leftist, left-handed, looking left, I left a place . . . I am often traveling in a left-handed direction—whether I'm walking with friend, or turning left on a road, or dancing, or flying. But I often seem to turn left or circle left. I even notice that I talk about being left in various places.

Clockwise

I couldn't believe it! Everything was clockwise! I drew each movement and they all went clockwise. I did some

Dreams . . . provide us with maps of regions which are inaccessible in waking consciousness. With these maps we are better able to follow the course of man's behavior, to understand why he selects one road rather than another, to anticipate the difficulties and obstacles he will encounter, and to predict his destinations.

—Calvin S. Hall
The Meaning of Dreams

reading in symbolism books and began to get ideas about what might be moving me in that direction.

"Clockwise"
Poster paint, sand and glue

Left to right

In dreams, things often move across my inner vision from left to right. Sometimes I don't even bother to write down which direction people are headed, but I'm going to from now on. I took a look at a batch of dreams from last year and here were some of the images: the V.P. of marketing is walking across a podium from left to right; I look from left to right lots of times; someone is surfing in toward a beach that is on the right; in one dream, I am even "left with a feeling of being right in the long run!" Isn't that incredible?

These dreams didn't seem to have anything tying them up with each other, until I started to look at the direction of movements. I still don't have a clue whether knowing this can help me, but I'm really paying attention and staying open. Maybe it has something to do with being logical—writing goes from left to right across a page.

Repeated directions lend themselves well to energy paintings and mandalas. Work with the gesture. Embody the direction and translate it into line form on the page. Let the hand wander or move from left to right. Let it fork or spiral. Mime it. What does this evoke in you? Does this feel familiar or new?

Tracing the Quality That Accompanies Action

Often, dream actions differ but share a common way in which they are being performed and described. Here is one dreamer's observation:

> **Fast!**
> Everything happens quickly—often too quickly in many of my dreams. And I end up missing something because it's all happening so fast. For example, my partner was talking so quickly I couldn't catch what she was saying in one dream; in another, I was running for the plane but it took off without me; in another, I'm told to "hold fast" but I can't. And in a lot of dreams, I'm having breakfast—*break-fast.*
>
> Maybe I'm making too much of it but it's made me think about how fast I seem to go in my life. I mean, I can't even catch my dreams!

There is a dream which I delight in and long for when I'm writing. It means to me that the work is going well. Or will go well. Or that I'm telling the truth and telling it well.

I dream of a very tall building. It's in the process of being built, and there are scaffolds and steps. It sort of looks like the inside of the Arc de Triomphe. I'm climbing it with alacrity and joy and laughter.

—Maya Angelou
In Naomi Epel's
Writers Dreaming

This dreamer made a list of the benefits and liabilities of being "fast" and saw that until now she had preferred to focus on the benefits—being a quick thinker, a quick mover, a quick study, a quick decision maker. She now needed to become more aware of its less helpful implications, such as "being impatient over others" (or with her own feelings), "not giving others a chance to speak in a conversation," "taking tasks away from my daughter because she takes too long. . . ."

Make a list of all the positive and negative things you associate with a repeated quality in your dreams to see what this quality is carrying for you. Then mime it. Exaggerate! Considering *how* we are or *how* we act in our dreams can be enlightening to our waking world.

Observing Repeated Feelings and Emotions

Patterns of feelings and emotions are often easy to recognize in a dream series. We are constantly puzzled, angry, caught out, frustrated, in love, sexually aroused, grieving.

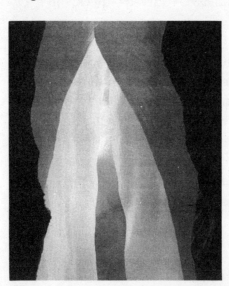

Explore the subtle variations in these feelings across time. For example, if you are often angry in your dreams, ask yourself: What touches off my anger? Is it always something minor? Does the trigger change over time? Am

"Birthing Dreams"
Collage

Can you imagine after writing all day, going to bed and dreaming something like "on the other hand, comma, it might be said . . ."

Borges, the great Argentine writer, said that it is written in the kabbala that when the words in a dream are loud and distinct and seem to come from no particular source, these words are from God. So all I can say is that my god is a god of punctuation marks and introductory adverbial clauses. And that it probably serves me right.

—John Barth
In Naomi Epel's
Writers Dreaming

I always feeling the same degree of anger? Does anyone respond to my anger? How?

Carla constantly dreamed of trying to make a place for herself professionally. She would crawl under tables groaning with food, trying not to disturb her coworkers while she tried to spy an empty chair. She would wait and wait to get her supervisor's attention, and then he would have to leave without speaking to her. Over a period of three years, she noticed, in reviewing these dreams, that she was gradually having to contend with fewer people occupying situations or doing things that she wanted to be doing. The intruders in the office lessened in number. Finally, she had a dream in which a woman spoke to her while Carla was talking with her supervisor. Carla turned to the woman, told her that she mustn't interrupt in the middle of a conversation, turned back to her supervisor, and continued talking.

After this dream, Carla had no more dreams about trying to make a place for herself at work. This ended the series. Certainly, in this series, it might seem that Carla was imaginatively trying out different scenarios for treating herself with more respect. Her outer behavior had been shifting over time, and the dreams acted as both a reflection of the outer changes she was already making and as preparation for future changes.

> *In listening to dreams, it is of primary importance to take the approach that anything is possible, and that our grasp of the dream world is about as advanced as a baboon's grasp of algebra.*
>
> —Robert Bosnak
> *A Little Course in Dreams*

Working with Images, Metaphors, and Symbols of Objects and Entities

The more an object or entity stands for itself in a particular time and place, the less it is a metaphor. The more it stands for something else, the more it takes on the function of metaphor. When it stands for something else consistently over a period of time, it becomes a symbol. The snake that appears once is an image with possible metaphoric and symbolic overtones; the snake that appears twice is beginning to stand for something in the soul; the snake that appears again and again takes on the authority of a personal symbol in our private mythology.

As you unearth these images that have earned the status of "symbol" in your inner realm, use the practices described earlier to pay homage to them in the outer realm, and to consolidate their place in consciousness: Find a stone that looks like the one in your dreams; buy a carving of that tiger; make a clay bird and paint it; make a collage of moon images; write a list poem including all the different situations in which this symbol has appeared in your dreams. In this way, you can explore the image without killing it; you can feed it so that it can continue to feed you.

Alternatively, choose one of the following ways of acknowledging and harnessing the energy of these symbols that orbit in your inner world:

- Make a mobile that includes pictures (photocopies) of several entities that have appeared in your dreams. Hang it near your bed (assuming no bellowing objections or ribald comments from others). Or hang it where you do your dream explorations during waking hours.

- Make a mandala that allows a formal place for several symbols. Draw a circle divided into pie slices on a white or colored board. Each section provides space for a symbol. Place each symbol in it at will, changing them every few days according to which symbol seems to belong in which space.

- Make a special box covered in simple but pleasing paper in which to keep photos or other visual replicas of your symbols. Every so often, add another, or quietly leaf through them.

- Collect a series of small figures from different tribal and cultural groups that somehow capture the spirit of your visiting spirit(s). Put them in a protected and private place.

- No time for any of these ideas, but the symbol is still haunting you? If you have a little spare money, visit a museum shop that sells carvings, paintings, and other art forms of different animals from different cultures, such as an African or Native American artifact gallery. Pick up a small version of your symbol that draws you. You might even find a pouch in which you could carry the replica to reinforce and remind you of the teaching, wisdom, humor, and mystery of that symbol.

Continue to work with repeated dream images until they lose efficacy, until you forget to look at them for a long while, or until they bore you. Your psychic connection to them will have lived a full life, and that internal energy has evolved. Don't hold on. Accept, be grateful, and move on.

The images provide access to the archetypal patterns underlying the contextual and emotional mental process by which we work on nonlinear levels of cognition. . . . This logos is very different from the linear, hierarchical, and dichotomizing modes of cognition that underlie Western, Judeo-Roman–based logic and grammar.

—Sylvia Brinton Perera
"Dream Design"

SNOW, GREEN ELEPHANTS, AND BUTTERFLIES: MAPPING RECURRING STRUCTURAL PATTERNS IN NARRATIVES

Repeated narrative structures in dreams seem to reflect patterns in outer and inner life. Recognizing them can sometimes free us from an unconscious need to follow grooves deepened over years; recognizing these grooves gives us choice to change.

According to Aboriginal thinking, dreaming is necessary for our recognition that we belong to a whole greater than our mere individual selves. It is a reflection of the future and our responsibility to continue as a species and as caretakers for the universe.

—Fred Alan Wolf
The Dreaming Universe

Claire spent months exploring many epic-length dreams. Each felt complete in itself with no apparent relationship to any other. Each seemed to be written by a different author. She explored the content of the dreams deeply, associating to the images at personal and archetypal levels, noting points of meaningful intersection between the life she lived and the dreams.

One foggy San Francisco morning, as she was mulling over yet another, she realized that there was something she was missing about these dreams. Certainly, she had paid attention to the content, themes, and symbols. And she had made good inner and outer use of her insights. But she believed there was "a deeper vein of gold in this series of dreams." She was silent a minute. She listened to what she had just said: "series." She began to ask herself: What does this series have in common if it's not symbols, images, feelings, or themes? Does it *need* to have anything in common?

Being able to ask new questions freed her from the templates of understanding she had laid over the dreams. She decided that the series did not have to have anything in common but that it certainly felt to her as though something wove the dreams together. Having a new question to ask opened the way for her to invent new answers (not right answers) that carried her contemplation into a different arena.

What she came to see was that her dreams had similar lines of development. She started to map out the energetic movements of the dreams. She quickly noticed that each began with a slow, nondirectional action followed by faster, direct action that was then cut across by a counterforce strong enough to permanently alter the original action. The counterforce would then disappear, but the narrative would continue in the new direction without much force.

How did this appear in Claire's dreams? There are questions we can ask to help us recognize energetic shifts in dreams. Here are some of Claire's responses to those questions:

- *Physical movement: Who went when where?* "I walked up the stairs to my parents' study and suddenly a breeze blew me down the stairs again."
- *Emotional movement: What was who feeling when and how did it change?* "I was feeling so happy about discovering a green elephant, and then my little sister walked into the room and made fun of me."
- *Natural movement: Was there a change in time, place, season, weather, or light?* "I woke up and was just getting ready to go for a jog when I looked outside and there was snow all over. I couldn't work out how, seeing it was summer."
- *Movement in buildings: Was there a change in the configuration of a room or structure?* "I went to leave by the front door, but instead of the door there was a big brick wall with ivy and butterflies all over it—right in the middle of the house."

One of the most important principles in the art of Japanese painting . . . is that called living movement . . . the transfusion into the work of the felt nature of the thing to be painted by the artist . . . Should his subject be a tree [the student] is urged when painting it to feel the strength which shoots through the branches and sustains the limbs.

—Henry P. Bowie
On the Laws of Japanese Painting

Claire stood up and walked around, embodying this energy pattern to see how it felt. She would move more and more quickly and surely, and then suddenly stop, change direction, and move lethargically. Her body felt young— perhaps twelve, perhaps eight. She felt angry, frustrated. Claire's images and body memories were doing good work, if she could just stay out of their way.

Then the insight came. "This is what always happened

to me with my uncle! I spent lots of time with him. He was a fine artist and I had an enormous crush on him! I wanted desperately to have him teach me how to draw, and to think I was great. And he did teach me.

"But he was a bad teacher, I realize now—so impatient! I'd start a drawing and take it to him all excited. You know what he'd do? He'd grab my pencil and change all my lines until the perspective was right and tell me to finish it.

"I learned a lot about art but I didn't want to draw anymore. I thought I wasn't much good.

"You know, I really lack confidence in my creativity in lots of areas—at work, with John [her husband]. Just when I'm getting in my stride, I let my own judgment get derailed so easily—by people I don't even trust! I've been letting this run my life without my knowing it!"

Over the ensuing months, this pattern lessened in frequency in Claire's dreams. Naturally, this insight was just a beginning: It was up to her to take quiet responsibility for her own creative capacities and to be an encouraging authority for herself. Claire could begin to be an advocate for her own creativity. Her recollection of her childhood experience and its anachronistic influence on her adult life began the long journey across psychological time zones to catch up with the rest of her adult conscious life.

Trusting the Image

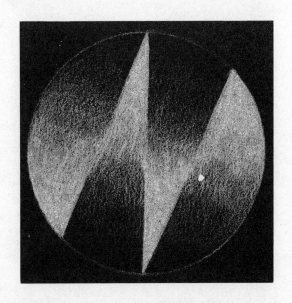

Two days after I finished this book, I had this dream:

I am at a community meeting being held in a large church. The community has met to discuss images.

A colleague (who has worked deeply with her dreams and painted them for years) stands up to speak. She is enthusiastic, full of quiet conviction. She addresses the community (none of whom are visible), saying: "Images themselves tell us how they want to be expressed—straight lines, circles, curves . . ."

Someone asks her how we can know whether to trust the image.

She replies, "All we have to do is look at what we have drawn to recognize that it is a perfect expression of itself. The lines we draw *are* the answer. The line itself tells us. All we need to do is attend to the images."

Those who lose dreaming are lost.
—Australian Aboriginal saying

My dream is far more succinct than I have been. The dream, dear fellow dreamer, contains all that I really needed to say.

)) ● ((

Appendix

Five Minute Practices

References

Achte, Kalle, and Taina Schakir. "Dreams in Different Cultures." *Psychiatria-Fennica*, 1981.

Adams, Michael V. "Image, Active Imagination, and the Imaginal Level: A Quadrant Interview with Robert Bosnak." *Quadrant XXV*, vol. 2 (1992).

Aristotle. *Parva Naturalia* (William David Ross, ed., J. Beare, Trans.). Oxford: Clarendon Press, 1955.

Arrien, Angeles. *Signs of Life: The Five Universal Shapes and How to Use Them*. Sonoma, Calif.: Arcus Publishing, 1992.

Boa, Fraser. *The Way of the Dream: Conversations on Jungian Dream Interpretation with Marie-Louise von Franz*. Boston and London: Shambhala, 1988, 1992, 1994.

Bosnak, Robert. *A Little Course in Dreams*. Boston and Shaftesbury: Shambhala, 1988.

Bowie, Henry P., *One the Laws of Japanese Painting*. New York: Dover Publications, Inc., [1911], 1952.

Cornell, Judith. *Mandalas: Luminous Symbols for Healing*. Wheaton, Ill.: Theosophical Publishing House, 1994.

Desjarlais, Robert R. "Dreams, Divination, and Yolmo Ways of Knowing." *Dreaming Journal of the Association for the Study of Dreams* 3, Vol. 1 (September 1991).

Downing, Jack, and Robert Marmorstein (eds.), *Dreams and Nightmares: A Book of Gestalt Therapy Sessions*. New York: Harper & Row, 1973.

Edinger, Edward F. *Ego and Archetype: Individuation and the Religious Function of the Psyche*. New York: Putnam, 1972.

Ellis, Havelock. *The World of Dreams*. Boston: Houghton Mifflin, 1911.

Emunah, Renée. *Acting for Real: Drama Therapy Process, Technique, and Performance*. New York: Brunner/Mazel Publishers, 1994.

Epel, Naomi. *Writers Dreaming*. New York: Carol Southern Books, 1993.

Fagan, Joel, and Irma Lee Shepherd, eds. *Gestalt Therapy Now: Theory, Techniques, Applications*. Palo Alto, Calif.: Science and Behavior Books, 1970.

Gendlin, Eugene T. *Let Your Body Interpret Your Dreams*. Wilmette, Ill.: Chiron Publications, 1986.

Gorer, Geoffrey. *African Dances: A Book About West African Negroes*. New York: Alfred A. Knopf, 1935.

Hall, Calvin S. *The Meaning of Dreams*. New York: McGraw-Hill, 1953, 1966.

Hall, Edward T. *The Hidden Dimension*. New York: Doubleday, 1966.

Handy, E. S. C. "Dreaming in Relation to Spirit Kindred and Sickness in Hawaii" in *Essays in Anthropology Presented to A. L. Kroeber in Celebration of His Sixtieth Birthday, June 11, 1936*. (Robert H. Lowie, ed.). New York: Kraus Reprint, 1969.

Hannah, Barbara. *Encounters with the Soul: Active Imagination as Developed by C. G. Jung*. Santa Monica, Calif.: Sigo Press, 1981.

Hillman, James. "An Inquiry into Image." *Spring*, 1977.

_____. "Further Notes on Images." *Spring*, 1978.

_____. *Healing Fiction*. Barrytown, N.Y.: Station Hill Press, 1983.

_____. "Image Sense." *Spring*, 1979.

_____. *The Dream and the Underworld*. New York, Hagerstown, San Francisco, London: Harper & Row, 1979.

Humbert, Elie G. "Dream Experience" in *Dreams in Analysis* (Nathan Schwartz-Salant and Murray Stein, eds., Robert Jalbert, trans.). Wilmette, Ill.: Chiron Publications, 1990.

Hunt, Harry T. *The Multiplicity of Dreams: Memory, Imagination and Consciousness*. New Haven and London: Yale University Press, 1989.

Johnson, Robert A. *Inner Work: Using Dreams and Active Imagination for Personal Growth*. San Francisco: Harper & Row, 1986.

_____. *We: Understanding the Psychology of Romantic Love*. San Francisco: Harper & Row, 1983.

_____. *She: A Contribution to Understanding Feminine Psychology*. New York: Harper & Row, 1976.

_____. *He: Understanding Masculine Psychology*. New York: Harper & Row, 1974.

Johnstone, Keith. *Impro: Improvisation and the Theatre*. New York: Routledge, 1979, 1981.

Jung, C. G. *Letters. Selected and Edited by Gerhard Adler, in Collaboration with Aniela Jaffe*. Vol. 1: 1906–1950. (R. F. C. Hull, trans.). Princeton: Princeton University Press, Bollingen Series XCV, 1973, 1975.

_____. *Collected Works of C. G. Jung*. Princeton: Princeton University Press, 1964, 1970.

_____. *Memories, Dreams, Reflections* (Recorded and edited by Aniela Jaffe). New York: Vintage Books, 1965.

Kiev, Ari. *Transcultural Psychiatry* (Erinnerungen, Traume, Gedanken, trans.). New York: The Free Press, A Division of MacMillan, 1972.

Keller, Helen. "The World I Live In" in *The World of Dreams* (Ralph Louis Woods, ed.). New York: Random House, 1947.

Laughlin, R. M. "Of Wonders Wild and New: Dreams from Zinacanta." *Smithsonian Contributions to Anthropology*, vol. 22. Washington: Smithsonian Institution Press, 1976.

Lowie, Robert H., ed. *Essays in Anthropology Presented to A. L. Kroeber in Celebration of His Sixtieth Birthday, June 11, 1936*. New York: Kraus Reprint, 1969.

Maritain, Jacques. *Creative Intuition in Art and Poetry*. Princeton: Princeton University Press, Bollingen Series XXXV. 1, 1953.

Martin, Stephen A. "Smaller Than Small, Bigger Than Big: The Role of the 'Little Dream' in Individuation." *Quadrant* XXV, vol. 2 (1992).

Matsumoto, Michihiro. *The Unspoken Way.* Tokyo and New York: Kodansha, 1988.

Matthews, June, "Child Studies Seminar," C. G. Jung Institute, San Francisco, 1993.

_____ , "Lecture," C. G. Jung Institute, San Francisco.

Mattoon, Mary Ann. *Applied Dream Analysis: A Jungian Approach.* Washington, D.C.: V. H. Winston and Sons, 1978.

Miller, Alice. *Pictures of a Childhood: Sixty-Six Watercolors and an Essay.* New York: Farrar, Straus & Giroux, 1986.

Mindell, Arnold. *The Shaman's Body: A New Shamanism for Transforming Health, Relationships, and Community.* San Francisco: Harper San Francisco, 1993.

_____ , *Dreambody: The Body's Role in Revealing the Self* (Sisa Sternback-Scott and Betty Goodman, eds.). Santa Monica, Calif.: Sigo Press, 1982.

Minh-ha, Trinh T. *Woman Native Other.* Bloomington and Indianapolis: Indiana University Press, 1989.

Nachmanovitch, Stephen. *Free Play: The Power of Improvisation in Lfe and the Arts.* New York: A Jeremy Tarcher/Putnam Book, 1990.

O'Nell, Carl W. *Dreams, Culture, and the Individual.* San Francisco: Chandler & Sharp, Publishers, 1976.

Perera, Sylvia Brinton. "Dream Design" in *Dreams in Analysis* (Nathan Schwartz-Salant and Murray Stein, eds.). Wilmette, Ill.: Chiron Publications, 1990.

Perls, Fritz. "Four Lectures" in *Gestalt Therapy Now: Theory, Techniques, Applications.* (Joen Fagan and Irma Lee Shepherd, eds.). Palo Alto, Calif.: Science and Behavior Books, 1970.

Petchkovsky, L., and J. Cawte. "The Dreams of the Yolngu Aborigines of Australia." *Journal of Analytical Psychology,* vol. 31 (4), 1986.

Reeves, Paula. *Stepping into the River.* Unpublished manuscript, 1996.

Rilke, Rainer Maria. *Sonnets to Orpheus* (C. F. MacIntyre, trans.). Berkeley and Los Angeles: University of California Press, 1960.

Sarris, Greg. *Keeping Slug Woman Alive: A Holistic Approach to American Indian Texts.* Berkeley, Los Angeles, Oxford: University of California Press, 1993.

Schwartz-Salant, Nathan, and Murray Stein, eds. *Dreams in Analysis.* Wilmette, Ill.: Chiron Publications, 1990.

Shlain, Leonard. *Art & Physics: Parallel Visions in Space, Time & Light.* New York: William Morrow, 1991.

Signell, Karen A. *Wisdom of the Heart: Working with Women's Dreams.* New York: Bantam, 1990.

Silko, Leslie Marmon. *Ceremony.* New York: Viking Press, 1977.

Singer, June. *Boundaries of the Soul: The Practice of Jung's Psychology.* New York: Anchor Books, Doubleday, 1972.

Stewart, Kilton. "Dream Theory in Malaya" in *Altered States of Consciousness* (Charles T. Tart, ed.). Garden City, N.Y.: A Doubleday Anchor Book, 1972.

Swentzell, Rina, and Sandra P. Edelman. "The Butterfly Effect: A Conversation with Rina Swentzell." *El Palacio* 1, vol. 95 (Fall/Winter 1989).

Tart, Charles T., ed. *Altered States of Consciousness.* Garden City, N.Y.: A Doubleday Anchor Book, 1972.

Tedlock, Barbara. "The Role of Dreams and Visionary Narratives in Mayan Cultural Survival." *Ethos* 4, vol. 20 (December 1992).

Van de Castle, Robert L. *Our Dreaming Mind.* New York: Ballantine Books, 1994.

Von Franz, Marie-Louise. *C. G. Jung: His Myth in Our Time* (William H. Kennedy, trans.). New York: Putnam, 1975.

Wilmer, Harry Aron. *Practical Jung: Nuts and Bolts of Jungian Psychotherapy.* Wilmette, Ill.: Chiron Publications, 1987.

Wolf, Fred Alan. *The Dreaming Universe: A Mind-Expanding Journey into the Realm Where Psyche and Physics Meet.* New York: Simon & Schuster, 1994.

Woodman, Marion. *Leaving My Father's House: A Journey to Conscious Femininity* (with Kate Danson, Mary Hamilton, and Rita Greer Allen). Boston: Shambhala, 1992.

———. (Speaker). *Dreams: Language of the Soul* (cassette recording no. A131). Boulder, Colo.: Sounds True Recordings, 1991.

———. *The Pregnant Virgin: A Process of Psychological Transformation.* Toronto: Inner City Books, 1985.

———. *Addiction to Perfection: The Still Unravished Bride.* Toronto: Inner City Books, 1982.

Woodman, Marion, Mary Hamilton, and Ann Skinner. *Unpublished manuscript.*

Wordsworth, William. *The Complete Poetical Works of Wordsworth* (Andrew J. George, ed.). Boston: Houghton Mifflin, 1932, 1904.

Zoja, Luigi. "Beyond Freud and Jung: Seven Analysts Discuss the Impact of New Ideas About Dreamwork." *Quadrant* XXV, vol. 2 (1992).

)) ● ((

Permissions Acknowledgments

The author wishes to thank the following for permission to reprint portions of the works indicated:

Excerpt from Maritain, Jacques: *Creative Intuition in Art and Poetry*. Copyright © 1953 by Trustees of National Gallery of Art renewed 1981 by Eveline Garnier. Reprinted by permission of Princeton University Press. From *The Way of the Dream: Conversations on Jungian Dream Interpretation With Marie-Louise Von Franz*, by Fraser Boa; © 1992; Reprinted by arrangement with Shambhala Publications, Inc, 300 Massachusetts Avenue, Boston, MA 02115. From *A Little Course on Dreams*, by Robert Bosnak; © 1992; Reprinted by arrangement with Shambhala Publications, Inc, 300 Massachusetts Avenue, Boston, MA 02115. Excerpt from *Image, Active Imagination, and the Imaginal Level* by Robert Bosnak, in QUADRANT XXV: 2, 1992. Copyright © 1992 by Robert Bosnak. Reprinted by permission of C.G. Jung Foundation. Excerpt from *Image Sense*, Spring 1979 by James Hillman. Copyright © 1979 by James Hillman. Reprinted by permission of Spring Publications, Inc. Selected excerpts to be used as margin quotes from *The Dream and the Underworld* by James Hillman. Copyright © 1979 by James Hillman. Reprinted by permission of HarperCollins Publishers, Inc. Excerpts from *The Multiplicity of Dreams: Memory, Imagination and Consciousness* by Harry T. Hunt. Copyright © 1989 by Harry T. Hunt. Reprinted by permission of Yale University Press. Excerpt from *Dreams, Culture, and the Individual* by Carl W. O'Nell. Copyright © 1976 by Carl W. O'Nell. Reprinted by permission of Chandler and Sharp Publishers, Inc. Excerpts from Sylvia Brinton Perera, *Dream Design*, in: Dreams in Analysis, © 1990 by Chiron Publications. Reprinted by permission of the publisher. Excerpt from *Smaller than Small, Bigger than Big* by Stephen Martin, in: QUADRANT XXV: 2, 1992. Copyright © 1992 by Stephen Martin. Reprinted by permission of C.G. Jung Foundation. Excerpt from *The Dreaming Universe* by Fred Alan Wolf, Ph.D. Copyright © 1994 by Fred Alan Wolf. Reprinted by permission of Simon & Schuster. Excerpt from *Writers Dreaming* by Naomi Epel. Copyright © 1993 by Naomi Epel. Reprinted by permission of Naomi Epel and the Sandra Dijkstra Literary Agency. Excerpt from *The Butterfly Effect: A Conversation with Rina Swentzell* by Rina Swentzell and Sandra P. Edelman in El Palacio, Vol 95, No. 1 Fall/Winter 1989. Copyright © 1989 by Rina Swentzell and Sandra P. Edelman. Reprinted by permission of the authors and El Palacio.

Index

Conari Press, established in 1987, publishes books on topics rang-
ing from spirituality and women's history to sexuality and personal growth. Our main goal is to publish quality books that will
make a difference in people's lives—both how we feel about ourselves and how we relate to one another. Our readers are or most
important resource, and we value your input, suggestions, and
ideas. We'd love to hear from you—after all, we are publishing
books for you!

For a complete catalog or to get on our mailing list, please contact
us at:

CONARI PRESS

2550 Ninth Street, Suite 101
Berkeley, CA 94710
(800)685-9595 · FAX (510)649-7190
E-MAIL conaripub@aol.com